KU-255-538

OPPOSITION IN THE GDR UNDER HONECKER, 1971–85

By the same author

ERNST JÜNGER AND THE NATURE OF POLITICAL COMMITMENT

OPPOSITION IN THE GDR UNDER HONECKER, 1971–85

An Introduction and Documentation

Roger Woods

Lecturer in German, Aston University

with translations by
Christopher Upward
Senior Lecturer in German, Aston University

St. Martin's Press New York

 For information, write:
Scholarly & Reference Division,
St. Martin's Press, Inc., 175 Fifth Avenue, New York, NY 10010

First published in the United States of America in 1986

Printed in Hong Kong

ISBN 0–312–58686–8

Library of Congress Cataloging-in-Publication Data
Woods, Roger, 1949–
Opposition in the GDR under Honecker.
Bibliography: p.
Includes index.
1. Opposition (Political science)—Germany (East)
2. Germany (East)—Politics and government. 3. Dissenters
—Germany (East) 4. Communism—Germany (East)
I. Title.
JN3971.5.A792068 1986 320.9431 85–22145
ISBN 0–312–58686–8

For Diana, Michael and Katherine

Contents

Preface

Apart from the fact that Western interest in the GDR has increased greatly during the Honecker period with as yet no English language survey of the various forms of opposition that exist there, this book was prompted by curiosity on two controversial points.

First, opposition in the GDR tends to be seen in the West either as activity restricted to a small, isolated and therefore insignificant group, or as the expression of the true opinions of the silent majority of East German citizens. At a time of heightened tension between East and West it is important to have a realistic view of just how widespread opposition is and whether it is a significant force in the GDR.

Secondly, forty years after the end of the Second World War, at a time when the majority of East German citizens have grown up under the new socialist regime, it is also worth asking to what extent opposition in the GDR today is the product of a clash between traditional and new political values, and to what extent it stems from conflicts generated within 'actually existing socialism' itself.

This introduction and documentation is intended to provide a conceptual framework and background information as well as a selection of primary sources, so that the reader will be able to draw his or her own conclusions on these points.

Most of the documents contained in the book have not been made available in English translation before and, with the exception of documents 16, 24, 29, 35 and 37, all have been translated by Christopher Upward. The documents (referred to in the introduction by numbers in brackets) have been selected as representative of the views of the individuals or groups from which they came.

Birmingham ROGER WOODS

Acknowledgements

The author and publishers wish to thank the following who have kindly given permission for the use of copyright material: Dietz Verlag; Rotbuch Verlag; Deutschland Archiv; Jürgen Wallmann; Spiegel Verlag; Jurek Becker; Verlag Junge Welt; Frankfurter Rundschau; New Left Review; Jürgen Kuczynski; Reuters; Frankfurter Allgemeine Zeitung; Peter Wensierski; Bund Verlag; Verlag Europäische Ideen; Rowohlt Verlag; Ullstein Verlag; Amnesty International; Akademie der Künste, West Berlin; Farrar, Straus & Giroux; Virago Press; END Journal; Walther Grunwald; Mecklenburgische Kirchenzeitung; Sinn und Form; Günter Kunert; Berliner Verlag; Buchverlag Der Morgen.

Introduction

1 The Official East German View

Officially there is 'no objective political or social basis for opposition' in the GDR since the working class is the main productive force in society and exercises political power with the aim of improving the material and cultural quality of life for the whole population. Opposition is thus only meaningful in bourgeois states, and here it comes typically from communist and workers' parties (1).

This basic premise permeates every aspect of political life in East Germany and provides the standard justification for the one-dimensional organisation of its political institutions under the leadership of the SED (Socialist Unity Party). Although the constitution guarantees freedom of expression, freedom of assembly and freedom of the press (but not the right to strike or the right to emigrate), these freedoms may only be exercised 'in accordance with the basic principles' of the constitution. These basic principles are that the GDR has taken the path of socialism and communism, and that the working class and its Marxist–Leninist party are the leading forces in East German society (2). East German commentaries on the constitution thus make it clear that there can be no freedom to indulge in anti-socialist agitation or to express 'counter-revolutionary' views, since these would be 'against the rule of the people, against the leading role of the working class and its party, against the socialist foundations of the social and political order, and hence against social progress'.[1]

In practice these provisos ensure that the SED has the option of condemning as unconstitutional any individual or group activity of which it disapproves, and taking legal action against East German citizens who group together to demand that their 'constitutional rights' be observed.

Within the general constitutional framework for dealing with opposition, the SED has developed a wide range of specific mechanisms to ensure that it retains its leading role in East German society. Elections to the East German parliament, the *Volkskammer*, are so designed as to limit the voter's choice basically to accepting or rejecting a single list of candidates drawn up by the National Front, a body which embraces all political parties and the mass organisations and which has acknowledged the leading role of the SED. The close attention paid to who does and does not turn out to vote ensures a high poll, and the right to cast one's assenting vote openly effectively inhibits those wishing to make use of the right to cast their vote in the privacy of a booth, the assumption being that a secret vote is a vote against the list. Thus, in the elections of 1976 the poll was 98.58 per cent, and 99.86 per cent of votes cast were in favour of the list.[2]

Seats in the 500 strong *Volkskammer* are allocated according to a formula which is unaffected by the election results. Although the SED has just 127 seats, the fact that many members of the *Volkskammer* who represent mass organisations such as the trade unions and the FDJ (Free German Youth) are also SED members, guarantees the SED an indirect majority (at the start of the seventies, 292 votes).[3] Obtaining a majority, however, is not essential for the SED, since the statutes of the mass organisations and the four non-communist parties expressly acknowledge the leading role of the SED. The *Volkskammer* is not regarded by delegates as a forum for airing dissenting views, and a glance at the reports on the proceedings of the Twelfth Party Congress of the NDPD (National Democratic Party of Germany) in April 1982 confirms that its loyalty to the SED line is beyond question, with Erich Honecker's speech to the Congress on the need to strengthen and protect the socialist state being paraphrased back to him by the NDPD delegates in their speech of welcome.[4] Similarly, despite the involvement of the Evangelical Church in the unofficial peace movement in the GDR, the party for Christians, the CDU (Christian Democratic Union), has been at pains to express its disapproval of the movement and thus to remain in step with the SED.[5]

The one-dimensional organisation of political institutions also means that party resolutions are binding on all other political groups in the GDR. In order to ensure that these resolutions are adhered to the SED has established the principle that party members should occupy senior posts in the state apparatus and the economy, and that the Central Committee of the SED 'steers the work of the elected central organs and organisations of the state and society through the party groups established within them'. Hence the chairmen of the Council of State and the Council of Ministers as well as the Minister of National Defence and the President of the *Volkskammer* are all members of the Politburo. The parallel structure of the state and the party and the presence of party groups as watchdogs at all levels in the state and mass organisations also help to ensure that party resolutions are put into practice (3). Although there is evidence that in the past these resolutions were not always acted upon with the zeal expected by the party,[6] there is at present no sign of any serious challenge to the authority of the party emerging from within the state apparatus or mass organisations. Essentially they are instruments in the hands of the SED.

The dominant principle of political life in the GDR is democratic centralism. In theory this involves regular elections of all party organs and free discussion of party policy on the one hand, and decisions which are absolutely binding for all lower level party organs on the other. Western observers of the GDR generally portray the practice as a system of 'consultative authoritarianism' in which the democratic element takes second place to the centralist principle and is focused on how best to achieve predetermined goals.[7] Democratic centralism is not restricted to the SED, however, for it is also the principle which determines how the state is run and, just as importantly, how it relates to the party. A hierarchy thus emerges which embraces the SED, the other parties and mass organisations, as well as the entire state apparatus. And at the head of this hierarchy stands the SED leadership.

The SED also ensures its supremacy by means of its cadre policy. Cadres are highly qualified and politically reliable individuals, selected and trained to take on key posts not just within the party but in all spheres of public life (4). An essential element of this policy is the system based on nomenclature – an index of those posts which may only be filled by candidates who have been scrutinised by the party. Examples from within the party range from members of the Central Committee down to the secretaries of the basic organisations. In the state apparatus the party monitors and controls appointments from the level of ministers down to that of bank managers, and in the economy directors of the largest combines and directors of small-scale enterprises alike have to be confirmed in office by the party.[8]

Within the considerable limitations imposed on its members, the SED allows, indeed officially encourages, 'criticism and self-criticism'. It is the right of every party member to criticise the actions of party functionaries, and anyone suppressing such criticism may be called to account (3, 5). Whenever the party feels that internal criticism is becoming excessive, however, it reminds the membership that although the SED is a party of revolutionaries and therefore indulges in criticism and self-criticism, it is not a 'party of mere critics'. Moreover, one must distinguish between criticism and anti-socialist criticism.

Ultimately, it is argued, criticism must be judged not according to its severity or quantity, but according to whether or not it is loyal to the party and strengthens the socialist order.[9] Yet the Honecker era began with an ideological shift at the highest level in apparent recognition of the tensions and conflicts in East German society: at the Eighth Party Congress of June 1971 the official concept of a socialist human community (*Menschengemeinschaft*) was abandoned because, as Politburo member Kurt Hager later explained, it overestimated the closeness of the various social classes and strata. This shift inevitably tended to erode the complementary concept of an identity of interests between the individual and society as a whole, a concept which in turn was a key element in the argument that there could be no justifiable opposition in the GDR. With the apparent blessing of the Soviet Union the idea of a non-harmonious dialectic under socialism also became respectable.[10]

These ideological adjustments seemed to be the green light for a more frank discussion of East Germany's problems, yet they also had a part to play in reaffirming the leading role of the party in the post-Ulbricht period. Under Ulbricht, it was suggested, Marxism–Leninism (and, by extension, the party itself) had tended to take second place to disciplines which projected society as a self-regulating mechanism.[11] Reasserting the primacy of Marxism–Leninism and of the party thus meant 'repoliticising' society, with party and state emerging more clearly as in charge of social development. This in turn posed potential problems for the SED, since the party became more readily identifiable as responsible for any shortcomings of the system.[12]

Such was the ambiguous ideological backdrop against which opposition was to unfold during the Honecker era.

2 The Challenge of the Seventies and Eighties

THE WESTERN CONNECTION

Since Honecker took over from Ulbricht as party leader in May 1971 the GDR has been subjected to social, economic and political strains, many of which originated outside its borders, but which were aggravated by the internal problems of East German society. The earliest of these strains in the Honecker era arose from the increased contact with the West. Against the background of growing hostility between the Soviet Union and China, and rapprochement between America and China, the Soviet Union pushed the GDR into détente with the West. Thus in Honecker's first years as SED leader East and West Germany concluded a whole series of agreements, the most important of which was the Basic Treaty, signed in December 1972. These agreements meant *de facto*, though not formal, recognition of the East German state by the Federal Republic, but they also opened up East Germany to the West. The Traffic Agreement which came into force in October 1972 meant that West Germans could visit acquaintances or simply go touring in East Germany (7, 8). Moreover, an agreement of November 1972 meant that journalists from the Federal Republic and West Berlin – who had previously relied on East German media or gathered information during brief trips to East Germany – were now allowed to set up their own offices in East Berlin.[13]

Against the background of the 'Prague Spring' of 1968, which the Soviet Union saw partly as the result of increased contacts between Czechoslovakia and the West, the GDR attempted to counter this potentially disruptive West German penetration of its borders. Having failed to get paragraphs written into the Basic

Treaty which would have stemmed the flow of 'undesirable information' from the Federal Republic and failed also to dissuade East German citizens from tuning into West German broadcasts,[14] the SED stepped up its policy of *Abgrenzung* (developing a separate identity), according to which peaceful co-existence and economic co-operation with West Germany did not mean abandoning ideological warfare. While the 1974 constitution dropped all references to a single German nation and stressed the existence of two independent German states, the GDR also drew closer to the Soviet Union with the October 1975 Treaty of Friendship, Co-operation and Mutual Aid. Yet the basic fact remains that 'political stability [in the GDR] depends on economic success, but this success can only be achieved by means of co-operation with the Western industrial states, primarily the FRG. This requires the opening up of borders, which in turn allows new ideas into the GDR and encourages the hope that the system can be changed'.[15]

The East German propaganda campaign against its West German capitalist neighbour had to counter a flood of West Germans taking advantage of the new opportunities for travel in the GDR. Whereas in the period between February 1968 and October 1972 there had been 6.1 million trips by West German citizens to the GDR, the period from November 1972 (i.e. after the Traffic Agreement) to December 1979 saw no fewer than 22.3 million trips. The 1972 agreement on journalism meant that West German television reporters could interview well-known dissidents such as Robert Havemann and Stefan Heym, and they could also record the discontent of East Germans on the streets about such controversial issues as the April 1979 restrictions on East German citizens buying in Intershops. These interviews would then be broadcast from the West back to the GDR where 80 per cent of the country can receive West German programmes and an estimated 80 to 90 per cent of potential viewers watch them.[16] When Rudolf Bahro's attack on 'actually existing socialism' and the anonymous 'Manifesto of the League of Democratic Communists of Germany' were published in the Federal Republic, their contents were discussed at some length on West German television. Wolf Biermann's concert performance in Cologne which, according to the SED, justified depriving him of East German citizenship, was broadcast in its entirety on West German television as was the film version of Reiner Kunze's *Die wunderbaren*

Jahre, a radical indictment of the East German political system. Although East German intellectuals have little difficulty in obtaining copies of critical books published in the West, the film adaptations of such books ensure that they are brought to the attention of a wider audience in the GDR. Stefan Heym, whose most critical work has been published only in the West, but who frequently appears on West German television, feels confident that he is the most popular East German writer in the GDR, and he attributes this popularity to the Western media.[17]

The West German media may provide a forum for East German citizens who wish to criticise their own society in public, yet many who do make use of this forum find that their message becomes distorted in the process. Rudolf Bahro complained that the West German magazine, *Der Spiegel*, conveyed a one-sided impression of his book by giving prominence to his criticisms of the party apparatus,[18] and the peace campaigner, Roland Jahn, resented the way the West German media tried to exploit him for their own anti-communist ends.[19] Just how problematic the Western connection can become for writers who do not wish to see themselves cast in the role of victims of the East German political system, let alone as its opponents, was made clear by the correspondence arising out of the projected broadcast of a selection from the work of the East German writer, Stephan Hermlin (9). And even when more extreme critics of the East German regime use West German media to further their cause, they often do so reluctantly (10), a fact which tends to be overlooked by Western reporters who can see themselves as the focal point for the hopes of a long-suffering East German population.[20]

When the GDR's internal critics do resort to publicising their views in the West they also provide the SED with a weapon for its counter-attack. Hartmut König, Secretary of the FDJ Central Council, makes great play of the anti-socialist goals of West German publishing houses which are prepared to market the critical writings of East German authors regardless of their literary merit (11).[21] This type of criticism can be echoed by the SED's critics themselves. Stefan Heym's character, Hans Collin, a disillusioned writer, finds no comfort in the idea that there are probably Western publishers with an eye for a sensation, eager to get their hands on his memoirs.[22] This problem encourages East German critics publishing in the West to emphasise that they are writing primarily for an East German, not a West German audience.[23] And indeed, they can be confident that their work will find its way back across the border, a fact which also helps explain why Politburo members can sometimes feel obliged to answer criticism published in the West (12).

Since the great majority of East Germans can receive both East and West German radio and television programmes, they are generally considered to be better informed than most of their Eastern bloc neighbours. Yet if the West German media are essentially negative and critical in their treatment of the GDR, they can also present West Germany in an unfavourable light,[24] and in this way the official East German image of West Germany as the home of neo-nazism, militarism and unemployment can be reinforced by West German television.

However, East German research published in 1970 showed a reluctance among schoolchildren to accept the official East German image of the other Germany: 54.6 per cent of those asked thought that they could only find out the truth about West Germany by going there and seeing for themselves, an attitude which the East German researcher traced back to what he seemed to regard as an unfortunate 'tendency to adopt an empirical approach towards arriving at the truth'.[25] East German research also suggests that young people object to the one-sided media presentation in the GDR, and that the image of West Germany as the enemy is far from generally accepted: even before the massive increase in the number of West German visitors to the East only half of the 15-year-olds asked agreed with a researcher's statement that the Bonn government and the West German *Bundeswehr* were the greatest enemies of the German people and a threat to all peace-loving people.[26]

Whatever GDR citizens' actual views may be, it is clear that the West German media invasion of East Germany has worried the SED. Amid talk of 'electronic imperialism'[27] and Western media exploiting the fact that East Germany is open to the world (11), West German journalists are accused of working on behalf of secret services and of aiming to stir up internal opposition in the GDR (13). Hartmut König has spoken out against a situation in which young East Germans are confronted with reactionary and trivial Western films in which the realistic and revealing elements are outweighed by their 'idyllic picture of conditions in late capitalist society' (11), and a Politburo resolution of May 1977 attacks capitalist mass media in the hands of the bourgeoisie for manipulating the masses, obscuring the realities of a capitalist order based on exploitation and spreading confusion on political issues.[28] East German reports openly state that official propaganda is not effective and blame this state of affairs on West German television and radio.[29] So concerned is the SED about the West German media as an alternative source of information on current affairs that East German television regularly broadcasts a programme which 'corrects the distortions' in West German news broadcasts. Rudolf Bahro sums up the problem when he says that the Western media occupy the near total vacuum left by the party (14).

This situation has encouraged some establishment figures to argue in favour of greater internal discussion and, in the process, to draw closer to critics of the regime who have fallen out of favour. Shortly before being expelled from the Writers' Union, Klaus Poche wrote an open letter (published in *Die Zeit*, 1 June 1979) in which he pointed out that East Germany's problems could not be solved by sweeping them under the carpet and condemning anyone who mentioned them as an enemy. Robert Weimann, Vice-President of the Academy of Arts of the GDR, argued at about the same time that the GDR had to expect constant interference from the West German media, and he concluded:

> Against this interference a partial or delayed or merely didactic correction will not suffice. What is needed is a superior, realistic perspective on the complex totality of the actual social background of our experience. As soon as a certain (perhaps problematic) area or subject is omitted, it is left for the other side to take up and occupy. There is no such thing as neutral ground in the public realm of social experience.[30]

Although Weimann acknowledges the need for Max Schulz's distinction between open and public discussion (for security reasons) he is clearly arguing in the same direction as Poche. Moreover, among establishment critics such as the economic historian Jürgen Kuczynski as well as those who have left the GDR for the West, the standard appeal for silence on internal problems – based on the contention that to break silence is to aid the class enemy – seems to be carrying ever less weight (15).[31]

The West German media are also a source of irritation to the SED because they help create material wishes which cannot be satisfied. Although the GDR is proud of the fact that it has the highest standard of living in the Eastern bloc, its citizens tend to take the Federal Republic as their point of comparison, and here the gap is considerable. Stefan Heym's impressions about East Germans' attitudes to the material aspects of life in West Germany (16) are confirmed by GDR researchers who have registered among young East Germans a preference for Western media, lifestyles and consumer goods.[32]

The East German authorities have responded to this challenge not just by stepping up their propaganda campaigns against the West,[33] but also by imposing restrictions on foreign journalists. According to a regulation introduced in February 1973, just four months after the agreement allowing Western journalists to open offices in East Berlin, foreign correspondents were obliged to give notice of any trips outside East Berlin and to obtain permission for visits to public offices and enterprises, as well as for interviews with leading figures. Foreign journalists were also forbidden to 'defame' the GDR, its institutions and leading figures,[34] and 1975 saw the first West German journalist expelled from East Berlin under this regulation.[35] Others followed, and in 1979 the street interviews conducted by West German journalists on the new Intershop ruling resulted in a further regulation obliging foreign correspondents to gain permission for interviews of any kind.[36] This led to the expulsion of ZDF reporter Peter van Loyen in May 1979 after he had recorded a 'statement' on censorship by Stefan Heym (17). The East German authorities saw van Loyen's action as contrary to the Helsinki principle of non-interference in the internal affairs of other states, while the protest from West German journalists and the expressions of concern from the Federal Government invoked the principle, also stated in the Helsinki agreement, that working conditions for foreign correspondents should be improved.[37]

THE POLISH FACTOR

The Western media ensure that the GDR has an alternative source of information about the latest unrest in Poland which began in July 1980 with strikes over price rises for meat and by August escalated into demands for free trade unions. Soon after this the SED took steps to reduce the flow of visitors to and from Poland to a trickle. The party newspaper, *Neues Deutschland*, quickly found it necessary to abandon its initial silence on the troubles in Poland and followed the Soviet line that Western imperialist circles were attempting to influence events there and to undermine a socialist state. While *Neues Deutschland* was busy attacking Solidarity leaders as 'counter-revolutionaries', Edward Gierek was replaced at the head of the Polish United Workers' Party (PUWP) by Stanislaw Kania who declared in public that the mass protests by the workers were not directed against socialism or the party but against violations of socialist principles, poor government and mistakes in party policy. Kania added that he was willing to work together with Solidarity.[38]

On these points the Polish leader had more in common with pro-Solidarity East German dissidents such as Stefan Heym than with the SED: in a statement broadcast on West German television and radio in January 1982 Heym argued that Solidarity was not the cause of the troubles but rather the consequence of shortcomings in the social and political system, and that with 9½ million members, Solidarity had to be regarded as the working class (18). Within the space of just a few months the PUWP had acknowledged the workers' right to strike and to form independent trade unions – concessions which were unthinkable for East Germany's political leaders. Moreover, within the PUWP the principle of democratic centralism was being called into question, and in the Polish parliament no-votes were being recorded. Poland seemed to be heading in the direction which the GDR's internal left-wing critics had been advocating for their own country for many years.

Yet despite reports in mid 1981 of clashes in the GDR between young demonstrators and police and of strikes and protests in support of Solidarity, the 'Polish fever' does not seem to be spreading to East Germany. Traditional anti-Polish sentiment in East Germany has been exploited by the SED,[39] and there is some evidence of resentment among the East German population over the economic aid it provides for Poland and over the disruption of production in the GDR when Polish factories supplying East German industry are unable to keep to their delivery dates.[40] For their part, the Poles appear to resent what they see as East Germany's total loyalty to the Soviet Union. Although there are some 20 000 Poles working in the GDR, traditional hostilities and an awareness of their relatively humble position (largely as unskilled workers) make them an unlikely catalyst for any large-scale protest movement within the East German workforce.

At a more subtle level, however, one can see how events in Poland have caused the SED to reflect upon its policies. Elected bodies at all levels are being urged to ensure that their decisions are fully discussed with constituents.[41] The initiative for this campaign stemmed from the Tenth Party Congress in April 1981 when Erich Honecker called for 'determined and imaginative public relations work to acquaint the individual with party and government policy and strengthen the bond between the electorate and its representatives'.[42] At a follow-up conference in Zwickau, in February 1982, speakers emphasised the need for the media to highlight the work of elected representatives and to show how suggestions from the electorate could change policies.[43]

THE ECONOMIC CHALLENGE

The record of opposition in Eastern bloc countries reveals a clear link between economic problems and political instability. The link has taken on particular significance in the GDR under Honecker which has seen a shift of emphasis from an ideological to an economic justification of the leading role of the party, followed by mounting problems for the economy.

The shift of emphasis has prompted observers to apply Antonin Liehm's concept of a 'new social contract' to the GDR. This is an unwritten agreement according to which the party guarantees the people a secure existence and a rising standard of living and in return expects them to accept certain limitations on their political freedom and to acknowledge, or at any rate passively accept, the supremacy of the party.[44] If Western commentators often interpret this switch as proof that the SED has been unable to justify its position in ideological terms to the population,[45] they also generally agree that the GDR has hitherto succeeded in keeping its end of the bargain, and that this success has probably been the single most important factor in preventing acute social discontent.[46]

However, whereas economic reports for the first half of the seventies showed healthy annual growth rates, the mid-seventies saw the start of dramatic price rises for the energy (particularly oil) the GDR imported from the Soviet Union. The targets for growth in national income set out in the five year plan for 1976–80 were not achieved, and living standards failed to rise in line with popular expectations. For 1983 the party settled for the lowest increase in national income since 1966 – 4.2 per cent.

Although talk in the West of the East German economy 'with its back to the wall' tends to underestimate its ability to survive crises, there is no denying that it faces a host of serious problems which are not susceptible to short-term solutions and which will at best probably rule out any significant rise in living standards for the rest of the eighties. Restrictions on the volume of oil available from the Soviet Union, delays in the installation of nuclear reactors, and cuts in investment expenditure tend to rule out any programme of economic expansion. Moreover the GDR's debts to the West and to the Soviet Union could only be managed in 1982 through drastic cuts in imports from the West, a policy which resulted in shortages at home for private consumers and industry alike.

The fact that the SED has been prepared to cut long-term investment programmes for the sake of maintaining living standards in the short term suggests that it is aware of the potential for unrest in the GDR.[47]

3 Defining Opposition

Discussions in the West about exactly what constitutes opposition in the Soviet bloc and about the most appropriate terms for the various forms of opposition have yet to produce a generally accepted model for the Soviet Union, let alone one which can be applied in its entirety to the East German situation. The problems which inevitably arise from any attempt to define opposition are not merely of semantic interest, for they reveal something about the way East German society works.

Definitions of opposition based on East German legal criteria follow on logically from the GDR view that there can be no justifiable opposition in socialist countries (1) and from the resultant one-dimensional organisation of political institutions.[48] Yet as a practical guide these definitions seem inadequate when one considers the open-ended nature of GDR laws on offences such as 'agitation against the State' or 'taking up illegal contacts', and their often unpredictable applicaton (6). After Wolf Biermann was deprived of East German citizenship, Jurek Becker (a signatory to the petition against the action who was subsequently expelled from the SED) argued that 'the inhabitants of a country have to be told precisely what kind of remarks might result in them having their citizenship withdrawn' (10). Becker's point is not made without irony, since it was widely felt at the time that the move against Biermann had been agreed upon even before his controversial concert performance in Cologne. Yet Becker does draw attention to the fact that the East German laws relating to 'anti-socialist activity' are defined and applied in different ways at different times. Moreover, the June 1979 reform of the Penal Code gave the courts greater freedom in interpreting and applying such laws by dispensing with the need to consider the 'subjective element', i.e. the intentions of the accused.[49]

The vagueness of legal criteria has left Western observers free to define opposition either as 'political resistance for the legal existence of which there is no basis',[50] or as an attempt at relatively open and relatively legal activity.[51]

Closely linked with the discussion of opposition based on notions of legality and illegality is the approach which focuses on the reaction of the SED as an indicator of opposition: opposition is whatever the party leadership takes action against at any given moment. Such a definition is useful since it implicitly acknowledges that the contents of opposition, the limits of what will be tolerated, are ever changing. Yet if a hostile reaction from the party can be taken as a sure guide to what is opposition, the absence of a hostile reaction cannot be taken as a sign that the party regards a certain activity as entirely acceptable. There can be little doubt that the unofficial peace movement is a considerable source of irritation to the SED, yet much of its activity is permitted: although the platform of the peace campaigners differs radically from that of the officially sponsored Peace Council, some unofficial peace groups have been allowed to join in demonstrations organised by the FDJ while others have been broken up forcibly.[52] Such inconsistency on the part of the authorities hardly means that the party does not see the unofficial peace movement as a source of opposition, but rather that it is confronted with the problem of dealing with a phenomenon which embraces not just a small group of intellectuals but some thousands of East German citizens whilst seeking to retain what Bahro has called 'a minimum of international reputation'.[53]

The party's reaction depends then only in part upon the contents of opposition activity. Apart from the scale of opposition and the fear of international repercussions, the social status of the individuals involved also influences the party's reaction. The point is illustrated by the very different treatment meted out to signatories of the Biermann petition (10, 19): while the less well-known signatories were imprisoned, more prominent intellectuals such as Stephan Hermlin escaped with a 'severe reprimand'.[54] A widely acknowledged past as an anti-fascist who has suffered at the hands of the Nazis also inhibits the party from taking legal action against an individual.[55]

Another kind of social status is prominence in the West: civil rights campaigners who do not have access to the Western media are more likely to be prosecuted than those who do.[56] There is clearly such a thing as excessive prominence in the West, however: Rudolf Bahro explained that he left East Germany partly because if he had stayed and supported certain reform activities the security service would have moved against those involved.[57]

The reaction of the party is also influenced by economic circumstances. In periods of economic experimentation 'ideological trial balloons', involving a measure of decentralisation and worker participation, may be permitted in the expectation that they could improve the performance of the GDR economy.[58]

The problem of opposition has also been approached by applying the term dissenter or dissident to 'anybody who holds a critical or heretical view compared to the official Party line'.[59] This definition avoids the problems associated with legal criteria and looks beyond the reaction of the party, yet it presupposes the existence of a clear official line which may in fact not always exist: under the impact of the unofficial peace movement it would be difficult to say, for example, what the official line is on pacifism. While it is traditionally scorned for rejecting the possiblity of a 'just war', the party's wish to avoid a confrontation with the Evangelical Church has led to a blurring of the official line and hints from the Politburo that there is room for collaboration between Marxists, Christians and pacifists.[60]

The notion of opposition as deviation from the official line becomes particularly awkward if one tries to set out in any detail what counts as deviation. A recent attempt by Shtromas to provide a theoretical framework for a study of opposition in the Soviet Union suggests that, regardless of what dissidents may say or how officialdom reacts, there is an objective criterion for assessing dissidence: those who advocate a socialist market economy, a system of strict socialist legality, creative freedom, or any other kind of genuine autonomy of social function or of a group from the total control of the party are objectively striving for 'system-rejective' change, although they may think they want 'within-system change'.[61] This approach is notable not least because it makes the valid point that it is insufficient to take critics' declarations of loyalty to the system at face value. Thus, while many of those involved in the unofficial peace movement characterise their stance not as opposition but as 'critical solidarity'[62] and Western observers have begun to portray the attitudes of peace, ecology and women's groups as signs not of opposition but of an 'alternative political culture',[63] it is essential to bear in mind the nature of the system in which they operate. The assumption is that in a society where the ruling party's demands are absolute, even the mildest forms of criticism are ultimately 'system-rejective' since they inevitably conflict with those demands.

Yet, when applied to the GDR, the idea that deviation from the party line in the form of advocacy of autonomy of social function can be taken as an indication of dissidence underestimates the scope for internal debate, and by this scheme most forms of 'criticism and self-criticism' would ultimately be classified as dissidence. In the Honecker period, many debates have taken place in which, for example, social scientists have taken up views which are quite clearly at odds with mainstream thinking, yet it would be wrong to label them dissidents. In fact, there is a sense in which their ideas are welcomed by the party, for they contribute to its standing by giving substance to the concept of criticism and self-criticism. Just as importantly, this approach tends to lump together at the radical end of the spectrum all forms of criticism, and thus to blur important distinctions such as that between individuals who make public their total rejection of the existing system and those who are intent on working behind the scenes to make that system more efficient or equitable.

It has been argued that there is a distinction to be drawn between opposition and dissent, with the former referring to those who wish to replace a communist regime by some other, and the latter to those who merely wish to assert the right freely to criticise the existing regime.[64] By these criteria there is virtually no opposition in the GDR today, only dissent. While this is a useful reminder that the GDR has changed since the June 1953 Uprising, it scarcely appeals to common sense to dispense entirely with the term opposition when discussing the current scene. Moreover, Shtromas's point, although overstated, does highlight the difficulty of establishing a dividing line between opposition and dissent.

Given the vagueness of legal criteria, the fact that the party may not always move against opposition, and the possibility of the 'official line' becoming flexible when challenged, opposition can perhaps best be thought of as unwelcome pressure for significant political change. In the GDR under Honecker, opposition has come from the following sources:

1. Dissident intellectuals who wish to stay in the GDR and who claim the right to criticise the regime (generally from a socialist standpoint), to recall it to its duty and to advocate alternative policies for it to pursue.[65] Dissident intellectuals find themselves in a more or less permanent public battle with the authorities and regularly make use of the Western media to state their case. Their position usually clashes so radically with mainstream party thinking that they are in fact striving for 'system-rejective' change even though they may claim to be seeking 'within-system' change. In the Honecker period, there have been just a few individuals who are readily classifiable as dissidents, but these few have attracted considerable attention in the West.

A grey area is occupied by a far larger group of intellectuals – mainly academics and writers – who, unlike the dissidents, are allowed to disseminate their ideas within the GDR, are often members of officially sponsored organisations and can receive public honours despite the fact that their views are controversial. Doubtless, the party regards this group with suspicion, and rightly finds what it has to say uncomfortably close to the dissidents' message. This group's claim not to be in opposition to the regime has more validity than similar claims coming from dissidents, but it will be necessary to consider what it has in common with the dissidents in order to appreciate the significance of opposition in the Honecker period.[66]

2. GDR citizens who wish to leave the GDR and to take up permanent residence in the West. Estimates of the numbers involved range from 150 000 to a staggering half a million out of a total population of around 17 million.[67] The motives of those wishing to renounce East German citizenship include hopes of a better economic future, rejection of the political system, often from a Christian or non-socialist standpoint, and the wish to be reunited with members of the family in the West. Some of those who are not permitted to leave the GDR form themselves into self-help groups.

3. The unofficial peace movement. Although the movement lacks central leadership, the involvement of the Evangelical and, to a

lesser extent, the Roman Catholic Church gives it a degree of independence from the state and cohesion to act as an autonomous group.[68]

Before looking at these in more detail it is worth noting that two forms of opposition which often feature in Western analyses of Eastern European socialist countries are virtually absent in the GDR under Honecker. The first is 'power struggle', involving one leader ousting another at national, local or regional level, and it is usually accompanied by some fundamental question of ideology or policy.[69] Honecker's own rise to power in 1971, followed by the consolidation of his position through promotion of his supporters to the Politburo, is the outstanding example in this category for the GDR, and the fundamental question of ideology was relations with the West. Honecker's elevation marked the resolution of this issue, and although it is likely that other members of the Politburo can influence Honecker via their private lines to the Kremlin, there has been no clear evidence of a power struggle at this level since he took office.[70]

The second form of opposition largely absent from the GDR in the seventies and eighties is 'pragmatic dissent'. This is pressure and resistance constantly exercised by scientists, technicians and experts in the name of greater efficiency, material progress and military might.[71]

As we have seen, one of the most distinctive ideological shifts following Honecker's rise to power was the reassertion of the primacy of Marxism-Leninism over the individual sciences. This included cybernetics, information theory and operational research, all of which were and are seen as crucial for increasing economic efficiency.[72] In practical terms this meant that new members of the Politburo tended to be political rather than economic experts,[73] and Politburo candidates who had served under Ulbricht as economic specialists lost their seats. At this level Honecker has been able to make use of economic experts such as Günter Mittag and Willi Stoph in times of economic difficulty without subjecting himself to unwelcome pressure for political reform.[74]

Western commentators have suggested that in highly developed societies such as the GDR economic experts become indispensable and tend to stimulate opposition. As long as the trend towards an elaborate consumer and highly technological economy persists, pragmatic dissent is likely to increase in the Eastern bloc. This theory began to take shape in the sixties around the concept of an 'institutionalised counter-élite',[75] yet in the seventies and eighties there are few signs of programmes for economic reform being formulated or implemented in ways which could be viewed as 'oppositional', and to portray them as such would be to underestimate the flexibility of the SED in matters of ideology and policy and to overestimate the impact of the technical élite.

There is certainly evidence of discontent among the 'scientific and technical intelligentsia', and one of their number, Rudolf Bahro, has provided the most coherent and persuasive attack of recent times on the GDR's economic system. Yet although fellow economists may privately share his views they have yet to translate their ideas into political action. Bahro's doctoral thesis sheds a revealing light on their attitude: whereas Bahro calls for fundamental reforms in the way work is organised, the cadre economists he interviewed in preparation for the thesis pursue the more modest and conformist goals of greater responsibility and less bureaucracy.[76] Although their dissatisfaction and their relative insusceptibility to the conditions of the new social contract[77] make it conceivable that, as has happened in other Eastern bloc countries during periods of upheaval, the 'technocrats' could sympathise with demands for political and economic reform, at present they are clearly reluctant to risk what has been termed 'politically and socially unprotected behaviour'.[78] Their 'minimal group solidarity' has been traced back to their dissimilar class backgrounds, educational experiences, salaries, relationships with authority and political orientation.[79]

In sum, there is little reason to revise the view formulated a decade ago that 'if, and as, the "technocrats" increase their numbers and influence in the centres of political decision it will be by quiet and gradual steps, of which the participants themselves will scarcely be aware. . . . The managerial revolution will be no revolution at all but a barely visible process of alliance building, infiltration and absorption'.[80]

4 The Major Forms of Opposition under Honecker

DISSIDENT INTELLECTUALS

The seventies and eighties have witnessed a high level of critical activity among left-wing intellectuals and often sharp reprisals from the party. In the seventies, the focus tended to be on the issues of intellectual freedom and the shortcomings of East German socialism. Following Wolf Biermann's expatriation in November 1976 for 'gross dereliction of his duties as a citizen of the GDR' and the protest petition (19), over one hundred well-known writers and artists made their way to the West, some after periods of imprisonment. Robert Havemann was placed under house arrest after writing an article for *Der Spiegel* in which he objected to Biermann's treatment (12), and in 1977 Rudolf Bahro was arrested after publishing his uncompromising account of 'actually existing socialism'. In 1979, Stefan Heym and Havemann were prosecuted and fined heavily for publishing in the West without permission, and the eight writers who protested against Heym's treatment, together with Heym himself, were expelled from the Writers' Union.[81]

In the 1980s, criticism from intellectuals has tended to be directed towards what is seen as the increasing militarisation of GDR society. The high points of this critical activity were the two Berlin meetings (December 1981 in East Berlin and April 1983 in West Berlin) of writers and scientists from East and West to discuss how to further the cause of peace. Both meetings were given extensive coverage on West German television, and many prominent East Germans aired their criticisms of GDR peace policy.

The three most prominent and coherent dissidents of the period are Robert Havemann, Rudolf Bahro and Stefan Heym. Havemann, a former member of the *Volkskammer* and Professor of Physical Chemistry at the Humboldt University in East Berlin, remained in the GDR until his death in 1982. Rudolf Bahro was a party member and economist whose attack on the SED's brand of socialism in *Die Alternative* resulted in his arrest and imprisonment. After his release in 1979 he moved to West Germany. Of the three, only Stefan Heym, the journalist and novelist, remains in the GDR and continues to arouse controversy as an outspoken critic of the regime. These three dissidents are distinctive because they published their radical criticisms in the West while they were still in the GDR, where they could publish nothing; they were intent on staying in the GDR for as long as possible, and all three were prosecuted.[82]

What are the main criticisms of the GDR from the dissident left? Bahro's argument that the establishment of 'socialism' in the GDR did not end the domination of one group of men over another and that alienation and subordination continue is echoed throughout the writings of the SED's radical critics (20).[83] Bahro contends that abolition of the private ownership of the means of production did not make them into 'the property of the people'. Instead the whole of East German society is dispossessed and confronted with a state apparatus which determines what will be produced and how it will be allocated.[84]

For Bahro, the working population in socialist countries can only exert a negative influence on events by the threat of a mass uprising.[85] Such sudden flare-ups result from the fact that the political and social order has no institutions for coping with tensions as they arise.[86] His characterisation of 'socialism as it actually exists' as an order based on the division of labour, social inequality, elimination of the rights obtained in the bourgeois period, and cadres with responsibility only to those in higher authority (21) parallels Havemann's criticism of the 'Stalinist superstructure'.[87] The reality of Eastern bloc socialism, it is argued, is damaging the cause of socialism in capitalist countries,[88] and is best described as protosocialism, socialism in the larval phase (21) or as the first stage of socialism.[89]

The experience of National Socialism and the idea of the GDR as a great experiment in socialism are recurring themes for Havemann and Heym. In 1943, Havemann was actually convicted of high treason and sentenced to death by the Nazis, and as a young socialist Stefan Heym had to leave Germany in 1933. These experiences make them genuine in their gratitude to the Soviet Union which they see as the conqueror of fascism.[90]

The Nazi experience led Havemann to believe for a long time after the war that Germany needed an 'energetic education towards democracy', a view which he later rejected as arrogant, dangerous and at the heart of the Stalinist system.[91] In practice this political conviction meant overlooking the realities of the early years of the GDR's existence and fixing one's gaze on the distant goal of communism.[92] Havemann agreed that he followed the official party line on the June 1953 Uprising (as inspired by Western secret service agencies) against his better knowledge,[93] and when he looked back on his time as a member of the *Volkskammer* he could condone the electoral system for the 'difficult' early years, but not for the present.[94] Jurek Becker characterises the mentality Havemann came to reject as 'wrong-headed solidarity' (10). Stefan Heym can acknowledge the progressive nature of the social and economic reforms in the immediate post-war period,[95] and where undemocratic methods were employed Heym was prepared to assume that these would be restricted to the period of transition.[96] Heym opted to live in the GDR in 1953, and he freely admits that he went there with many illusions. He is perhaps more willing than Havemann to argue in favour of the rough justice of the fifties which he sees in retrospect as a necessary response to the concerted anti-socialist campaigns of the period.[97]

The events which prompted critical intellectuals to abandon such thinking are the turning points in the GDR's history. The June 1953 Uprising destroyed Heym's illusions,[98] and for Havemann the crunch came with Khrushchev's denunciation of Stalin's crimes at the Twentieth CPSU Congress of 1956.[99] For the younger generation of critics, the invasion of Czechoslovakia in 1968 marked the end of an 'experiment in democratic socialism' and the onset of disillusionment.[100]

Yet the early reluctance to speak out against the realities of socialism in the GDR was rarely immediately replaced by simple anti-party polemic. Bahro, Havemann and Heym all passed through intermediate positions, attempting to expand the area of permissible debate. Their particular attempts ended in failure, however, and Bahro eventually switched to the view that East German society could not be helped by helping the Politburo apparatus. Instead, criticism should be aimed at the apparatus itself.[101]

Among the SED's radical critics it is striking just how consistently religious imagery is invoked. Bahro writes of the 'quasi-theocratic' state,[102] and the party is presented as a church in need of a Reformation.[103] Its claim to understand the future is mocked as 'divine omniscience'.[104] Propaganda is likened to prayer,[105] 'revisionism' to a 'mortal sin', and critics such as Biermann are characterised as heretics in the eyes of the party.[106] Heym depicts senior party members as 'high priests',[107] and Jürgen Fuchs, a supporter of the Biermann petition, attacks party leaders by comparing them to a pope who comes to believe he is Jesus Christ in person.[108] This criticism in religious terms suggests that the GDR's dissidents share a cause with the Eurocommunists: in a famous speech at the Conference of Communist and Workers' Parties in East Berlin (June 1976) the General Secretary of the Spanish Communist Party, Santiago Carillo, declared that 'for years Moscow . . . was our Rome. We talked of the Great Socialist October Revolution as if it were our Christmas. Those were our childhood years. Now we have grown up'.[109]

If this religious imagery implicitly opposes the party's claim to have instituted the rule of the majority according to a rational ideology with the suggestion that it has in fact established an authoritarian, irrational order, the recent involvement of the Evangelical and Catholic Churches in the unofficial peace movement has made left-wing intellectuals think again. The critical habit of comparing the party to a church must have made many socialists wary of seeing the churches in the GDR as advocates of liberal reform, yet Stefan Heym asserts that in East Germany the clerics are now talking like revolutionaries while the functionaries are talking like priests.[110]

A common theme in left-wing criticism of the GDR is that it takes its lead from capitalism. Havemann made out this case, seeing East Germany struggling to follow capitalism at the very time when the capitalist order was revealing itself as inadequate and even starting to crumble. He saw definitions of communism based on wealth as a dead end. East Germany had taken to worshipping the idols of the consumer society, and its ultimate goal was the convergence of socialism and capitalism (22, 23).[111] This criticism of the GDR is extended into spheres other than the economy: taking its economic lead from capitalism means for Bahro that the social structure of East Germany is essentially the same as under capitalism, the shared characteristics being division of labour and division into classes.[112] Havemann saw the economic rivalry with the West as responsible for the drive for higher levels of production which in turn were achieved by capitalist-style exploitation of the workforce.[113]

The capitalist orientation of the East German economy is not seen as restricted to the decision-makers. Although Havemann could at one point argue that the East German population wanted more freedom, not more consumer goods,[114] he could elsewhere scarcely conceal his distaste for the materialism of the *Kleinbürger und Spießer*.[115] This ambiguous attitude reflects an awareness among many intellectuals that they might be out of step with the majority of the population, and it is interesting to note that, according to East German research, the car, object of so much scorn from the dissidents (22), features near the top of the list of priorities for GDR citizens.[116] Bahro acknowledges the enormity of the task facing any would-be reformers of East German society when he insists on the need for a 'revolution in people's requirements',[117] and he fears that the growing material expectations among the population will mean that the GDR will always regard itself as too poor to progress to communism (21).[118] He interprets the SED's linking of economic and social policy as an attempt to cultivate materialism in order to direct the population away from social reform.[119] The party also works towards this end unintentionally inasmuch as East Germans 'switch off' as soon as the official mouthpieces start up. The tragedy is that the party has turned the population against revolutionary Marxism and left it in an ideological vacuum which is then promptly filled by Western ideology (14).[120]

True socialism, Havemann argued, had aims which were fundamentally different from those of capitalism,[121] and Bahro makes a plea for self-development to take priority over the promises of 'bread and circuses' contained in every five-year plan.[122] Criticism of the capitalist path can be extended into an environmentalist attack on wasted resources and the ideology of unlimited growth,[123] yet it is interesting to note the occasional positive references to capitalist efficiency as a point of contrast with the accounts of the inefficiencies of the GDR economy.[124]

As a general principle, however, left-wing critics in the GDR are also harsh critics of the West. Bahro describes the capitalist economic system as anarchy,[125] and Havemann had little doubt that it was time for the bourgeoisie to leave the stage of history, since socialism offered the only hope of a solution to the world's problems.[126] Stefan Heym agrees that there is no reasonable alternative to socialism (18). In his polemic against the Federal Republic Havemann was just as vehement as in anything he had to say about the GDR, the main targets in the West being mass unemployment, anti-communism, the revival of fascism, and *Berufsverbote*.[127] Havemann remained convinced that the GDR was 'the better German state',[128] and that it was one step nearer socialism than the West because the means of production were no longer in private hands.[129]

Left-wing critics who dismiss any pro-Western attacks on the GDR as 'anachronistic'[130] look instead to the Czechoslovakia of 1968 and to Eurocommunism for their models. The 'Prague Spring' is seized upon as an attempt to fuse socialism and democracy,[131] as a step towards completing the socialist revolution which had the support of the population,[132] and as a step which the GDR now needs to take.[133] The two models for reform in Czechoslovakia, one emanating from party members under Dubček and based on single-party rule, the other popular among Czech intellectuals and proposing a multi-party state,[134] are reflected in the differences among the left in East Germany about a possible future political framework: whereas Bahro argues that a multi-party system would serve no purpose in a post-capitalist society,[135] Havemann advocated at least one opposition party.[136]

If 1968 is a model it is an ambiguous one: Havemann described it as both a victory and a defeat.[137] It generated optimism, since it showed that 'Stalinism' could be overcome and showed too how quickly socialist democracy could grow.[138] Bahro claims that the effect of 1968 extended into the SED, with hundreds of thousands of party members in sympathy with its aims, and he concludes from this that the potential for similar change exists in the GDR.[139]

Yet Biermann points out that the abrupt end to the Czech experiment made many abandon hope of political change and seek an entirely private form of satisfaction,[140] and Bahro is forced to agree.[141]

Left-wing dissidents in the GDR have often been encouraged and supported in their conflicts with the party by the Eurocommunists of Italy, France and Spain. For the Spanish Communist Party, Carillo argued in public that Bahro should be allowed to express his views without fear of reprisals,[142] and the communist parties of Spain, France and Italy all protested at Biermann's expatriation. The Conference of Communist and Workers' Parties in 1976 and the Karl Marx Conference of 1983, both held in East Berlin, must have done much to stimulate debate in the GDR on Eurocommunism, for at these conferences Western European and Japanese communists made it clear that political and ideological pluralism were essential elements of socialism. Moreover, the proceedings of these conferences were published in *Neues Deutschland*.[143]

Havemann and Bahro insist on the need to apply Marxist methods in their analyses of East German society. What both claim to offer is not merely a list of reforms East German socialism ideally needs to undergo, but an account of the forces currently at work in society which will establish 'genuine' socialism.[144] The message is that their criticisms of the present and projections of a future society are significant because they are based on a Marxist analysis of how society will develop. For Bahro it is the 'intellectualising' of the workforce which generates 'emancipatory interests' (21), and Western observers saw this non-Utopianism as the most important feature of his *Alternative*.[145] For Havemann it is the tension between the 'state and the masses' which will bring about the 'second phase' of the socialist revolution.[146]

Yet Bahro and Havemann are aware of the shortcomings of their analyses: in *Die Alternative* Bahro asserts that Marx's categorical imperative that any order must be overthrown in which man is a degraded, enslaved, abandoned, humiliated being must take precedence over any scientific proof that such a revolution is possible.[147] Bahro also reflects that his strategy for a communist alternative in *Die Alternative* is the shakiest and most incomplete part of his book, and that it runs the risk of Utopianism.[148] And it is interesting to note that after the initial enthusiasm for Bahro's theories had given way to an assessment of their validity, Western observers of the GDR found it difficult to go along with his account of precisely where the pressure for political reform would come from.[149]

The term 'Utopianism' in the sense of non-Marxist speculation on a better future also pervades Havemann's work, and on occasion he could apply the term to his own suggested reforms for East German society (23). He could go further still and argue that *Bahro* was indulging in pipe-dreams when he called for a League of Communists to be established (23). Bahro implicitly returned the compliment, for whereas Havemann saw the call for individual freedom growing louder as the standard of living rises, Bahro looked with dismay at the 'material insatiability' in the GDR which gets in the way of political progress.[150] There is then an element of morale boosting as well as of Marxist conviction underlying Bahro's objections to what he calls defeatist social analysis,[151] and Havemann's conclusion that a Prague Spring is a historical inevitability in all socialist countries.[152]

Perhaps because of their uncertainty about the validity of their 'Marxist' analyses of the long-term changes coming to East German society, Havemann and Bahro also put forward a series of specific suggestions for the short term. Havemann's 'policy of small steps' is an appeal to the party to permit more open and wide-ranging discussion, and it follows on from his fear that Bahro's large-scale reforms are totally unrealistic (23). Essentially it is an appeal for liberalisation rather than democratisation. Bahro himself criticises reform efforts which focus on human or civil rights as 'superficial', since they do not go to the socio-economic base of the existing order,[153] yet he is obliged to acknowledge the contribution such movements make towards more thoroughgoing change, and he advises would-be reformers in the GDR to insist on their civil rights (21).

In the context of the GDR under Honecker it has not been possible for the left-wing critics we have looked at to gain acceptance for what they saw as positions of critical solidarity. Ultimately frustrated by the constraints on permissible debate, they took on the characteristics of the dissident.

REJECTION OF THE GDR

The GDR is a signatory to various international agreements which many of its citizens view as granting them rights which go beyond those laid down in the East German constitution. The main agreement of this kind in the Honecker period is the Final Act of August 1975 which emerged as the end product of the Helsinki Conference on Security and Co-operation in Europe. The conference was attended by the Soviet Union, the USA and East and West European countries, including the two Germanies, and the Final Act confirmed that human rights were to be respected, and applications from individuals wishing to be reunited with their families abroad would be dealt with in a positive and humanitarian spirit (24). In addition, the UN Universal Declaration of Human Rights (Article 13) and the International Covenant on Civil and Political Rights (Article 12) state that individuals have the right to leave their own country.[154]

In a sense, the wish of the 1 to 3 per cent of the East German population to quit their country for the West can perhaps best be described not as opposition, but as an alternative to opposition since they do not aim to change the system. To this extent the Western tendency to apply the label 'civil rights movement' to this group is misleading, and the possibility of leaving one Germany for the other is in fact crucially important in explaining the general *absence* of a large-scale civil rights movement in the GDR.[155] Yet the majority of those wishing to leave have not been allowed to do so, and some have resorted to oppositional methods such as publicising their cause in the West, criticising the GDR's record on basic rights, forming themselves into self-help groups and attempting to leave the GDR illegally. As a result many are charged with taking up illegal contacts, agitation against the state and attempting to cross the border illegally. The sentences handed out for these offences range from one to five years,[156] and this group of citizens trying to get to the West forms the majority of the political prisoners in the GDR.[157] Moreover, the growth in the number of East Germans wishing to 'vote with their feet' has sparked off an awkward discussion within the Evangelical Church, with church synods not merely urging their parishioners to stay, but also urging the authorities to create the social and political conditions which will encourage them to do so.[158]

The pro-Western attitude of many of those wishing to leave the GDR marks them off from the dissidents (25). They regard the Federal Republic not only as a forum for presenting their criticisms of East Germany, but also as the better Germany. The dissidents can look favourably upon the thoroughgoing social, political and economic reforms in the early stages of the GDR's existence, viewing them as necessary steps to prevent any recurrence of fascism, and they can criticise 'neo-fascism' in West Germany. Some of those who wish to leave, however, argue that the GDR is continuing many of the traditions of Nazi Germany. They are often anti-communist, referring to the GDR as the 'zone' (i.e. Soviet Zone of Occupation), and interpreting the population's compliance as the result of a rule of terror (26). Not surprisingly, these fundamental differences between dissidents and those applying to leave the GDR mean that there is little solidarity between the two groups, and a decision to try to leave can meet with hostility from the dissidents.[159]

The GDR citizens who wish to go to the West come from all walks of life and all age groups. Statistical information compiled on the West German side about the 31 194 East Germans who emigrated to the Federal Republic in the first half of 1984 suggests that their motives may not have been exclusively political or to do with being reunited with family members living in the West.[160] The largest single group (8178) was made up of 25–34-year-olds, and the second largest (5911) of 35–44-year-olds. Seventy per cent of those who left were of employable age, a figure which is appreciably higher than for the East German population as a whole (64 per cent in 1982). In terms of occupation, the largest groups were mechanics, fitters, administrators, engineers, health service workers, salespersons and transport workers, and most came from the lower grades of these jobs. Given the fact that up to 1 million skilled workers in the GDR are currently not able to obtain employment which matches their relatively high level of qualifications, and that pay levels in many service industries are notoriously low, these figures suggest that many of those who left did so because they thought their economic prospects would be better in the Federal Republic.[161]

The statistics also show that 52 per cent of those who gave details were members of the Evangelical Church. This figure is also appreciably higher than the most optimistic church estimates for the East German population as a whole (47 per cent), and it seems reasonable to conclude that religious motives featured in the thinking of many who left for the West. This may also be tied in with economics, however, since members of religious communities in the GDR often do not have the same career prospects as others. Reports from church workers in the GDR also suggest that many applicants are financially motivated but turn to their minister for advice on motives which they feel will carry more weight with the authorities.[162]

One of the best known collective attempts to leave the GDR was organised by a group of thirty-three East German citizens from Riesa, near Dresden, in July 1976. They submitted a 'Petition to Secure Full Human Rights' to the UN Division of Human Rights and to the signatories of the Helsinki Final Act, seeking support for their applications to renounce East German citizenship and move to West Germany (27). Another forty-six East Germans added their names to the petition in the following weeks. One of the suspected initiators of the petition, Dr Karl-Heinz Nitschke, was arrested in August 1977 after having been demoted at work and temporarily detained by the State Security Police on suspicion of attempting to escape from the GDR. Six further signatories of the petition were also arrested and the rest were interviewed and urged to give up their applications to leave. On this occasion the state dealt with the initiators of the petition by releasing them to the West.[163]

The reaction from the authorities is often unpredictable (28), but frequently involves demotion and non-payment of premiums at work, and restrictions on movement. Pressure can also be brought to bear on an applicant's acquaintances with the aim of socially isolating him or her.[164] Arrest for agitation against the state is not uncommon in the case of East German citizens who persist with their applications after receiving either no official response or a verbal rejection, and some East Germans whose cases have been publicised in the West are prosecuted for 'treasonable communication of information' (6).[165] Yet the silent demonstrations in Jena by some 200 East Germans in the summer of 1983 resulted in some of them being permitted to leave the GDR, not least because West German television had reported on their action.[166]

Immediately after the signing of the Helsinki Final Act senior

East German politicians set about providing an interpretation of the agreement which laid great emphasis on the principles of the sovereign equality of states, their territorial integrity, the inviolability of their frontiers and non-intervention in the internal affairs of other states. These principles, which are set out in the first section of the agreement, were accorded greater weight than those in the section dealing with 'co-operation in humanitarian and other fields'.[167] In practice, this means that the support which East Germans may receive from West Germany in their efforts to leave the GDR can be condemned as 'intervention in the internal affairs of another state'. At the first follow-up conference to Helsinki, held in Belgrade from October 1977 to March 1978, criticism of the human rights record of the Eastern bloc states was rejected on the same grounds.[168]

The reform of the Penal Code in April 1977 made it illegal to 'obstruct the activity of organs of state' (6), and this clause has been invoked against GDR citizens who refuse to abandon their efforts to leave East Germany (29). In a further reform of the Penal Code of June 1979 the maximum sentence for this offence was increased from two to three years. The maximum sentences for agitation against the state, taking up illegal contacts and 'public vilification' (paragraph 220) were also increased substantially.

Yet the official reaction to applications for exit visas has fluctuated dramatically during the Honecker period. The numbers permitted to leave the GDR for West Germany each year did not rise significantly immediately after the Helsinki agreement and actually fell in 1977 and 1978.[169] But 1984 saw the largest number of East Germans allowed out since the Wall was built. The criteria for selecting those permitted to leave also remain obscure, with the result that while some GDR citizens were being allowed to leave by legal means, others were resorting to entering Western embassies in East Berlin and Prague in their bid to get to the West.[170]

The connection between Western loans and relatively minor concessions from the GDR on formalities at the border between the two Germanies is fairly well established: even as Honecker was busy denying it, *Pravda* went out of its way to confirm the connection.[171] But the financial argument is less convincing in the case of those wishing to leave the GDR for good, and it seems more likely that East Germany is exporting potential opposition.

Also, the fact that it has declared the issuing of exit permits to be in accordance with the Madrid agreement (the result of a follow-up conference to Helsinki) suggests that it has been influenced by international pressure.[172]

THE UNOFFICIAL PEACE MOVEMENT

The main facts about the unofficial peace movement can be stated quickly. The term 'peace movement' began to be applied to peace initiatives not originating within the party when the Dresden Peace Forum was held in February 1982. The Evangelical Church organised the event in the Dresden Kreuzkirche, and some 5000 (mainly young) East Germans took the opportunity to discuss the question of peace in ways which challenged the official view that 'peace must be armed'.

Though some observers see the movement as a response to Western peace movements, most trace it back to the introduction in the summer of 1978 of compulsory pre-military training in schools for 15 and 16-year-olds. The governing body of the Evangelical Churches in the GDR made public its reservations about this move, arguing that it would undermine education for peace as well as the credibility of the GDR's peace policies (30). Pre-military training was nevertheless introduced, and the Evangelical Church launched a series of discussions around the theme of 'Education for Peace'.[173] In May 1981, members of the Evangelical Church produced their proposal for 'social service for peace'. The proposal, which was eventually backed by church synods, went further than the principle of the construction units which came into being in 1964 as a form of military service without weapons for potential conscientious objectors. Social service for peace was envisaged as an alternative to military service, involving socially useful work for those who did not wish to serve in the National People's Army (31).

Like the objections to the introduction of pre-military training, this suggestion was totally rejected by the SED. The SED Secretary for Church Affairs, Klaus Gysi, argued that the construction units already offered an alternative to bearing arms, and he reminded his audience from the Theology Department of the Humboldt University that the GDR had military obligations as a member of the Warsaw Pact. Gysi also made it clear that the Evangelical Church was on the point of incurring the party's wrath when he stressed that anyone who did not agree with the state's position was clearly bent on confrontation. Similarly, Werner Walde, a senior SED member, declared that the initiative for an alternative to military service was anti-socialist and hostile to the constitution.

In February 1982, Reiner Eppelmann, an East Berlin minister involved in youth work, was taken into custody for two days after publishing with Robert Havemann the 'Berlin Appeal', a statement which was eventually signed by more than 2000 East Germans. The Appeal was more radical than most statements emanating from church circles, since it called for the withdrawal of all 'occupation troops from Germany', a formulation which clearly and consciously included the 400 000 strong Red Army contingent in the GDR (officially known as the Group of Soviet Armed Forces in Germany). The Appeal also sought to re-open the discussions on the issues of social service for peace and pre-military training in schools – discussions which the SED clearly regarded as over (32).

There followed the Dresden Peace Forum, and in March 1982 the official ban on wearing in public the peace groups' badge which bore the biblical quotation 'Swords into Ploughshares'. Midst accusations from within that it was paying too high a price for its continued existence, the Evangelical Church abandoned public use of the badge 'for the sake of peace', and the SED stepped up its propaganda campaign, based on the principle that peace is best guaranteed if socialism is strong.

The problematic link between the issues of peace and 'equal rights for women' was demonstrated in an open letter to Erich Honecker in which several hundred East German women objected to the March 1982 military service law which provided for female conscription if the need should arise (33).

East German intellectuals joined in the controversial discussions on peace at two meetings of writers and scientists from East and West.[174] At these meetings established figures such as Stephan Hermlin and Günter de Bruyn praised the unofficial peace movement and urged the government to show more tolerance towards independent peace initiatives (34). At about the same time, Christa Wolf, perhaps the most respected East German writer today, argued that there could be no such thing as 'armed peace' and went public with her view that unilateral disarmament by the East might well be the best hope for survival (35).

The unofficial peace movement has sparked off a host of key debates about the fundamentals of East German socialism. The obligatory distinction between the defensive, peace-keeping forces of socialism and the aggressive, reactionary forces of imperialism has been abandoned by many of those associated with the unofficial peace movement. Instead criticism is aimed at both sides in equal measure (35).[175] The idea that peace can be maintained by the threat of nuclear force has been singled out as the key element of military thinking in East and West alike, and it has been compared with the 'atavistic delusions' in Germany which led to the Second World War.[176] The notion that socialism must be armed in order to prevent a recurrence of 1939[177] has been challenged by the thought that all who stand ready to launch nuclear missiles are potential brothers of Eichmann.[178]

The unofficial peace movement has also provoked a discussion of the human rights situation in the GDR. In numerous peace movement statements human rights issues are seen as inextricably bound up with the commitment to peace (36, 37).[179] In order to achieve peace, it is argued, the 'whole social context' must be considered.[180] Freedom to work for peace in one's own way is an essential human right,[181] and if wars are to be prevented, individuals must criticise the shortcomings of their own societies. 'The atomic threat, if it has brought us to the brink of annihilation, must then have brought us to the brink of silence too, to the brink of endurance, to the brink of reserve about our fear and anxiety, and our true opinions' (35).

Christa Wolf's idea of a link between excessive efforts in the sphere of armament and patriarchal patterns of thought and government has also been taken up in the GDR by groups of women for peace who feel they have a specifically female contribution to make in public affairs.[182]

The positions taken up in peace initiatives within the churches can be influenced by the fact that both the Evangelical Church and the Roman Catholic Church have international links. The September 1982 Conference of the League of Evangelical Churches in the GDR, which had as its theme the Christian's responsibility for peace, took account of the Oecumenical Council's report, drawn up in Amsterdam in 1981, in which churches were called upon to condemn the production, possession and use of nuclear weapons as a crime against humanity.[183] Similarly, the long-awaited statement in January 1983 by Catholic bishops which took issue with many aspects of official peace policy in the GDR was prompted not least by their audience with the pope.[184]

The party's response to the unofficial peace movement has been mixed. While some peace campaigners have been permitted to join in officially sponsored FDJ peace rallies, others have been arrested and charged with 'hooliganism' or 'riotous assembly'. Others who attempt to establish contacts with Western European peace movements can be charged with taking up illegal contacts. Sentences range from seven months to three years and nine months.[185] The authorities have also responded by presenting peace activists with the choice between trial and imprisonment or leaving the GDR,[186] an offer, incidentally, which has encouraged some of the East German citizens who do wish to leave the country to become involved in the unofficial peace movement. In their harsher treatment of peace activists the authorities were helped by the stationing of Cruise and Pershing missiles in the Federal Republic at the end of 1983.

Yet the SED has also attempted to avoid confrontation by prevailing upon the Evangelical Church to restrain 'problematic and dangerous peace groups'.[187] It has also dropped the ban on the 'Swords into Ploughshares' symbol and, more importantly, signalled its willingness to make ideological compromises for the sake of superficial harmony. When the synod of the Evangelical Church in Saxony passed a resolution in November 1979 which welcomed government peace initiatives but also criticised the militarisation of East German society, *Neues Deutschland* was content to misrepresent the synod's position as one of unqualified support for the party's policies.[188] Similarly, the Catholic bishops' statement on the issue of peace in January 1983 goes so far as to suggest that where the educational aims of parents and state may differ, the parents have the right to ensure that their views prevail.[189] This is clearly at odds with the harmonious formulation in the East German 'Family Code' which sees parents educating their children in co-operation with political and social institutions to make them 'constructors of socialism'. Yet the SED has equally clearly acknowledged the realities of ideological consciousness in the GDR and not risen to this challenge to its authority.

The party's desire to avoid confrontation has also led to a reappraisal of official attitudes towards construction soldiers and pacifism. For the first time since the construction units were established in 1964 a Minister of Defence – Heinz Hoffmann – has mildly praised their work. Compared with the 1982 statement from the *Gesellschaft für Sport und Technik* (a mass organisation providing young people with pre-military training) that anyone who is not prepared to bear arms is objectively weakening socialism and supporting imperialist aggression,[190] Hoffmann's conciliatory tone represents a considerable concession. And whereas official East German dogma once only saw pacifism as acceptable in Western countries, Politburo member Kurt Hager has recently spoken of the possibility of an alliance between Marxists, Christians and pacifists,[191] and Honecker himself has emphasised that pacifists are not to be scorned.[192]

Rudolf Bahro has characterised the unofficial peace movement in the GDR as a counter-movement and a cultural conversion movement rather than a source of opposition, but at the same time he sees the Evangelical Church's denial that it is an opposition movement as a matter of tactics as much as of conviction.[193] Such denials feature regularly in statements not just from the milder church-dominated peace groups but also from more controversial figures such as Reiner Eppelmann (from whose 'Berlin Appeal' the Evangelical Church expressly disassociated itself).[194] Moreover, those who speak out on behalf of the unofficial peace movement while they are in the GDR are more likely to place their support in an anti-Western and pro-GDR framework when they are outside their country.[195]

If one pushes the point further, however, the debates conducted around the principle of the 'Church in Socialism' show how involved the opposition question has become, with Evangelical Church representatives arguing that the principle could not be taken to mean that the church uncritically approved of all state decisions.[196] Basically, however, the Evangelical Church has shown itself eager to avoid a confrontation with the SED (38). It urged young people to think of other ways of demonstrating their commitment to peace after the state had made it clear that the 'social work for peace' scheme could not be implemented.[197]

This eagerness to avoid a confrontation exists on both sides, then, with the SED projecting a superficial unity between church and state, and the church seeking to stake out a position of critical solidarity for itself. This is a convenient posture for both sides, and it is maintained in particular by the party as the most efficient way of containing the more moderate peace initiatives. Yet, objectively, the positions taken up by the two sides are far removed from each other, even irreconcilable.

Within the movement there are signs that the convenient posture has been abandoned by some as too convenient. It is seen as having the effect of depriving the peace activists' work of any impact. At the Dresden Peace Forum it was clear that many young people were more radical than the church representatives who fielded their questions. Their enthusiasm for Eppelmann's 'Berlin Appeal' was particularly noticeable,[198] and the association with illegality was strengthened when young people wearing peace badges attended Robert Havemann's funeral some two months later. The idea of an alliance between unofficial and official peace groups has been dropped by the more radical wing of the movement: instead of seeking to win governments over, it is argued, the aim must be to create a mass movement. It is seen as essential to reduce church influence on the peace movement and to concentrate on political analysis, thought and action.[199] Talk of a European peace movement which would provide a bridge between the two blocs (36), involving unofficial peace movements in East and West making common cause, tends not only to undermine the basis for the East German regime's praise of the Western peace movement, but also to make confrontation between state and the more radical peace campaigners in the GDR more likely.

5 The Significance of Opposition

Anyone considering the GDR's home-grown critics must sooner or later ask in what ways they are significant and what value can be attached to their activities. Significance and value can be assessed in terms of the size of opposition groups, how widespread their attitudes are among the East German population as a whole, the level of solidarity within and between opposition groups, their relationship to power, and how the party reacts to them – in particular, whether it sees them as a serious threat. It is also necessary to consider whether opposition has any effect on party policy and whether the criticisms levelled against the regime reflect major concerns and debates within the GDR.[200]

There have been just a handful of dissident intellectuals in the Honecker era, and although it has been argued of the peace movement that 5000 in the GDR are the equivalent of sixty times that number in West Germany,[201] the fact remains that the movement involves thousands, not hundreds of thousands. Purely in terms of numbers, those who have applied to leave the GDR are the most significant group, yet this significance is qualified by the fact that, unlike the dissidents and peace activists, their energies are not primarily directed towards reforming major features of East Germany's social and political system.

Opinions and evidence on how widespread opposition attitudes are among the East German population as a whole vary dramatically. A typical East German response to its radical critics is to dismiss them as a 'tiny group of individuals who represent nothing and nobody'.[202] In May 1979, shortly after Heym's novel, *Collin*, and Rolf Schneider's *November* had appeared in West Germany, and Joachim Seyppel had protested against the authorities' treatment of Havemann (12), the writer Dieter Noll assured Erich

Honecker that 'a few worn out types like Heym, Seyppel or Schneider who co-operate so eagerly with the class enemy to obtain cheap recognition for themselves . . . certainly do not represent the writers of our Republic. And the Party can be sure that working people throughout the country approve of the government's actions'.[203]

In the West, intellectual dissent within the GDR is sometimes viewed as activity confined to a tiny group which is 'completely isolated from the mass of the population',[204] but more usually dissidents' opinions about the regime are portrayed as typical of the views of the East German population as a whole. This response is encountered not just in the Western press but also in some Western academic studies of the GDR. Havemann's brand of democratic communism is said to reflect a widespread feeling of opposition among the East German population,[205] and when *Der Spiegel* published the anonymous *Manifest der Opposition* in 1978 the debate over its authenticity on occasion gave way to the idea that, authentic or not, it could be regarded as a summary of popular feeling in the GDR.[206] More generally it is argued that the majority of the East German population rejects the existing regime, and that the absence of larger-scale protest in the GDR is not a sign of social harmony but of political resignation.[207]

The Western assumption that the views of highly critical intellectuals are representative appears to be backed up by some of the findings of research into popular opinion in East Germany. There have been some ingenious attempts to find out just what the East German population does think of its political system: Gebhard Schweigler related findings of surveys conducted in the 1960s in which West Berliners returning from East Germany were questioned about the views of the East Germans they had spoken to.[208] Mleczkowski bases his assessment of popular opinion in the GDR on public opinion polls undertaken in Czechoslovakia in 1968,[209] and the economist Hans Apel conducted his own small-scale polls in East Germany in the 1960s.[210] Ingenious though some of these surveys may be, however, they are all ultimately unsatisfactory, and the unscientific methods used are underlined by the radically different results each survey produced: estimated support for the system during the sixties ranges from 7 to 15 to over 50 per cent (Mleczkowski, Schweigler, Apel).[211]

The confusion is not entirely dispelled if one looks at what critics of the regime have to say about their significance. At one point Heym can argue that writers are paid more attention than in the West,[212] and that as far as the East German population is concerned he is the most popular East German writer of the day.[213] Yet elsewhere he fears that those who think as he does may turn against him because they do not have his freedom to travel in the West and to speak out.[214] Moreover, popular or not, Heym senses a political indifference among the great majority of the East German population.[215]

Similarly, Havemann was at one stage not prepared to assume that most East Germans thought as he did,[216] yet at another he claimed that the 200 signatories to his open letter to Brezhnev were representative of the majority of the East German population.[217] We have seen too that there is an unresolved tension running through Havemann's work over what he considers to be the aspirations of East Germans, and that this tension reflects a suspicion that intellectuals' aims may not be shared by a majority of the population.

For his part, Bahro points out that demands for greater democracy such as were heard in Czechoslovakia in 1968 are superficial, limiting any reform movement to the special interests of intellectuals, and he rightly adds that the party can and does make use of popular anti-intellectualism in combating any such demands.[218] We have seen too that Bahro's radicalism marks him off from the ranks of the cadre economists from which he came. This uncertainty among dissident intellectuals qualifies the widespread assumption that intellectuals are important because they articulate the discontent of a larger sector of the population.[219]

Perhaps because there is some doubt in their own minds about how representative they are, dissident intellectuals can develop a fall-back position: although their commitment to what they see as genuine socialism is obviously sincere, their insistence on applying Marxist methods (implying inevitable social change) seems to stem in part from a need to provide their analyses with an alternative significance.[220]

Unofficial peace activists claim that their views are widespread among the East German population (37), yet they are also aware that their image may have suffered in the eyes of the East German public since it has become clear that some GDR citizens joined the movement in the hope that the authorities would regard them as trouble-makers and push them over the border into West Berlin.[221]

Balanced against this are reports of ever larger audiences (up to 30 000) attending Evangelical Church events at which the government is urged to soften its line on peace initiatives. Congregations of 100 000 for open-air services are also not uncommon.[222]

Officially sponsored research into aspects of public opinion in the GDR provides some further information on how opposition views might be regarded by the population.[223] One of the recurring demands from the unofficial peace movement is that the *Feindbild* ('enemy-image') of the West should be overcome. Research from the early seventies indicates that as East German children grow older they become less inclined to accept the view of West Germany as the enemy of peace.[224] A 1972 study of attitudes towards military matters revealed that although 90 per cent of pupils who were asked agreed that it was necessary to protect peace by military means, only 54.5 per cent agreed that service in pre-military organisations was an expression of their 'willingness to protect the fatherland against the class enemy's onslaughts'. A reluctance to learn about military matters was registered among 19 per cent of the 16-year-olds questioned, and, as they grew older, there was a sharp drop in the number of young people willing to serve as professional soldiers (39.9 per cent of 12-year-olds, but 6.8 per cent of 16-year-olds).[225]

If these particular findings suggest that the views of unofficial peace activists may be received sympathetically by significant numbers of young people just around the age when their pre-military training begins, it is more usual for East German research on young people to indicate a low level of interest in politics and a tendency to withdraw from social and political activity.[226] Although young East Germans have come out top of the Eastern European league in terms of 'socialisation potential' when assessed on the basis of the percentage of young people in youth organisations, numbers of officials in these organisations serving in top party bodies and circulation of youth organisations' newspapers,[227] the significance of such information seems open to question in view of a survey of 1200 political prisoners released to the Federal Republic in 1975 and 1976, which found that almost all had been members of political organisations for young people.[228]

It is unlikely that the 'official values, orientations and perceptions actually dominate the minds of the majority of the citizens'.[229] Yet if published East German sources suggest that dissatisfaction is widespread among the working population,[230] this dissatisfaction generally expresses itself in what Bahro calls subservient reactions and attitudes such as reluctance to exert oneself, indifference and hypocrisy, and it will not provoke radical change (21).

It is true that the ties between the technical intelligentsia, workers and dissident intellectuals are weak,[231] and dissident intellectuals can expend much energy arguing among themselves.[232] Yet intellectuals in the Honecker era have shown group solidarity, most notably in the protest of over a hundred writers and artists against the expatriation of Wolf Biermann in November 1976, and on a smaller scale when eight East German writers protested after currency charges had been brought against Stefan Heym. This solidarity between a small number of dissident intellectuals and a far larger number of intellectuals who are still in favour is a crucial point and indicates the pyramidal structure of criticism from intellectuals in the GDR, with support for a few outspoken critics coming from a broader base which occupies a grey area between acceptable criticism and unacceptable opposition (39).

Although those wishing to leave the GDR have on occasion banded together to form self-help groups, issue joint petitions or organise public demonstrations, they generally approach the authorities as individuals or families. Reports from the GDR suggest that peace groups and critical intellectuals tend to look down on them and are not eager to help them obtain what they see as their right to leave the country.[233]

Solidarity between peace activists and intellectuals has grown, on the other hand, and the latter have often acted as unofficial spokesmen of the unofficial peace movement. Havemann and Heym's provocative and challenging stance placed them nearer many young East German peace campaigners who grew increasingly impatient with the circumspection of the Evangelical and Catholic Churches. Moreover, the praise for the movement expressed by Stephan Hermlin and Volker Braun makes it more difficult for the party to draw its usual distinction between its radical critics and its valued but 'difficult' intellectuals.[234]

How significant a force is opposition in the eyes of the SED? Despite its denials that radical critics are in any way a representative group in East German society, the severity of the official reaction is a clear sign that the party takes its critics seriously. One of the main aims of the June 1979 revision of the Penal Code was to silence East German intellectuals who had resorted to publishing their critical writings abroad. The strengthening of the cultural contingent on the Central Committee elected in 1981 also reflects a growing awareness of the potential for conflict in the cultural sphere,[235] as does the frequency of Honecker's personal interventions in the debates surrounding critical intellectuals. Honecker's interview with Stephan Hermlin, generally regarded as the instigator of the Biermann petition, is perhaps the most dramatic proof of how seriously the party takes unrest among intellectuals.[236] Similarly, the SED's often vigorous reaction to the unofficial peace movement suggests how concerned the party is about independent initiatives. More generally, the often heard assumption that the party feels it has many enemies[237] is echoed within the SED by Erich Mielke in his secret speech to propaganda officers from his Ministry of State Security in October 1978 (13). At the start of 1981 Western intelligence sources reported that Mielke had presented an extremely gloomy dossier on the potential for public unrest to the SED and this was accompanied by an intensified propaganda campaign calling for a new ideological offensive and increased vigilance against counter-revolutionary activity.[238]

It has been argued that one of the main purposes of studying opposition under communism is to establish to what extent and in what direction political decisions and processes are influenced by the relationship between government and opposition.[239] Judged by this criterion, the dissident intellectuals and the peace movement seem relatively insignificant. Far from heeding objections to the 'militarisation' of East German society, the SED pushed ahead with the introduction of pre-military training in schools and revised the statute of the 600 000 strong *Gesellschaft für Sport und Technik* to ensure that its members are more specifically prepared for service in the *Nationale Volksarmee*.[240] Weighed against this is the fact that the party responded to church pressure in 1964 when it agreed to establish the construction units. More recently, observers have noted that these units have been engaged in non-military tasks to a greater extent than in the past, and this has been interpreted as a concession to the suggestion of a social service for peace.

At a more subtle level the peace movement has also affected SED thinking. The upgrading of pacifism should be recognised for what it is, i.e. a shift in ideology, not in policy, yet even this says something about the party's eagerness to avoid confrontation.

The fact that so many East Germans who wanted to leave the GDR were allowed to do so in 1984 cannot simply be explained as the result of any direct influence of large numbers on SED policy. While it is likely that some of those East Germans who entered West German embassies in other Eastern European countries succeeded in their bid to move to the Federal Republic because of their own efforts and the SED's wish to avoid a protracted public wrangle, the party's motives for allowing so many East Germans to leave on the basis of an application are still unclear. The SED's more liberal policy in 1984 was not directly linked with the number of applicants, nor was it a response to any concerted campaign from applicants.

But there is good reason to believe that a different kind of dissent, potential dissent, strongly influences party policy. Fear of potential dissent seems the most likely reason for the party soft-pedalling on the introduction of the 'scientific organisation of work' at the start of the seventies. Workers successfully resisted the scheme because they were concerned that it would involve an unfavourable recalculation of work norms. Where new technology or the scientific organisation of work scheme has been introduced, the workforce has exerted pressure to have new norms calculated in reverse, with the old pay levels taken as the starting point.[241]

The question of the significance of opposition can also be answered in terms of internal resonance. Do the criticisms and reform programmes of opponents of the regime reflect major concerns and debates within official circles in the GDR? To anticipate the conclusion, it is clear that these criticisms and programmes do indeed tie in with internal discussions. While some of these discussions are conducted by groups far-removed from the decision-making process, others are conducted by those responsible for formulating policy and shaping East German society. It is here that the 'tiny group' of dissident intellectuals plays a key role and it is perhaps this role which justifies the amount of attention their ideas receive.[242] To pinpoint the various discussions is to establish the existence of a continuum, of areas of overlap between permissible debate and what the SED rejects as anti-socialist opposition.

The most readily accessible area in which dissident ideas are aired within official circles is the area of *Selbstkritik*, which is largely concerned with inefficiencies in the economy. Although it is generally sandwiched between thick slices of self-congratulation on the achievements of socialism, this criticism can often provide unambiguous confirmation of what, for example, Bahro has to say. Anyone familiar with Politburo reports on poor morale at work, on resources being wasted, laws being ignored and unpleasant truths being concealed,[243] will realise that Mielke's secret speech[244] contains much less that is new (or for that matter secret) than is generally supposed. The malpractices noted by the Politburo can be dwelt upon at some length in published surveys. In one such survey directors of industrial enterprises complain about the complexity of East German labour law and state that if it were necessary they would ignore legal stipulations in order to meet their targets.[245]

When Bahro describes how workers give less than their best because the pressure to perform well is not as great as in the West,[246] he is doing no more than echoing the account in the FDJ newspaper of how a visit to a Berlin building site revealed poor productivity: 'We did not pick a bad day – the practice is common. Perhaps it is because of the simple socialist truth: in this country you live in the comforting knowledge that your job is safe and that society will look after you.'[247] Elsewhere Honecker himself can publicly blame government ministers for failing to ensure uninterrupted supplies of electricity and fuel.[248] Bahro's point that the cadre economists he interviewed for his thesis showed signs of disappointment and discouragement because they were over-qualified for the tasks they actually performed is directly confirmed for a wider section of the working population by East German research: a 1980 study by the Central Labour Research Institute reveals that almost 20 per cent of skilled workers are in jobs which do not make proper use of their training. East German sources estimate that approximately 1 million skilled workers do not have sufficient opportunity to utilise their training and qualifications, and conclude that this problem can result in dissatisfaction, frequent changes of job, disappointment and a resigned attitude.[249]

When Bahro questions the effectiveness of financial incentives in work and argues instead for greater responsibility to be given at the level of individual enterprises, he is able to back up his case by referring to surveys conducted not only in the Soviet Union but also in the GDR.[250] East German academic sources also echo Bahro's plea for technologists to be given more say in the overall running of enterprises, and his arguments against excessive centralisation.[251] Similarly, the journal *Sinn und Form* recently published an interview with the director of an agricultural collective in which he blamed the shortfalls in the food supply on central planners and their inhibiting effects on local initiatives.[252] Although the Honecker years have generally witnessed a recentralisation in industry and agriculture, East Germany's economic planners have shown themselves willing to take on board such objections, as for example when poor results in agriculture led to a positive reappraisal of small-scale farming.[253]

In these areas then there is clearly an overlap between Bahro's pragmatic criticisms and public self-criticism within East Germany. And indeed, Bahro placed his thesis within this framework of acceptable self-criticism. Although it was ultimately rejected, the positive response the thesis received from its first three assessors (two of whom were SED members) shows that his idea of what was acceptable was not that far off the mark.[254] Yet echoes of Bahro are to be heard not merely in this area of pragmatic criticism aimed at greater economic efficiency. Bahro himself points the way when he refers to economists and sociologists in the Soviet Union homing in on the crucial issues, and Soviet artists, social scientists and journalists dismantling the official image of their country to reveal a very different reality. There are clear signs that the same process is at work in the GDR.

In his thesis, Bahro argues that the divison of labour retained in East Germany hinders the development of the personality.[255] In *Die Alternative*, the idea resurfaces in more aggressive form, with Bahro arguing that self-development is a worthier goal than the economic growth which the SED accords such high priority, and that material insatiability is costing East Germany its freedom to develop into a higher form.[256] That these points were also being raised within the SED close to the time when *Die Alternative* appeared is suggested by a report in which a Central Committee head of section responsible for agitation took issue with the argument that increasing material prosperity was paralysing the social energy and activity of East German citizens. Shortly before that, Politburo member Konrad Naumann had attacked what he called radical left-wing critics who accused the party of pursuing its consumer policies at the expense of ideology,[257] and Honecker had reaffirmed his commitment to the linking of economic and social policy in the face of critics who were reminding him that 'man cannot live by bread alone'.[258]

The debate in the late seventies between Harry Maier, Deputy Director of the Central Institute of Economic Science, and Harry Nick, Research Director of the Academy of Social Sciences, underlines the fact that Honecker's remarks are not merely directed against his critics abroad. Maier stresses that material wealth is only the means enabling members of a society to develop all aspects of their character and that the economic goal of socialism should be to increase the amount of free time available for individual development and to pay particular attention to the quality of work. Ranged against Maier, and very much in the majority, Nick adamantly rejects any such arguments since they seem to him to call into question the goal of economic expansion.[259]

A similar debate, which also ties in with what Bahro had to say, was conducted in 1978 over how to measure social progress. Jürgen Kuczynski and others argued that social progress could be assessed in terms of the increase in leisure time, thereby suggesting that under the conditions prevailing in socialist society self-fulfilment was not to be found in work. Kuczynski's critics accused him of blindness for failing to distinguish between work under capitalism, in which self-fulfilment was indeed impossible, and work under socialism which had succeeded in bringing forth 'new socialist man'.[260]

The concern for the environment expressed by dissidents, church and unofficial ecology groups has also been voiced in official circles. Adolf Bauer and Horst Paucke have called into question the notion of a harmonious relationship between communism and nature, and suggested that socialism needs to develop new methods for coping with the demands of the environment.[261] With their forthright criticism of the profit-driven destruction of the environment under capitalism, Bauer and Paucke stand midway between traditional official thinking and the more provocative stance taken up by Günter Kunert when he recalled a conversation with the Greek writer Yannis Ritsos about the 'symmetrical' development of modern industrial society and its devastating consequences.[262] When criticised, he went on to argue that pollution of the environment was in some respects worse under socialism than under capitalism (40).

Havemann's advocacy of some measure of political pluralism and his rejection of Soviet domination of Eastern Europe mean that he had much in common with the Eurocommunism of the Communist Parties of Spain, France and Italy. This Eurocommunism in its turn has given the SED cause for concern since it appears to have raised its head within the party itself. In December 1979, the Central Committee passed a resolution to review the state of the party by interviewing all of its 2 130 671 members and candidates. Whereas the previous party review of 1970 had resulted in expulsions for simple inactivity, the 3944 members expelled in 1980 were said to have been unwilling to observe the party statute, and the expulsions were preceded by warnings from Erich Mückenberger, head of the Central Party Control Commission, against false and damaging ideas, hostile influences, reformism, revisionism, anti-Soviet attitudes and ideas of a third way,[263] a reference to the path between social democracy and Soviet communism which the Communist Parties of Italy and Spain were advocating.[264] At a confidential meeting of party members in the Academy of Sciences Professor Gerhard Ziegengeist spoke after the Biermann affair about the popularity Eurocommunism enjoyed among East German writers, and he concluded that 'the Berlinguer model is getting a sympathetic hearing. Among large numbers of artists an image of socialism has become entrenched consisting of left-wing, revisionist and SPD elements'.[265]

It has often been argued, and not infrequently by establishment figures in the GDR, that East German writers provide a more realistic account of GDR socialism than the social scientists (15), and it is perhaps in the area of East German literature that voices are heard which are most strikingly reminiscent not only of the themes but sometimes also of the viewpoints of dissident intellectuals. Thus it is not just Heym who can mock socialist realism in art, where, as he puts it in *Collin*, the men all have massive hands and tiny heads, and the women all look six months pregnant.[266] Jurij Brězan complains that a significant number of talented young writers not only do not take socialist realism as their model, they actually wish to be seen in conflict with it (41). Similarly, Hartmut König has spoken out against young East German writers who announced in a journal for literature, aesthetics and cultural theory – the reference is to *Weimarer Beiträge* – that literature is a form of opposition and resistance, initially to parents and school and then later in ideology. König is obviously dismayed that not enough young writers are praising achievements such as the completion of the building programme with songs like '*In Potsdam wird gebaut*' ('They're building in Potsdam'). He objects to young East German writers suggesting that the constraints of socialism made the free development of the personality impossible and that the individual develops not through East German society but against it (11).

The concern dissidents show for the individual *vis-à-vis* the state is clearly shared by many writers whose work is published in East Germany. These writers can thus meet with terms of disapproval which are very similar to those applied to more extreme critics of East German society and to 'pessimistic' Western literature. Where Reiner Kunze was condemned for adopting the standpoint of a 'critical individualist' in work he published in the West, Klaus Höpcke, Deputy Minister of Cultural Affairs, has more recently registered with regret the subjective views put forward by some young GDR writers,[267] and a discussion in *Weimarer Beiträge* about Doris Paschiller's *Die Würde* is typical of many reviews critical of new literary developments which have little to do with the SED's exhortations to East German writers to help 'strengthen the love and loyalty of young people towards our socialist fatherland'.[268] Paschiller is said not to be greatly concerned with examining the possibility of self-fulfilment in society, and to view with scepticism the individual's chances of helping to shape society. The heroine instead seeks self-fulfilment by withdrawing from society, regarding her environment as mysterious and threatening.[269]

The recent anthology of works by GDR writers born after 1946, *Kein Duft von wilder Minze*, is criticised for its lack of appreciation of social issues, for its apparent failure to appreciate the critical point reached in the struggle between imperialism and socialism, for the excessive interest the writers show in their own individual problems and an entirely private form of self-fulfilment (41). Other young writers are taken to task for portraying the relationship between the individual and the state as antagonistic (11), and in the journal, *Temperamente*, Sylvia Kögler makes a similar attack on young authors for their individualism, their disillusionment and their lack of revolutionary commitment.[270] This tendency to withdraw from the social and political arena is in fact at odds with the dissidents' highly political reactions to political problems, but the idea of an antagonism between the individual and the state remains a link between them and young writers publishing in the GDR.

Weimarer Beiträge has recently attempted a defence of this rising tide of individualism, arguing that it is a trend one can afford since the figures portrayed by young writers are all in agreement about the basic social issues.[271] Yet this argument tends to underestimate the potential for conflict underlying what has been described as the growing understanding among East German intellectuals that only a literature which describes and intensifies social contradictions can help the GDR out of its problems.[272]

This development in literature is expressly acknowledged by the legal theorist Uwe Jens-Heuer. Heuer notes that the themes of personality and individuality loomed ever larger in East German literature of the seventies and provided one inspiration for discussions in legal circles. He detects a trend away from the idea that under socialism the interests of the individual and the state are identical and towards recognition of the fact that individual and state are separate, that even under socialism there should be 'subjective rights', i.e. rights of the individual in his dealings with the state. Heuer argues that if society does not solve its problems collectively, and if the existence of contradictions under socialism is denied, then people will seek their own private solutions. Individualism will spread at the expense of progress towards communism.[273]

There are signs that, on this point, Heuer may be doing more than airing a theory about the future. For sociological research conducted in the GDR has revealed a tendency for young people to withdraw from social and political activity and to favour informal groups outside state-controlled organisations.[274]

On these issues Heuer is at odds with East German legal theorists such as Haney who sees implicit in Heuer's position the danger of a confrontation between society and the individual, and of a pluralistic fragmentation of society.[275] Yet Heuer makes his points at a time when the party had already abandoned the harmonious notion of a socialist human community. In the cultural sphere Honecker had declared that, in his opinion, there could be no taboos in the realm of art and literature if one proceeded from the solid premises of socialism, and a decade later indicated that it was the writer's task to understand and give artistic form to the revolutionary reshaping of society, including its conflicts.[276]

Of course, such statements did not translate into an intellectual free-for-all: Volker Braun took up Honecker's words when he announced at the March 1972 meeting of the Berlin section of the Writers' Union that it was pointless saying there were no taboos for writers if in fact there were, and that the taboos had to be faced.[277] That there were indeed narrow limits to Honecker's 'no taboos' policy soon became clear, and Hartmut König summed up the objections of hard-liners when he took issue with literary historians who described the main literary and artistic development after the Eighth Party Congress as crucially influenced by the shedding of illusions, since this suggested that the history of the struggle for socialism could be divided into periods of illusion and sobriety (11). Nevertheless, the Eighth Party Congress did clear the way for the publication of many critical works such as Ulrich Plenzdorf's *Die neuen Leiden des jungen W* (1972) which had been written 'for the desk drawer', and which was reminiscent of the dissidents' views on the conflict between the individual and society.

In the social sphere a lively debate is gathering pace over the issue of the emancipation of women. Although dissidents generally have remarkably little to say on the subject, Bahro is certainly critical of the patriarchal tradition and of the subordinate role played by women in the GDR.[278] In many ways recent developments in the internal discussion go beyond what Bahro has to say.

Whereas work and family tasks are traditionally portrayed as complementary in East German society, with the woman deriving important stimulation for motherhood from her employment and a more mature relationship developing between mother and child,[279] the literary historian Karin Hirdina has taken up Brigitte

Martin's simple question: 'why, for all the equality between men and women, are there more dissatisfied women than men?', thus starting a public discussion on the issue of women in the columns of *Für Dich*, the mass circulation women's magazine. Emancipation, Hirdina points out, seems to have become a burden, and she cites the many East German women writers who portray the demands of work as a danger to personal relationships, to the survival of the family and to the well-being of the children (42). Similarly, Irene Dölling, a lecturer in cultural theory at the Humboldt University, describes the situation of East German women with the term 'double-bind', a more subtle and critical label than the more usual double-burden (*Doppelbelastung*), for it means that women are not simply weighed down with responsibilities in two areas, but that they are involved in contradictory, not complementary, activities. Social norms encouraged by socialist states emphasise marriage, family and motherhood as essential to women's happiness, yet they do not draw the necessary conclusions for other female aspirations. Dölling argues that emancipation can only be a genuine liberation if women can bring their qualities and values into all spheres of productive activity and thus bring about changes in the nature and the aims of this activity. Dölling's rejection of the idea that work equals emancipation seems to be a criticism of SED policy on women which is so concerned to create the conditions for women to combine motherhood and employment.[280]

In her preface to Maxie Wander's best-selling '*Guten Morgen, du Schöne*', Christa Wolf writes that East German society gave women the opportunity of doing what men do, and that this eventually led women to ask whether this was in fact what they wanted for themselves (43). Just what practical effect such a question might have on public life was demonstrated in the women's open letter to Erich Honecker on military service (33).

Although feminism is rejected by East German critics of the current situation of women, the often heard complaints about the dominance of male standards and male institutions have been interpreted in the GDR as evidence of an 'anti-male attitude', and this in turn is regarded by more conformist East German sociologists as an essential element of feminism.[281] There is then a growing feeling among writers and academics that the issue of emancipation, declared by Ulbricht to have been resolved in his own time,[282] is more complex and subtle than originally thought, and that the time has come to throw it back in the melting-pot.

It is true that many of these debates on social, economic, political and legal issues are conducted in specialist and cultural journals and works of literature which are generally produced in small editions (10).[283] SED policy towards those who promote such ideas has been described as repressive tolerance, as a technique applied to intellectuals who are not readily susceptible to the new social contract. The authorities, so it is suggested, have politically co-opted intellectuals by granting them a measure of freedom of expression, but only on a circumscribed public agenda and in a sanitised social space that fosters the illusion of critical involvement at little real cost to the regime.[284] This interpretation can seem justified when one considers the amount of intellectual energy which goes into formulating and presenting controversial ideas and registers the minimal impact these ideas seem to have upon SED policy. Yet in the case of the unofficial peace movement the ties between intellectuals and peace groups and the extension of debate into the area of human rights show that the sanitised social space and the circumscribed public agenda are proving hard to maintain. More generally, the continuity of criticism between the regime's opponents and the critics it tolerates or even encourages shows that the opposition has raised issues which the party realises it cannot afford to ignore.

Notes and References

1. Quoted by S. Mampel in *Die sozialistische Verfassung der Deutschen Demokratischen Republik: Text und Kommentar*, 3rd ed. (Frankfurt a. M., 1972) p. 648. See also U. Arens, *Die andere Freiheit: Die Freiheit in Theorie und Praxis der Sozialistischen Einheitspartei Deutschlands*, 2nd ed. (Munich, 1980), p. 206; K. Löw, *Die Grundrechte: Verständnis und Wirklichkeit in beiden Teilen Deutschlands* (Munich, 1977) pp. 258–70.
2. Since the revision of the electoral law in 1963 the number of candidates on the list has exceeded the number of seats available in the *Volkskammer*, and the voter has the opportunity of rejecting individual candidates. If rejected by more than 50 per cent of voters, the candidate is not elected. See B. Vogel *et al., Wahlen in Deutschland* (Berlin, New York, 1971) pp. 270–5.
3. See Arens, *Die andere Freiheit*, p. 189. The fixed formula for allocating seats is as follows: 127 seats for the SED; 52 seats for each of the four other parties (CDU, LDPD, NDPD, DBD); 68 seats for the FDGB (trade union organisation); 35 for the DFD (the Democratic Women's League of Germany); 40 for the FDJ (Free German Youth); 22 for the *Kulturbund* (Cultural League).
4. Honecker: 'In the struggle to further strengthen the socialist state and its military defences the Central Committee of the SED recognises that it has at its side reliable comrades-in-arms in the members of your party.' NDPD delegates greeted Honecker thus: 'Our Twelfth Party Congress declares that in the new phase of achieving the programme for the further construction of our developed socialist society the members of the NDPD, as responsible comrades at the side of the communists of our country, will make every effort to strengthen our socialist fatherland, the GDR, in every way' (*Neues Deutschland*, 22 and 23 April 1982).
5. See the statement by CDU Deputy Chairman, Wolfgang Heyl, quoted in Friedrich-Ebert-Stiftung, *Die Friedensbewegung in der DDR* (Bonn, 1982) p. 41.
6. See G. Neugebauer, *Partei und Staatsapparat in der DDR* (Opladen, 1978) p. 127.
7. Ibid., p. 27; H. Weber, *Die SED nach Ulbricht* (Hanover, 1974) p. 17.

8. On cadre policy see G.-J. Glaeßner, *Herrschaft durch Kader* (Opladen, 1977) esp. p. 240.
9. K. Höpcke, 'Zwei gegensätzliche Ströme von Texten', *Forum*, no. 3 (February 1979) p. 4f.; 'Phantasie für das Wirkliche', *Einheit*, no. 2, 1982, pp. 173–9.
10. See G. Gleserman, 'Widersprüche der gesellschaftlichen Entwicklung im Sozialismus', *Probleme des Friedens und des Sozialismus*, no. 3 (March 1972) pp. 381–9.
11. See M. McCauley, *The German Democratic Republic since 1945* (London, 1983) pp. 152–5; K. Hager, *Zur Theorie und Politik des Sozialismus: Reden und Aufsätze* (Berlin, 1972).
12. See D. Staritz, 'Formen und Wandlungen der Austragung innerer Konflikte in der DDR', *Deutschland Archiv Sonderheft* (Cologne, 1979) p. 100.
13. See D. Schulz, 'Korrespondentenarbeit in der DDR: Wie entsteht das DDR-Bild der Presse?' in J.-P. Picaper (ed.) *DDR-Bild im Wandel* (Berlin, 1982) pp. 75–100.
14. See G. Wettig, 'Der östliche Kampf gegen den Informationsfluß aus der Bundesrepublik', *Deutschland Archiv*, no. 10 (October 1976) pp. 1039–62.
15. H. Weber, *Kleine Geschichte der DDR* (Cologne, 1980) p. 169.
16. See A. J. Goss, *Deutschlandbilder im Fernsehen* (Cologne, 1980) p. 218; W. Mleczkowski, 'In Search of the Forbidden Nation', *Government and Opposition*, no. 2 (Spring 1983) p. 182. There is general agreement that it is not technically possible to jam West German television broadcasts. See L. Loewe, *Abends kommt der Klassenfeind* (Frankfurt a. M., 1977); D. Schulz, 'Korrespondentenarbeit in der DDR', p. 99.
17. H. Wolfschütz, 'Gespräch mit Stefan Heym', *GDR Monitor*, no. 8 (Winter 1982/83) p. 1.
18. In Komitee gegen die politische Unterdrückung, *Freiheit heißt die heiße Ware* (Cologne, 1978) p. 99.
19. *Der Spiegel*, no. 25, 20 June 1983, p. 78f.
20. See, for example, Lothar Loewe's account of the Western media involvement in the Biermann affair, pp. 102–7.
21. Similarly, Hermann Kant at the Eighth Writers' Congress of May 1978, quoted by M. Jäger, *Kultur und Politik in der DDR* (Cologne, 1982) p. 163, and Kurt Hager in *Neues Deutschland*, 23–24 October 1982.
22. S. Heym, *Collin* (Munich, 1979), p. 383.
23. See, for example, Robert Havemann in *Berliner Schriften*, ed. by A. Mytze (Munich, 1977) p. 31, and in *Ein Marxist in der DDR*, ed. by H. Jäckel (Munich and Zurich, 1980) p. 195.
24. See Goss, *Deutschlandbilder im Fernsehen*, pp. 51–60.
25. Research results reported in K. Schmitt, *Politische Erziehung in der DDR* (Paderborn, 1980) p. 182.
26. Ibid., pp. 182, 203f.
27. Goss, *Deutschlandbilder im Fernsehen*, p. 17.

28. Politburo resolution of 18 May 1977, *Neues Deutschland*, 21–22 May 1977, p. 3f.
29. E.g. K. Bühn, 'Gedanken zur Verbesserung der kommunistischen Erziehung im Staatsbürgerkundeunterricht', *Pädagogik*, no. 10 (October 1980) pp. 806–9.
30. 'Kunst and Öffentlichkeit in der sozialistischen Gesellschaft', *Sinn und Form*, no. 2 (March/April 1979) p. 240.
31. See also E. Loest, *Der vierte Zensor* (Cologne, 1984) p. 14f.
32. D. Voigt, 'Freizeitforschung in der DDR', *Deutschland Archiv*, no. 5 (May 1974) pp. 503–20.
33. See the Politburo resolution of 18 May 1977 in *Neues Deutschland*, 21–22 May 1977 and the speech by Kurt Hager in *Neues Deutschland*, 23–24 October 1982.
34. *Gesetzblatt der DDR 1*, 1973, p. 99f.
35. Jörg Mettke, the *Spiegel* correspondent, was expelled in December 1975 after the magazine had published an article by another *Spiegel* reporter on how the children of East Germans who tried to escape to the West were put up for adoption.
36. See *Neues Deutschland*, 14–15 April 1979.
37. The Helsinki Final Document on Security and Co-operation in Europe was signed in August 1975 by thirty-five states, including the FRG and the GDR. Documents on the van Loyen expulsion in *Deutschland Archiv*, no. 7 (July 1979) pp. 782–4.
38. On the East German reaction to events in Poland see the series of articles by P. J. Winters in *Deutschland Archiv*, 1980, no. 10 (October 1980) pp. 1013–18; no. 1 (January 1981) pp. 4–8; no. 7 (July 1981) pp. 686–9; no. 10 (October 1981) pp. 1009–12; no. 10 (October 1983) pp. 1012–17.
39. See 'Zwei Anträge des Pfarrers Friedrich Schorlemmer', in W. Büscher, P. Wensierski and K. Wolschner (eds), *Friedensbewegung in der DDR* (Hattingen, 1982) pp. 202–4. This was a reaction to the reports on events in Poland such as the item in *Neues Deutschland* on 8 September 1981.
40. See H.-D. Schulz, 'Zusätzliche Hilfe für Polen', *Deutschland Archiv*, no. 10 (October 1980) p. 1012f.
41. See the recommendations of the Council of State in *Neues Deutschland*, 19–20 June 1982, p. 5; Gerhard Francke, 'Neue Erfahrungen mit den Oranienburger Familiengesprächen', in *Organisation*, no. 3 (May/June 1982) p. 9f. Further articles on 'public relations' work are listed at the end of Francke's contribution.
42. *Bericht des Zentralkomitees der Sozialistischen Einheitspartei Deutschlands an den X. Parteitag der SED* (Berlin, 1981) p. 117.
43. Reported in *Organisation*, no. 3 (May/June 1982) pp. 11–14.
44. See, for example, H. Timmermann, *Reformkommunisten in West und Ost: Konzeptionen, Querverbindungen und Perspektiven* (Berichte des Bundesinstituts für ostwissenschaftliche und internationale Studien, no. 31, 1980) p. 14f. A similar case is made for the Soviet Union by A. Y. Shtromas, 'Dissent and Political Change in the

Soviet Union', *Studies in Comparative Communism*, vol. 12, nos. 2 and 3 (1979) pp. 212–44.

45. P. C. Ludz, *Deutschlands doppelte Zukunft*, 3rd ed. (Munich, 1974) pp. 80–83.
46. See M. Sodaro, 'Limits to Dissent in the GDR', in J. L. Curry (ed.), *Dissent in Eastern Europe* (New York, 1983) pp. 82–116 (108f.); M. McCauley, *The German Democratic Republic since 1945*, p. 193.
47. See M. McCauley, 'Social Policy under Honecker', in I. Wallace (ed.), *The GDR under Honecker 1971–1981* (Dundee, 1981) pp. 3–20.
48. The absence of 'institutionalised, recognised and legitimate' political opposition can lead to the conclusion that communist states are 'oppositionless'. The point is discussed by H. G. Skilling in 'Background to the Study of Opposition in Communist Eastern Europe', in L. Schapiro (ed.), *Political Opposition in One-Party States* (London, 1972) pp. 72–103.
49. See J. B. Bilke, 'Menschenrechte im SED-Staat', *Aus Politik und Zeitgeschichte*, 15 November 1980, pp. 3–18.
50. Bundesministerium für innerdeutsche Beziehungen (ed.), *DDR Handbuch*, 2nd ed. (Cologne, 1979) p. 775.
51. K. W. Fricke, *Opposition und Widerstand in der DDR* (Cologne, 1984) p. 13. Fricke reserves the term resistance for illegal activity (ibid).
52. See the reports in *Der Spiegel*, no. 26, 27 June and no. 42, 17 October 1983.
53. 'Ein deutsches Ereignis' (manuscript, 1982), p. 25.
54. By 1980 Hermlin was back in favour: on the occasion of his 65th birthday *Neues Deutschland* (12–13 April and 2 May 1980) carried a lengthy account of his work, and he was awarded the National Order of Merit. See also K.-H. Jakobs, *Das endlose Jahr* (Düsseldorf, 1983) pp. 123, 201.
55. See the account of a party meeting in the Academy of Sciences in *Die Zeit*, 20 May 1977.
56. Havemann, *Berliner Schriften*, p. 90. See also details of the non-prominent East Germans who were arrested for protesting against Biermann's expatriation in Komitee gegen die politische Unterdrückung, *Freiheit heißt die heiße Ware*, pp. 88–91.
57. Interview in *Le Monde*, 23 October 1979.
58. See T. A. Baylis, *The Technical Intelligentsia and the East German Elite* (Berkeley, Los Angeles; London, 1974) p. 151.
59. W. Volkmer, 'East Germany: Dissenting Views during the Last Decade', in R. Tökés (ed.), *Opposition in Eastern Europe*, (London, 1979) p. 138.
60. See J. Kuppe, H. Buck, 'Keine neuen Akzente', *Deutschland Archiv*, no. 8 (August 1982) p. 787n.
61. Shtromas, 'Dissent and Political Change in the Soviet Union', p. 213.

62. Bishop Krusche applied the expression to the Evangelical Church. It was also Biermann's characterisation of the contents of his Cologne concert performance. See P. Roos (ed.), *Exil: Die Ausbürgerung Wolf Biermanns aus der DDR* (Cologne, 1977) p. 41.
63. C. Lemke, 'Departure from Conformity? Political Socialization and Political Change in the GDR' (manuscript, 1984). Similarly, A. J. Liehm on the 'parallel polity' in Czechoslovakia, in Curry, *Dissent in Eastern Europe*, p. 176f.
64. Schapiro, *Political Opposition in One-Party States*, p. 3.
65. Ibid.
66. See the section on the significance of opposition.
67. T. Ammer, 'Bürgerrechtsbewegung in Riesa – ein Versuch', *Politische Studien*, no. 234 (1977) pp. 382–90; W. Seiffert, 'Die DDR kämpft um ihre Existenz', *Der Spiegel*, no. 41, 10 October 1983, pp. 64–7.
68. See Schapiro – *Political Opposition in One-Party States* – on pressure groups, p. 7.
69. Ibid., p. 4f.
70. See Sodaro, 'Limits to Dissent in the GDR', p. 85f. and D. Childs, *The GDR: Moscow's German Ally* (London, 1983) p. 103.
71. Schapiro, *Political Opposition in One-Party States*, p. 9f. This category corresponds to Shtromas's 'positive intrastructural dissent' which comes from technocrats looking for freedom from the detrimental control of the 'partocratic' bureaucracy over their professional activities (p. 228).
72. See the speech by Kurt Hager quoted in H. Weber, *Die SED nach Ulbricht*, p. 36.
73. See H. Weber, *Kleine Geschichte der DDR*, p. 148.
74. See Childs, *The GDR: Moscow's German Ally*, p. 99f. and P. C. Ludz, 'Die Neuordnung der Führungsspitze der DDR', *Europa Archiv*, no. 4 (1977) pp. 113–20. In October 1976, Willi Stoph became Chairman of the Council of Ministers and Günter Mittag was made Central Committee Secretary for the Economy.
75. See P. C. Ludz, *The Changing Party Elite in East Germany* (Massachusetts, 1972) esp. pp. 51, 148–55; Timmermann, *Reformkommunisten in West und Ost* p. 29f.; Schapiro, *Political Opposition in One-Party States*, p. 12; Skilling, 'Background to the Study of Opposition in Communist Eastern Europe', p. 91.
76. R. Bahro, *Plädoyer für schöpferische Initiative* (Cologne, 1980) p. 32n.
77. See the research findings by Schellenberger, quoted by Bahro, *Plädoyer*, p. 134n.
78. P. C. Ludz, 'Experts and Critical Intellectuals in East Germany', in E. J. Feuchtwanger (ed.), *Upheaval and Continuity* (London, 1973) pp. 166–82.
79. Baylis, *The Technical Intelligentsia and the East German Elite* pp. 73–82; Ludz, 'Experts and Critical Intellectuals', p. 174f.; See

also Sodaro, 'Limits to Dissent in the GDR', on 'reformist technocrats' in the Ulbricht era, p. 89.

80. Baylis, *The Technical Intelligentsia and the East German Elite*, p. 277. See also Werner Rossade's criticism of Ludz's original theory of the 'institutionalised counter-elite' in 'Kulturpolitik als Herrschaftsinstrument', *Deutschland Archiv*, no. 3 (March 1977) pp. 288–304.
81. See the documentation in *Deutschland Archiv*, no. 9 (September 1979) pp. 983–96.
82. Since our focus is on opposition in the GDR the attitudes of the many intellectuals who went public with their criticisms largely after leaving East Germany are not considered here.
83. Bahro, *Die Alternative* (Hamburg, 1980) p. 7; Havemann, *Berliner Schriften*, p. 26f.; P. Lübbe, *Der staatlich etablierte Sozialismus* (Hamburg, 1975) p. 53.
84. Bahro, *Die Alternative*, p. 10.
85. Ibid., p. 127.
86. Ibid., p. 276.
87. *Berliner Schriften*, p. 17.
88. Havemann, 'Über die Notwendigkeit eines demokratischen Sozialismus', in H. Vogt, *Parlamentarische und außerparlamentarische Opposition* (Opladen, 1972) p. 161.
89. Havemann, *Ein Marxist in der DDR*, p. 195.
90. Havemann, *Ein deutscher Kommunist* (Hamburg, 1978) p. 112; H. Wolfschütz 'Gespräch mit Stefan Heym', p. 3.
91. *Berliner Schriften*, p. 145.
92. Havemann, *Ein deutscher Kommunist*, p. 72.
93. Ibid., p. 76f.
94. *Berliner Schriften*, p. 141f.
95. S. Heym, 'Leben in Ostdeutschland', in *Wege und Umwege*. ed. P. Mallwitz (Munich, 1980) p. 339.
96. Wolfschütz 'Gespräch mit Stefan Heym', p. 3f. Biermann also stresses that the GDR took steps to ensure that National Socialism would never return: *Nachlaß I* (Cologne, 1977) p. 90.
97. Wolfschütz, 'Gespräch mit Stefan Heym', p. 3.
98. Heym, 'Leben in Ostdeutschland', p. 341.
99. Havemann, *Ein deutscher Kommunist*, p. 112f.
100. Rudolf Bahro, *Ich werde meinen Weg fortsetzen*, 2nd ed. (Cologne, Frankfurt, a. M., 1979) p. 71.
101. *Plädoyer*, p. 7f. Bahro's change of attitude illustrates what Shtromas describes as the tendency for 'overt dissidents' to be former 'intrastructural dissidents' (p. 237).
102. Bahro *Die Alternative*, p. 12.
103. Ibid., pp. 201, 286. See also Lübbe, *Der staatlich etablierte Sozialismus*, p. 26.
104. Bahro *Die Alternative*, p. 203.
105. Ibid., p. 205; Havemann, *Berliner Schriften*, p. 192; Heym, *Collin*, p. 180.

106. *Berliner Schriften*, pp. 38, 146. The *Manifest der Opposition*, allegedly written by party functionaries, is also shot through with religious imagery. G. Johannes and U. Schwarz (eds), *DDR. Das Manifest der Opposition* (Munich, 1978). Continuing doubts over its authenticity mean that it will not be considered here in any detail.
107. Heym, *Collin*, p. 228.
108. In *Ein Marxist in der DDR*, p. 77. See also the account by Irene Böhme of party disciplinary hearings at which rebels are urged in religious terms to find their faith again; *Die da drüben* (Berlin, 1982) p. 59. Irene Böhme was editor of the weekly *Sonntag* and dramatic advisor to an East Berlin theatre before moving to West Berlin in 1980.
109. Reported in *Neues Deutschland*, 30 June 1976.
110. 'Plötzlich hebt sich der Boden', *Der Spiegel*. no. 22, 31 May 1982, p. 100.
111. See also Wolf Biermann, *Nachlaß I*, p. 469. Similar arguments are now coming from the Evangelical Church. See W. Büscher and P. Wensierski, *Null Bock auf DDR* (Reinbek, 1984) pp. 44–7.
112. Bahro, *Die Alternative*, pp. 118, 138f.
113. Havemann, *Ein deutscher Kommunist*, p. 85.
114. *Berliner Schriften*, p. 142.
115. Ibid., p. 109.
116. See P. C. Ludz, 'An Overview of Survey Research in the German Democratic Republic', in W. A. Welsh (ed.), *Survey Research and Public Attitudes in Eastern Europe and the Soviet Union* (New York, 1981) p. 287.
117. Bahro, *Die Alternative*, p. 224.
118. Similarly in ibid., p. 219.
119. Ibid., p. 263.
120. Similarly Nico Hübner in *Die Welt*, 31 March 1978. Hübner was imprisoned for refusing to do military service and eventually released to the West at the end of 1979.
121. Havemann, *Ein deutscher Kommunist*, p. 87.
122. Bahro, *Die Alternative*, p. 8.
123. Ibid., p. 216f.
124. Ibid., p. 184.
125. Ibid., p. 134.
126. *Berliner Schriften*, p. 52; *Ein Marxist in der DDR*, p. 202.
127. *Berliner Schriften*, pp. 43, 92.
128. Ibid., p. 161.
129. Ibid., p. 52.
130. Bahro, 'Ein deutsches Ereignis', p. 4.
131. Havemann, 'Über die Notwendigkeit eines demokratischen Sozialismus', p. 159.
132. *Berliner Schriften*, p. 13.
133. Havemann, *Ein Marxist in der DDR*, p. 195.
134. See P. C. Burens, *Die DDR und der Prager Frühling* (Berlin, 1981) p. 34.

135. Bahro, *Die Alternative*, p. 289f.
136. *Berliner Schriften*, p. 163.
137. Ibid., p. 84.
138. Wolf Biermann in *Berliner Schriften*, p. 92; Havemann, p. 13.
139. Bahro, 'Ein deutsches Ereignis', p. 10.
140. *Berliner Schriften*, p. 109.
141. Bahro, *Ich werde meinen Weg fortsetzen*, p. 69.
142. Quoted in H. Bussiek, *Notizen aus der DDR* (Frankfurt a. M., 1979) p. 165.
143. Although there is a considerable area of overlap in the attitudes of the Eurocommunists and the GDR's left-wing dissidents, the common assumption that their aims are the same (see, for example, Weber in *Ein Marxist in der DDR*, p. 173) falls down in Bahro's case over the issue of a multi-party state. See Carillo's speech in *Neues Deutschland*, 30 June 1976.
144. *Berliner Schriften*, p. 17; Bahro, *Die Alternative*, p. 206.
145. See, for example, Raymond Williams, *Problems in Materialism and Culture* (London, 1980) p. 261.
146. *Berliner Schriften*, p. 17.
147. Ibid., p. 22.
148. Ibid., p. 209.
149. See, for example, the discussion of this point in *Deutschland Archiv*, no. 11 (November 1978) pp. 1160–81, particularly the contributions by D. Waterkamp and G.-J. Glaeßner.
150. *Berliner Schriften*, p. 26; Bahro, *Die Alternative*, p. 335.
151. *Die Zeit*, 16 January 1981.
152. *Berliner Schriften*, p. 28.
153. Bahro, *Die Alternative*, pp. 254–7.
154. Neither the Helsinki Agreement nor the Universal Declaration of Human Rights is legally binding on the GDR, however, and the International Covenant on Civil and Political Rights (which is), contains the proviso that human rights can be restricted in the interests of national security or public order. See W. Bruns, 'Menschenrechtspakte und DDR', *Deutschland Archiv*, no. 8 (August 1978) pp. 848–53.
155. See Sodaro, 'Limits to Dissent in the GDR', p. 84.
156. In practice, many of those convicted do not serve the full sentence, but are 'bought free' by the Federal Republic under the controversial *Freikauf* arrangements and thus also eventually make their way across the border.
157. Estimates of the total number of political prisoners in the GDR range from 2000 to 6000. Finn takes a figure of 3000 for the years 1973–9. *Politischer Strafvollzug in der DDR* (Cologne, 1981) p. 121.
158. See W. Büscher, ' "Warum bleibe ich eigentlich?" ', *Deutschland Archiv*, no. 7 (July 1984) pp. 683–8; *Kirche im Sozialismus*, no. 2 (June 1984) p. 48.
159. Siegmar Faust writes that Biermann and Havemann regarded him as 'having died' when he pressed the authorities to let him leave in

1976. *In welchem Lande lebt Mephisto?* (Munich and Vienna, 1980) p. 172. On anti-communism among would-be emigrants see also the result of a very useful West German survey of 500 emigrants who left the GDR in 1984 by A. Köhler and V. Ronge, ' "Einmal BRD – einfach", Die DDR-Ausreisewelle im Frühjahr 1984', *Deutschland Archiv*, no. 12 (December 1984) pp. 1280–6.

160. Statistics from the Bundesausgleichsamt (1/3 – Vt 6838/6943/1). See also Fricke, *Opposition und Widerstand in der DDR*, pp. 162–74. Köhler and Ronge discuss the problems of interpreting their survey result that 71 per cent counted 'lack of freedom of opinion' and 66 per cent counted 'political pressure' among their motives for leaving (p. 1281f.).
161. See Jan Kuhnert, 'Überqualifikation oder Bildungsvorlauf?' *Deutschland Archiv*, no. 5 (May 1983), pp. 497–520, and the survey by Köhler and Ronge which revealed that nearly 70 per cent of those asked expected working conditions to be better in the Federal Republic than in the GDR (p. 1284).
162. See G. Rein, 'Zum Bleiben ermuntert', *Kirche in Sozialismus*, no. 4 (September 1984) pp. 9–14.
163. See T. Ammer, 'Bürgerrechtsbewegung in Riesa – ein Versuch', *Politische Studien* no. 234, 1977, pp. 381–90; Bilke, 'Menschenrechte im SED-Staat'.
164. See the account by Nico Hübner, 'Letter from Berlin', *Encounter*, July 1978, pp. 84–8 and the results of the Köhler/Ronge survey, p. 1283.
165. *Amnesty International Briefing EUR 22/01/82*, p. 2.
166. See Fricke, *Opposition und Widerstand in der DDR*, p. 172f.
167. See G. Wettig, *Die Folgen der KSZE aus östlicher Sicht* (Berichte des Bundesinstituts für ostwissenschaftliche and internationale Studien, no. 7, 1977) p. 20f.
168. See R. Dirnecker, 'Die Ergebnisse der Belgrader Überprüfungskonferenz der KSZE', in Göttinger Arbeitskreis (ed.), *Studien zur Deutschland-Frage*, vol. 3 (Berlin, 1979) pp. 73–85.
169. See the official West German figures compiled by the Federal Ministry of the Interior, document no. VtK15 934000 VII.
170. In October 1984, it was reported that up to 130 East Germans had taken refuge in the West German embassy in Prague.
171. See the reports in *Frankfurter Allgemeine Zeitung*, 26 July 1984 and the *Financial Times*, 1 August 1984.
172. See Ilse Spittmann, 'Die deutsche Option', *Deutschland Archiv*, no. 5 (May 1984) pp. 449–55.
173. See Büscher *et al.*, *Friedensbewegung*, pp. 81–96.
174. The first of these meetings was held in East Berlin in December 1981, the second in West Berlin in April 1983. The proceedings of the meetings were published as *Berliner Begegnung zur Friedensförderung* (Darmstadt and Neuwied, 1982) and *Zweite Berliner Begegnung: Den Frieden erklären* (Darmstadt and Neuwied, 1983).
175. See also the debate between Stefan Heym and Hermann Kant in

Zweite Berliner Begegnung, pp. 51–6, and Heym on the Soviet SS20s in *Berliner Begegnung zur Friedensförderung*, p. 66.

176. Speech by Hans Tschiche, head of the Evangelical Academy in Magdeburg in Büscher *et al., Friedensbewegung*, p. 155.
177. Erik Neutsch, *Berliner Begegnung*, p. 151.
178. Stefan Heym, *Zweite Berliner Begegnung*, pp. 50f., 177.
179. At the second Berlin meeting of writers the Hungarian, György Konrad, declared that the democratic movement and the peace movement in Eastern Europe were the same thing (*Zweite Berliner Begegnung*, p. 172).
180. 'Zur Friedensbewegung in der DDR', *Papiere aus Osteuropa zur Vorbereitung der END-Konferenz in Perugia vom 17–21 Juli 1984.*
181. Heym, *Zweite Berliner Begegnung*, p. 177.
182. *Voraussetzungen einer Erzählung: Kassandra*, 6th ed. (Darmstadt and Neuwied, 1984) p. 122. See the account of the women's meeting in East Berlin in September 1983 in W. Büscher and P. Wensierski, *Null Bock auf DDR*, pp. 125–7.
183. See the documentation in *Deutschland Archiv*, no. 11 (November 1982) pp. 1219–27.
184. See the report in *Der Spiegel*, no. 2, 3 January 1983, pp. 41–4 and the *Neues Deutschland* report (7 January 1983) on East German dignitaries who are 'controlled from Rome'.
185. See the *Amnesty International Briefing EUR/22/06/84.*
186. See *Der Spiegel*, no. 17, 23 April 1984, p. 44; no. 22, 30 May 1983, p. 25.
187. See W. Büscher, ' "Warum bleibe ich eigentlich?" '.
188. See Büscher *et al., Friedensbewegung*, pp. 106–8. Soviet sources were similarly selective in their reporting of the first Berlin meeting of writers and scientists.
189. Statement reproduced in *Der Spiegel*, no. 2, 10 January 1983, p. 44.
190. See Bernd Eisenfeld, 'Spaten-Soldaten: 20 Jahre Bausoldaten in der DDR', in *Kirche im Sozialismus*, no. 4 (September 1984) pp. 20–29.
191. Speech in *Neues Deutschland*, 19–20 June 1982.
192. Interview with *Stern*, reprinted in *Deutschland Archiv*, no. 1 (January 1984) pp. 86–93. See also Rolf Schneider's commentary on the official GDR meaning of pacifism in *Zweite Berliner Begegnung*, p. 42f.
193. Bahro, 'Ein deutsches Ereignis', p. 15.
194. Bahro quotes Eppelmann's statement in 'Ein deutsches Ereignis', p. 15. See the church's response to the Berlin Appeal in Büscher *et al., Friedensbewegung*, p. 283f.
195. See, for example, Stephan Hermlin's contribution to the Second Berlin Meeting, in *Zweite Berliner Begegnung*, p. 29f.
196. *Der Spiegel*, no. 17, 23 April 1984. See also Bishop Werner Krusche in Büscher *et al., Friedensbewegung*, p. 233f.
197. Letter reproduced in Büscher *et al., Friedensbewegung*, p. 209f.
198. See the transcript of the discussion in K. Ehring and M. Dallwitz, *Schwerter zu Pflugscharen* (Reinbek, 1982) pp. 76–87.

199. Paper 7 of the *Papiere aus Osteuropa*.
200. For a general discussion of the purposes of studying opposition under communism see V. Kusin, 'Typology of Opposition', *Soviet Studies*, no. 1 (July 1973) pp. 125–9.
201. Bahro, 'Ein deutsches Ereignis', p. 13. See also Heym, 'Plötzlich hebt sich der Boden', p. 100.
202. Quoted from *Militärwesen* by Bussiek, p. 257.
203. *Neues Deutschland*, 22 May 1979. The government actions referred to were the bringing of currency charges against Heym and Havemann.
204. R. Sharlet, 'Varieties of Dissent and Regularities of Repression in the European Communist States: An Overview', in Curry, *Dissent in Eastern Europe*, p. 5.
205. H. Weber, 'Demokratischer Kommunismus', in *Ein Marxist in der DDR*, p. 172.
206. See Volkmer, 'East Germany: Dissenting Views during the Last Decade', p. 137f. Similarly Ilse Spittmann, quoted by Wolfgang Mleczkowski in 'Der neue Moralismus – Zur politisch-geistigen Alternative in der DDR', *Liberal*, no. 4, 1979, p. 272.
207. Fricke, *Opposition und Widerstand in der DDR*, p. 206.
208. *Nationalbewußtsein in der BRD und der DDR*, 2nd ed. (Düsseldorf, 1974) p. 94.
209. 'Grenzprobleme regimekritischen Denkens', *Liberal*, no. 21, 1979, pp. 552–4.
210. Apel's findings summarised in H. Rudolph, *Die Gesellschaft der DDR – eine deutsche Möglichkeit?* (Munich, 1972) p. 17f.
211. Peter Ludz estimates that in 1975 25 per cent of the East German population accepted the political system and 20 per cent rejected it. *Die DDR zwischen Ost und West* (Munich, 1977) p. 224. Ludz gives his source as Bonn, suggesting that surveys of the type Schweigler refers to are still being conducted on behalf of the Federal Government, but that the findings are not being made generally available.
212. Quoted by Bilke, 'Menschenrechte im SED-Staat', p. 8.
213. Wolfschütz, 'Gespräch mit Stefan Heym', p. 1.
214. *Der Spiegel*, no. 22, 31 May 1982, p. 97.
215. Heym, *Collin*, p. 227f.
216. *Berliner Schriften*, p. 22.
217. See the interview with Havemann in Büscher *et al.*, *Friedensbewegung*, p. 186.
218. Bahro, *Die Alternative*, p. 271.
219. See, for example, J. Pelikán and M. Wilke (eds), *Menschenrechte: Ein Jahrbuch zu Osteuropa* (Hamburg, 1977) p. 17.
220. In Bahro's case this is balanced by a reluctance to define Marxism as a method which makes it possible to predict social development since this would put him in the same category as the SED whose notion of scientific Marxism he rejects as simplistic (*Die Alternative*, p. 202).

221. See *Der Spiegel*, no. 26, 27 June 1983, p. 68 and no. 42, 17 October 1983, pp. 106–33.
222. See *Kirche im Sozialismus*, no. 4, 1983, p. 68.
223. The problems of interpreting the findings of such research are discussed by Schmitt, *Politische Erziehung in der DDR*, p. 167.
224. Ibid., p. 182.
225. Ibid., pp. 200–2.
226. Ibid., p. 173f.; D. Voigt, 'Freizeitforschung in der DDR'.
227. See the analysis by I. Volgyes, 'Political Socialization in Eastern Europe', *Problems of Communism* (January/February 1974) pp. 46ff.
228. See J. Lolland and F. Rödiger (eds), *Gesicht zur Wand!* (Stuttgart, 1977) p. 22.
229. This is Archie Brown's question about official political culture in the Soviet Union. A. Brown and J. Gray (eds), *Political Culture and Political Change in Communist States*, 2nd ed. (London, 1979) p. 8.
230. See H. Zimmermann, 'Power Distribution and Opportunities for Participation: Aspects of the Socio-Political System of the GDR', in H. Zimmermann and K. von Beyme (eds), *Policymaking in the German Democratic Republic* (Aldershot, 1984) p. 79.
231. See N. Naimark, 'Is it true what they're saying about East Germany?' *Orbis*, no. 3 (Fall, 1979) p. 570; Baylis, *The Technical Intelligentsia and the East German Elite*, p. 271f. See also A. Bust-Bartels, *Herrschaft und Widerstand in den DDR-Betrieben* (Frankfurt a. M.; New York, 1980) p. 134 on antagonism between workers and enterprise directors.
232. See, for example, Hermlin on Havemann's non-attendance at the first peace meeting of writers and scientists in East Berlin (*Berliner Begegnung*, p. 86).
233. Büscher and Wensierski, *Null Bock auf DDR*, p. 155.
234. See the contributions by Hermlin and Braun in *Berliner Begegnung*, pp. 38, 161.
235. See Zimmermann's analysis of the composition of the Central Committee, *Policymaking in the German Democratic Republic*, p. 24.
236. See the graphic account of Hermlin's dealings with Honecker by Karl-Heinz Jakobs, 'Wir werden ihre Schnauzen nicht vergessen', *Der Spiegel*, no. 48, 23 November 1981, pp. 86–108.
237. Havemann, *Ein Marxist in der DDR*, p. 199.
238. See the report in the *Daily Telegraph*, 16 February 1981.
239. Kusin, 'Typology of Opposition', p. 127.
240. See K. W. Fricke, 'Forcierte Militarisierung im Erziehungswesen der DDR', *Deutschland Archiv*, no. 10 (October 1982) pp. 1057–62.
241. See Bust-Bartels, *Herrschaft und Widerstand in den DDR-Betrieben*, pp. 114–33. On the category of potential dissent see Shtromas, 'Dissent and Political Change in the Soviet Union', p. 221f.
242. Shtromas puts forward a similar argument for the Soviet Union,

suggesting that it is wrong to see 'overt dissidents' as an isolated, powerless group unable to influence the country's social and political life. Overt dissent represents 'positive intrastructural dissent' which, although inconspicuous, is really a mass phenomenon (p. 239). See also Zimmermann on the East German discussion of the term 'political system' (pp. 2–6).

243. See, for example, the Politburo resolution of 18 May 1977 in *Neues Deutschland*, 21–22 May 1977, p. 3f.
244. See in particular the second half of Mielke's speech in *Deutschland Archiv*, no. 6 (June 1979) pp. 666–8.
245. Details in U. Jens-Heuer, *Recht und Wirtschaftsleitung im Sozialismus* (Berlin, 1982) p. 196f.
246. Bahro, *Die Alternative*, p. 172.
247. *Junge Welt*, 8–9 December 1979.
248. *Neues Deutschland*, 28–29 April 1979, p. 3.
249. See Jan Kuhnert, 'Überqualifikation oder Bildungsvorlauf?' *Deutschland Archiv*, no. 5 (May 1983) pp. 497–520.
250. Bahro, *Plädoyer*, pp. 33, 82, 134.
251. Ibid., pp. 53n., 142.
252. Gabriele Eckart, 'Zwei Tonbandprotokolle aus dem 'Havelobst'', *Sinn und Form*, no. 2 (March/April 1984) pp. 290–313.
253. This discussion summarised in *DDR Report*, no. 7, 1983. On the critical discussion following centralisation see *DDR Report,* no. 7, 1980.
254. Heym also placed his *5 Tage im Juni* within the framework of acceptable debate by prefacing it with a quotation from the party statute on the duty to encourage criticism and self-criticism. In his statement on Poland (18) Heym stressed that the trade union Solidarity was a consequence of social and political defects ('*Mißstände*'), a term taken from the party statute (3).
255. Bahro, *Plädoyer*, p. 46.
256. Bahro, *Die Alternative*, pp. 218, 335.
257. See the report in *Süddeutsche Zeitung*, 14 November 1978.
258. *Die Zeit*, 21 April 1978.
259. The debate is summarised in K. M. Gyöngyösi *et al.* (eds), *Der Bahro-Kongreß* (Berlin, 1979) pp. 233–5.
260. See *Forum*, nos. 8, 15 and 16, 1978.
261. 'Einheit und Kampf zwischen Natur und Gesellschaft', *Deutsche Zeitschrift für Philosophie*, no. 5 (May 1979) pp. 593–602.
262. 'Antäus', *Sinn und Form*, no. 2 (March/April 1979) p. 403.
263. See K. W. Fricke, 'Die SED nach der Überprüfung', *Deutschland Archiv*, no. 7 (July 1980) pp. 680–3.
264. See H. Timmermann, 'Reformkommunisten', p. 25.
265. Minutes of the meeting were published in *Die Zeit*, 20 May 1977.
266. Heym, *Collin*, p. 117.
267. 'Phantasie für das Wirkliche', *Einheit*, no. 2 (February 1982) p. 178.
268. Kurt Hager's speech to the FDJ's Conference on Culture, October 1982, reported in *Frankfurter Allgemeine Zeitung*, 23 October 1982.

269. W. Gabler, 'Doris Paschiller: Die Würde', *Weimarer Beiträge*, no.1 (January 1983) p. 16.
270. 'Zur Diskussion junger Künstler', *Temperamente*, no. 2, 1980, pp. 140–4.
271. R. Bernhardt, 'Die Sonderlinge der Debütanten', *Weimarer Beiträge*, no. 1 (January 1983) p. 7.
272. Alexander Stephan, 'Cultural Politics in the GDR under Honecker', in I. Wallace (ed.), *The GDR under Honecker 1971–1981,* p. 39f. See also Christa Wolf's contribution in *Berliner Begegnung zur Friedensförderung*, p. 119.
273. *Gesellschaftliche Gesetze und politische Organisation* (Berlin, 1974) p. 41f. Heuer returns to the issue of possible conflicts of interest in *Recht und Wirtschaftsleitung im Sozialismus*, p. 219.
274. See Voigt, 'Freizeitforschung in der DDR'.
275. See W. Biermann, *Demokratisierung in der DDR?* (Cologne, 1978) p. 27.
276. E. Honecker, *Die Kulturpolitik unserer Partei wird erfolgreich verwirklicht* (Berlin, 1982) pp. 44, 307.
277. 'Tabus', *Es genügt nicht die einfache Wahrheit* (Leipzig, 1979), p. 103.
278. Bahro, *Die Alternative*, pp. 367–9.
279. H. Kuhrig and W. Speigner, *Zur gesellschaftlichen Stellung der Frau in der DDR* (Leipzig, 1978) p. 56.
280. 'Zur kulturtheoretischen Analyse von Geschlechterbeziehungen', *Weimarer Beiträge*, no. 1 (January 1980) pp. 59–88.
281. See, for example, Kuhrig and Speigner, *Zur gesellschaftlichen Stellung der Frau in der DDR*, p. 14.
282. See G. Helwig, 'Frauen in der DDR', *Deutschland Archiv*, no. 7 (July 1979) pp. 754–8.
283. See the account by Peter Huchel, one-time editor of *Sinn und Form*, of the hostility from the party towards the journal in the sixties. 'Der Fall Sinn und Form', *Deutschland Archiv*, no. 10 (October 1975) p. 1023f.
284. Sharlet, in Curry, *Dissent in Eastern Europe,* p. 11.

Documents

The Official East German View

1. OPPOSITION

Conflict, antagonism, resistance: in bourgeois political life, resistance by certain political movements and organisations to a government, or ruling class, or party. In bourgeois states the most consistent opposition policy is pursued by communist and workers' parties, in alliance with other democratic forces, to defend peace and the vital interests of the working people. The ruling classes use the coercive powers of the state, including legal prohibition, in their efforts to suppress all genuine opposition. Their class rule is disguised by a show of opposition, which prevents the majority of the people seeing the realities of power: in such circumstances, opposition parties do not aim at a fundamental change in prevailing political and economic conditions, nor to establish social conditions in keeping with the wishes and interests of working people. They are often a manifestation of differences within the ruling classes. In socialist countries there is no objective political or social basis for opposition, since the working class, allied with all other working people, is at once the class which holds power and the main productive force in society, whose fundamental interests basically coincide with those of the other classes and strata. Its policy is to continue improving the material and cultural quality of life of the people, and this requires the further development of fraternal and amicable relations with other classes and categories of working people.

SOURCE: G. Schütz (ed.), *Kleines Politisches Wörterbuch*, 4th ed. (Berlin, 1983) p. 694f.

2. THE CONSTITUTION

In pursuance of the revolutionary traditions of the German working class and basing themselves on their liberation from fascism, the people of the German Democratic Republic have realised their right to socio-economic, political and national self-determination, in accordance with the processes of historical development of our age, and are giving shape to a developed socialist society.

Inspired by the will freely to determine their own future and to continue unswervingly along the path of socialism and communism, peace, democracy, and friendship between peoples, the people of the German Democratic Republic have given themselves this socialist constitution.

ARTICLE 1

The German Democratic Republic is a socialist state of workers and farmers. It is the political organisation of the working people in town and country under the leadership of the working class and its Marxist-Leninist Party.

ARTICLE 27

1. Every citizen of the German Democratic Republic has the right, in accordance with the basic principles of this constitution, to express his opinion freely and in public. This right is not limited by any contract of service or employment. No one may suffer disadvantage from exercising this right.
2. Freedom of the press, radio and television is guaranteed.

ARTICLE 28

1. All citizens have the right of peaceful assembly, within the principles and aims of the constitution.

ARTICLE 29

The citizens of the German Democratic Republic have the right of association for the purpose of pursuing their interests by communal action in political parties, social organisations, associations and collectives, in accordance with the principles and aims of the constitution.

ARTICLE 39

1. Every citizen of the German Democratic Republic has the right to declare allegiance to a religious confession and to carry out religious acts.
2. The churches and other religious communities order their affairs and conduct their activities in accordance with the constitution and the legal provisions of the German Democratic Republic. Further details may be determined by agreement.

SOURCE: *Constitution of the German Democratic Republic* (amended version of 7.10.74).

3. STATUTE OF THE SOCIALIST UNITY PARTY OF GERMANY

The Socialist Unity Party of Germany is the conscious and organised vanguard of the working class and the working people in the socialist German Democratic Republic. As a voluntary fighting alliance of like-minded people, it unites in its ranks the most progressive members of the working class, the class of co-operative farmers, the intelligentsia and other working people.

The Socialist Unity Party of Germany embodies and is continuing the best revolutionary traditions of more than a hundred years of the history of the German workers' movement.

In keeping with the historical development of our epoch, it is fulfilling in the German Democratic Republic the tasks and aims of the working class as set out by Marx, Engels and Lenin. Under the leadership of the Socialist Unity Party of Germany the working class, in alliance with the working farmers and the progressive intelligentsia and other working people, has, in a combined revolutionary process, completed the anti-fascist, democratic upheaval and led the socialist revolution to victory in the German Democratic Republic.

The Socialist Unity Party of Germany, as the highest form of socio-political organisation of the working class, as its battle-hardened vanguard, is the leading force of socialist society, of all organisations of the working class and of the working people, and of organisations of the state and society.

On the basis of Marxism-Leninism, and its creative application and further development, the party steers and leads the shaping of developed socialist society, which is laying the foundations for the gradual transition to communism in the German Democratic Republic. It leads the people along the road to socialism and communism, and to the securing of peace and democracy. It sets the direction and goals for this struggle.

The Socialist Unity Party of Germany contributes to the enrichment of Marxism-Leninism. It wages an uncompromising fight against all manifestations of bourgeois ideology, against anti-communism and anti-sovietism, against nationalism and racism, and against all revisionist distortions of Marxist-Leninist theory.

The party ensures strict adherence to democratic centralism and the Leninist norms of party life, collective leadership and inner-party democracy. It develops the activity and creative initiative of all members and encourages criticism and self-criticism in all circumstances.

All manifestations of factionalism and group formation conflict fundamentally with the basic principles of our Marxist-Leninist party and are incompatible with membership of the party. The party shall disown all persons who disregard the Programme or the Statute of the Socialist Unity Party of Germany and who demonstrate by their conduct that they are unworthy to bear the honourable name of communist.

I Party Members, their Duties and Rights

2. Party members have the duty:

(h) fearlessly to make known shortcomings and to commit themselves to eliminating them; to take a stand against subjectivism, disregard for the collective, egoism and the glossing over of shortcomings, and against the tendency to become intoxicated with success; to combat all attempts at suppressing criticism and making things seem better than they are and giving exaggerated praise, as well as in every way to encourage criticism and self-criticism from below; to inform the leading organs of the party, up to the Central Committee, of shortcomings, regardless of the individuals involved.

No party member may conceal shortcomings, nor pass over in

silence actions which damage the interests of the party and the state.

Every party member shall consistently fight for the preservation of socialist legality, order, discipline and security;

(i) be sincere and honest towards the party and not permit the truth to be concealed or distorted.

Dishonesty of a party member towards the party is a serious offence.

3. Party members have the right:

(a) within their party organisation, at party meetings and in the party press, to participate in discussing all questions of party policy and its practical work, to put forward proposals, and to express their opinions freely, until the organisation has reached its decision.

(b) at party meetings, at plenary sessions of the leading organs of the party, as well as at party conferences and congresses, to criticise the activity of party members and officials, regardless of their position. Party members who suppress criticism or consciously tolerate the suppression of criticism, are to be held accountable.

8. Members who offend against the unity and purity of the party, do not carry out its decisions, do not respect inner-party democracy, violate the discipline of the party and state or abuse their membership and the functions vested in them, or show themselves in their public or personal life to be unworthy of membership of the party, shall be held accountable by the local organisation or a higher organ of the party.

   According to the nature of the offence, the following party penalties may be imposed:

(a) A reprimand.
(b) A severe reprimand
(c) Expulsion from the party.

III The Structure of the Party and Inner-Party Democracy

23. The organisational structure of the party is based on the principle of democratic centralism. By this principle:

(a) all organs of the party, from the lowest to the highest, are democratically elected;

(b) the elected organs of the party have the duty to report regularly on their activity to the organisations that elected them;

(c) all decisions of the higher organs of the party are binding on lower organs, strict party discipline is to be observed, and both minorities and individuals are to submit in a disciplined fashion to the decisions of the majority.

24. Collectivity is the overriding principle governing the work of the leading organs of the party. All leading bodies must collectively discuss and take decisions on the problems facing the party, its tasks and the planning of work.

The principle of collectivity includes personal responsibility of the individual. The cult of personality and the violation of inner-party democracy thereby entailed are incompatible with the Leninist norms of party life and cannot be tolerated in the party.

30. Inner-party democracy ensures that all members of the party and all candidates have the right to express their views freely and objectively within the party organisations on all questions of the party's policy.

31. Inner-party democracy is the basis for the development of criticism and self-criticism, for the consolidation of party discipline, which is a form of discipline that is consciously and voluntarily adopted, and for the healthy evolution and constant strengthening of the party.

32. Every party organisation, every member and every candidate shall defend the party against influences and elements hostile to the party, as well as against factionalism, and shall be committed to the unity and purity of the party on the basis of

Marxism–Leninism. Party members have the duty to prevent inner-party democracy being exploited by the enemies of the working class to distort the party line, to impose the wishes of an insignificant minority on the majority of the party or to destroy the unity of the party and attempt to create splits by the formation of factions.

IV The Supreme Organs of the Party

39. The Central Committee carries out the decisions of the party Congress, is the supreme organ of the party between party Congresses, and leads all its activity. It represents the party in its dealings with other parties and organisations.

The Central Committee places representatives of the party in the supreme leading organs of the apparatus of the state and the economy, and confirms its candidates for the *Volkskammer*.

The Central Committee steers the work of the elected central organs and organisations of the state and society through the party groups established within them.

V Regional, Municipal, District and City Borough Organisations of the Party

49. The regional, municipal, district and city borough organisations of the party are guided in their work by the Programme and Statute of the party, and within their own area organise the implementation of the decisions and directives of the party Congress, the Central Committee and its elected organs.

Their most important duties are:

(a) to give political leadership in the social development of their area on the basis of the party's decisions; to develop systematic political, ideological and organisational work to persuade all working people consciously to participate in shaping developed socialist society, in favour of a rapid development of socialist production, the raising of efficiency, scientific and technical progress, the growth of labour productivity, and in favour of the fulfilment, by all sectors, of the economic plan to raise the material and cultural standard of living of the people;

(b) to organise ideological work, propaganda for Marxism–Leninism in the party and among the masses; continually to consolidate socialist consciousness, love of the socialist fatherland and readiness to defend socialism; to control the press; to control the activity of all cultural and educational institutions in their area;

(c) to provide guidance for the organs of state and support for them in implementing the decisions and directives of the party and higher ranking organs of state, guidance for the trade union, and the youth and women's organisations, as well as for all other social organisations through the party groups established within them, with the aim of drawing ever broader masses of the working people into the work of these organisations and encouraging their initiative and activity. The leading organs of the party ensure that the party organisations do not take over the tasks of the organs of state and social organisations, because their responsibility would thereby be restricted;

(d) to select and deploy the leading cadres, to educate them to loyalty towards Marxism–Leninism, honesty and modesty, to a high sense of responsibility towards the party, the working class and the people of the German Democratic Republic for the tasks that have been entrusted to them.

VI The Local Party Organisations

56. The party's local organisations represent its foundations. They are formed in individual enterprises in industry, building, transport and communications, agriculture, forestry and food, trade, in state and academic bodies and institutions, in urban and rural residential areas, as well as in armed units, provided that they contain at least three members of the party.

57. The local party organisation is guided in all its activities by the Programme, Statute, and decisions of the party Congress, of the Central Committee and of its elected organs.

It unites the working people closely round the party, and organises the masses for the implementation of the party's policy of shaping a developed socialist society. The tasks of the local organisations therefore include:

(a) continually intensifying the militancy and activity of all party members and candidates; ensuring the political, ideological and organisational influence of the party so as to realise its leading role in all spheres of society; conducting propaganda activity and political work among the masses, in accordance with the party's decisions and watchwords; running the press and radio within individual enterprises;

(b) ideological toughening of members and candidates; organisation of systematic political training and making use of all opportunities for acquiring Marxist–Leninist theory, as well as applying it in practice; waging an unrelenting struggle against all the influences of imperialist and bourgeois ideology, as well as against all petty bourgeois deviations in the party and among the working people;

(c) helping strengthen the German Democratic Republic in every way, consolidate the fraternal alliance with the Soviet Union and reinforce the socialist community of states. This is at the same time its most important contribution to securing peace and to further shifting the balance of forces in favour of socialism;

(d) selecting the best candidates for entry to the party;

(e) carefully and punctually carrying out the tasks decided upon by the leadership of the party;

(f) mobilising and organising the masses to carry out tasks within the state, the economy and the cultural field, leading our comrades and supervising their activity in the mass organisations, the social organs and residential areas.

63. The party organisations in enterprises in the fields of production, trade, transport and communications, in the agricultural co-operatives and state farms, co-operative sections of crop production and other communal and co-operative institutions, in craft production co-operatives, as well as in planning and design offices, the academic research institutes,

teaching institutes, cultural and educational institutions, medical institutions, as well as in other institutions and organisations, have the right of control over the activities of the management, in order to fulfil their responsibilities for the political leadership of social development in their field.

The party organisations in the ministries and other central and local organs of state and institutions have the right to exercise control over the activity of the administration in implementing decisions of the party and government, with due regard to the norms of socialist law. They have the duty actively to ensure the rational and effective organisation of work as well as the considerate conduct of colleagues towards citizens and the encouragement of democratic collaboration.

4. CADRES

In a socialist society these are the people who have the responsibility of leading a collective; full-time or honorary workers who are confirmed in their posts by election within a social institution, or are appointed by a leader entrusted with this task by the party of the working class or by the government. Through their work as leaders or as members of the leadership collective, they bear personal responsibility for implementing decisions taken by the party of the working class, and the laws and decrees of the organs of state. Cadres are also young people of promise, and working people with a university degree or technical qualification, who are systematically groomed for leadership tasks on account of their political and specialist knowledge and abilities. The pre-eminent qualities of cadres are: unconditional loyalty to the working class, its party and to Marxism–Leninism, as well as their unflagging determination to ensure decisions are implemented; pride in the achievements of socialism, love of the socialist homeland, unshakeable friendship with the CPSU and the peoples of the Soviet Union and loyalty to proletarian internationalism; sound practical knowledge of Marxism–Leninism and of specialist fields, uncompromising struggle against all manifestations of bourgeois ideology: partisanship, specialist knowledge, discipline and creativity, modesty and exemplary conduct at work and in private life, cultivation of criticism and self-criticism; the capacity to lead collectives and, when working with others, to develop their creative initiatives and talents to the full and encourage the formation of socialist consciousness.

SOURCE: *Kleines Politisches Wörterbuch*, p. 420.

5. CRITICISM AND SELF-CRITICISM

A method based on dialectical materialism, for revealing and creatively resolving contradictions between objective demands of social development in the different spheres of life on the one hand, and outdated, subjective conceptions and attitudes, as well as patterns of behaviour and working practices on the other. Criticism and self-criticism are therefore quite distinct from that destructive form of criticism which arises from a nihilistic and sceptical outlook, and never transcends the purely negative. Criticism and self-criticism are developed, in the first place, as one of the norms of party life propounded by Lenin within the Marxist–Leninist party as a special way of systematically applying the dialectic of contradictions, and consciously used as a method of education in the party and to raise its militancy. Under socialism the conditions are created for using criticism and self-criticism systematically, within the framework of society as a whole, as a means of accelerating social progress and for the socialist education of collectives and individuals. Criticism and self-criticism are an important driving-force behind social development under socialism. The constant aim is constructively to overcome outdated conditions, shortcomings, misconceptions, etc, to encourage the activity and initiative of the working people, and thereby to contribute to the positive development of socialist society.

SOURCE: *Kleines Politisches Wörterbuch*, p. 530.

6. THE EAST GERMAN PENAL CODE

§97

Espionage

1. Persons who, to the detriment of the German Democratic Republic's interests, collect, betray, deliver or otherwise make available information or objects which are classified as secret, for an alien power, its institutions or representatives or for a secret service or for foreign organisations or their helpers, shall be sentenced to not less than five years' imprisonment.
2. Preparing and attempting such acts is punishable.
3. In particularly serious cases the sentence may be life-imprisonment or death.

§99

Treasonable Communication of Information

1. Persons who, to the detriment of the German Democratic Republic's interests, pass on, collect or make available information that is not classified as secret, to the organisations or persons named in §97, shall be sentenced to between two and twelve years' imprisonment.

§106

Agitation against the State

1. Persons who attack the constitutional foundations of the socialist order of state and society in the German Democratic Republic or incite opposition to them by

(1) derogating the social conditions, representatives or other citizens of the German Democratic Republic on account of their activity on behalf of the state or society;
(2) producing, importing, disseminating, or displaying written material, objects or symbols to derogate the social conditions, representatives or other citizens;
(3) derogating the German Democratic Republic's friendly relations and alliances;

(4) threatening to commit crimes against the state or calling on others to oppose the socialist order of state and society of the German Democratic Republic:

shall be sentenced to between one and eight years' imprisonment.

2. Persons who, in order to commit such a crime, collaborate with organisations, institutions or persons who are engaged in activities against the German Democratic Republic, or who wilfully commit such a crime, shall be sentenced to between two and ten years' imprisonment.

§214

Obstructing the Activity of the State or Society

1. Persons who obstruct the activity of organs of state by force or threats, or who demonstrate disregard for the laws in a manner deleterious to public order, or who call upon others to disregard the laws, shall be sentenced to up to three years' imprisonment, or given a suspended sentence, detention, a fine or public reprimand.
2. Persons will be similarly punished who take action, or threaten to do so, to oppose citizens on account of their activity on behalf of the state or society or their support for public order and security.
3. Persons who together with others commit an act as described in sections 1 and 2 shall be sentenced to up to five years' imprisonment.
4. If complicity is only slight, the offender may receive a suspended sentence, detention or a fine.

§219

Taking up Illegal Contacts

1. Persons who take up contact with organisations, institutions or persons whose aim is to act against the order of state of the German Democratic Republic, in the knowledge of such aims or actions, shall be sentenced to up to five years' imprisonment, a suspended sentence or a fine.
2. Persons will be similarly sentenced

(1) who as citizens of the German Democratic Republic disseminate abroad or cause so to be disseminated information which may harm the interests of the German Democratic Republic, or who record anything in writing or cause anything so to be recorded for this purpose;
(2) who pass on or cause to be passed on to organisations, institutions or persons abroad written material, manuscripts or other material which may harm the interests of the German Democratic Republic, in circumvention of regulations.

SOURCE: *Strafgesetzbuch der Deutschen Demokratischen Republik mit den Änderungen vom 28.6.1979.*

The Western Connection

7. THE TRAFFIC AGREEMENT

Secretary of State to the Council of Ministers
of the German Democratic Republic

102 Berlin,
26 May 1972

Secretary of State
in the Federal Chancellory
of the Federal Republic of Germany
Herr
Egon Bahr
Bonn

Dear Herr Bahr

I have the honour to inform you as follows:

The Traffic Agreement between the German Democratic Republic and the Federal Republic of Germany has come into effect, and travel arrangements between the two states will now be made easier than has hitherto usually been the case. On application from citizens of the German Democratic Republic, the competent authorities in the German Democratic Republic will permit relatives and friends from the Federal Republic of Germany to enter the German Democratic Republic several times a year for the purpose of visiting. Citizens of the Federal Republic of Germany can also enter the German Democratic Republic for commercial, cultural, sporting or religious reasons, if invitations are issued for this purpose by the appropriate institutions or organisations in the German Democratic Republic. In addition, tourists from the Federal Republic of Germany will be allowed to travel to the German Democratic Republic on the basis of agreements between the travel agencies of the two states. Travellers to the German Democratic Republic will also be allowed to use private cars more frequently than before. The limit for duty-free presents that can be taken by travellers to the German Democratic Republic will be raised. The Government of the German Democratic Republic will make it possible for citizens of the German Democratic Republic to travel to the Federal Republic of Germany on urgent family business.

Please communicate this information to your Government.

Yours faithfully

Michael Kohl

SOURCE: Bundesministerium für innerdeutsche Beziehungen (ed.), *Zehn Jahre Deutschlandpolitik* (Bonn, 1980) p. 188.

8. US AND THEM

The host changes the subject. He asks about work, working conditions, about how people behave towards each other at work. People are always talking about work in the East, it is a favourite topic and always good for a moan. The Zoni talks about difficulties and suggestions for improvements, tactical tricks, production figures and meeting targets, qualifications and personal successes. He demonstrates that he is someone who knows his subject and knows his way around. He gives the appearance of having a responsible position, asks about technical 'know how', proudly announces how unsatisfactory the set-up is in his factory, and how cunningly he and his like achieve German standards of quality in these circumstances. The GDR citizen is in his element. His guest listens in astonishment, asks occasional questions, and tries to understand. By the end he is only taking in a heartfelt account of appalling conditions. It begins to bore him. It's more or less as he imagined. What he can't imagine, is that someone should enjoy endlessly ruminating about it in his spare time. For the West German, work is something you do with zip and verve. Work is the source of one's success and money-supply, not a subject for social occasions. At most you make a passing remark about a successful deal, or a coup that came off. If you've got problems at work, you maybe admit it to your spouse, but hardly to your best friends. If you didn't take early retirement entirely voluntarily, you keep that inside the immediate family circle. Western man is programmed for success, he must always appear fighting fit and hide his weak points. If he then encounters someone who positively savours the opportunity to expound the problems he has at work, he is shaken and horrified. The only explanation he can think of is that in the GDR people are totally destroyed by the state. If he says as much, his host suddenly becomes a passionate defender of the system. He had been talking about how he was feeling, his low spirits, the way in which, deep within himself, he enjoyed conflict, he had wanted to show how the pleasure he took in fatalism was an optimistic attitude to life, he had uncovered the complexities of his self-image. His guest can't have been listening if he now talks about the state and tries to force a political interpretation on personal feelings.

Our tragic search for what we have in common obliges us to play down this situation too. Conversation is diverted to other areas, preferably to cars, that's something you can always agree about. But the West German will be unable to forget that he has had to look into the soul of a broken man, and how abruptly this downtrodden creature began defending the state. And the East German will not be able to forget that he has bared his soul to a philistine, and tried to discuss the meaning of life with someone who is unwilling to give it a moment's thought. Both repress how uncomfortable they feel. Again it is the impression of similarity that prevails, as though the discrepancies between them came from outside and arose purely by chance. The one is unaware just how much the Slav has already entered into his character. The other is unaware of just how much, in certain matters, he thinks and feels like an American. Both have a sense of something alien, and brush it aside, without thinking or speaking about it. Each regards his behaviour as normal, and it doesn't occur to him that he is different because for thirty-five years he has been living a different everyday life in a different Germany. Us and them: there shouldn't be this distinction. They cling desperately to each other, so restricting each other's normal range of movements, and the fraternal embrace threatens to suffocate them.

Astonished at what he has seen, the West German returns home, satisfied with his good deed. He never said that he found the streets stank, he turned a blind eye to dirt and disorder, he enjoyed the countryside, and the art and architecture of the past. If he was perturbed, he kept the feeling under control, adopting a mien of provincial imperturbability. He has been a good guest, though it was a strain on his nerves and his purse. He decides to visit the GDR again, because he has come to understand how important his visit is for his compatriots. He has shaken off a few prejudices, but his opinion of the country has been confirmed. He shudders when he recalls how careful he had to be in his dealings with people, how much he could not say openly, how alien everything was to him. He now knows, with greater certainty, that he prefers his own cares and worries, and that not just his standard of living, but his way of living is better. He crosses the frontier, takes a deep breath, he's home again. He's carrying no objects of value in his suitcase, but a sense of value has stirred within him.

The Easterner waves goodbye to the parting visitor, contentedly feeling that he's been a good host, that he's offered something that cannot be found elsewhere. It has been a strain on his nerves and his purse. He has shaken off a few prejudices, his opinion of these Westerners has been confirmed, you can't speak freely and openly with them. After this visit he knows with greater certainty that although he is poorer, his way of living is better. He takes a deep breath, he is home again. He sees these wall-skimmers on their way, as the farmer does the migrant birds. They come once a year, pecking and chirping, and then fly on.

Source: I. Böhme, *Die da drüben* (Berlin, 1982) pp. 15–17.

9. EAST/WEST 'CO-OPERATION'

26 January 1976

Dear Herr Hermlin,

As I told you over the phone, I am interested in broadcasting some of your *Urban Ballads* in my magazine programme on GDR culture. Unfortunately I can't yet send you my commentary as it's never put together until very shortly before the broadcast, when all the spoken and musical items are ready. But I can send you a criticism of the Claassen edition of your book, by Jürgen P. Wallmann, which I have since received. I would very much like to link this review with your reading, as I can then dispense with a lengthy introduction.

Yours sincerely

Dr Karl Corino

Jürgen P. Wallmann, *The Early Works of Stephan Hermlin*; Stephan Hermlin, *Städte-Balladen*. With eight colour-woodcuts by H. A. P. Grieshaber. Düsseldorf: Claassen Verlag, 1975.

In the last few months it has been striking just how often the writer Stephan Hermlin has been mentioned in the GDR. In its week-end edition of 12–13 April 1975 the central organ of the SED, *Neues Deutschland* (ND), published a telegram of congratulations, signed by Erich Honecker, on Hermlin's sixtieth birthday, which included these words: 'Your life and your creative activity are inseparably linked with the working class and its revolutionary party.' On 25 September 1975 ND printed a lengthy conversation between Hermlin and Horst Simon; on 2 October 1975 the same newspaper announced that the writer had been awarded the National Prize, First Class, for Art and Literature; and finally, on 9 October 1975, ND reported that, on the GDR's Day of National Celebration, in the Small Comedy Auditorium of the Deutsches Theater, Hermlin had read from the manuscript of the volume *Deutsches Lesebuch*, an anthology that he had been commissioned by the East Berlin Academy of the Arts to collect and which Reclam (Leipzig) is to publish in 1976.

So much benevolent official and semi-official attention might lead one to conclude that the writer Stephan Hermlin is one of the GDR's compliant, and therefore pampered, party bards. But that is not so. True, his communist convictions are beyond all doubt: at the early age of sixteen Rudolf Leder of Chemnitz, who later took Stephan Hermlin as his pseudonym, joined the communist youth league, and his friendship with Erich Honecker dates from that time; he worked in the anti-fascist resistance, emigrated, and after a two-year interlude when he worked for the radio in Frankfurt am Main, he settled in the GDR in 1947 – what better credentials could there be for a functionary of the SED?

And yet one also senses from the long birthday article that Kurt Stern published in ND on 12–13 April 1975 that Hermlin is by no means as uncontroversial a figure in the country of his choice as might appear from the reports first mentioned. Hermlin is defended against the criticism of being a supporter of aestheticism and *l'art pour l'art*, and there is reference to Hermlin's 'brightly scintillating personality', and to him having opponents and critics 'in our own country too'. And indeed this eminent author, who has often used his influence and prestige to protect colleagues under pressure in the GDR, is not easy for the dogmatists to come to terms with. And in fact in the past decades they have made sure that he could not exercise any immediate influence on the direction of the GDR's cultural policy, they reined him in when he pleaded for greater liberalism in cultural policy, and forced him to give up the offices he once held.

And in the sixties Hermlin practised self-criticism, as required by party discipline, but he did so without degrading himself or betraying his principles. So for all his fame, even he is not protected from petty bureaucratic harassment: thus in the summer of 1975, when he was invited to spend a semester as visiting lecturer at the University of Cincinnati (Ohio/USA), he was not allowed to take his son with him as he had wished; whereupon he decided rather to cancel his trip to the USA.

We have not heard much of Hermlin the creative writer in recent times. It is idle to speculate why Hermlin has for several years scarcely published anything that you could really call literature or poetry. There may be political or ideological reasons why he has fallen silent. However it is more probable that he rather had scruples of a specifically technical–aesthetic kind which prevented him from continuing to write in a manner which appeared dubious not just to a few critics but subsequently to himself as well. Thus in Honecker's congratulatory telegram it is symptomatic that there is scarcely any mention of Hermlin's current writing, but of works which 'delighted the builders of the infant German Democratic Republic' – and that after all is quite some while ago now.

SOURCE: *Deutschland Archiv*, no. 4 (April 1976) pp. 418ff.

12 February 1976

Dear Dr Corino

You tell me you are wanting to 'link' a broadcast of my poems on Hesse Radio with a criticism by a Herr Wallmann – that is the expression you chose to use. It is out of the question.

Herr Wallmann is not a critic, he neither has the knowledge nor the sensitivity to language which are indispensable for criticising lyric poetry. He is just a mediocre journalist who is waging the Cold War in the field of GDR literature. I do not follow his work, nor that of his fellow warriors, but we hear and read these things occasionally here, and find them difficult to pass judgment on.

I shall not go into the many inaccuracies in Wallmann's article. However, something I do regard as particularly malicious is the lie that the powers that be in the GDR prevented me from taking up a visiting professorship in the USA. The truth is that the authorities concerned immediately granted me and my family permission to leave the country for six months. The reasons why I cancelled my contract in June 1975 were purely personal and were my own decision.

In this connection I would mention that for several years the authorities have placed no obstacles of any kind in the way of colleagues or friends of mine, or myself, travelling to Western countries. Several of these colleagues have travelled with their families. Wallmann is perfectly well aware of that; he is deliberately lying. The writers I am thinking of include Stefan Heym, Christa Wolf, Ulrich Plenzdorf, Reiner Kunze, Günter Kunert, Heiner Müller.

If you want to give a proper commentary on my poems, there are plenty to choose from. Real critics such as Max Rychner and Hans Mayer have written about my work; as have a number of writers such as Ilya Ehrenburg, Peter Huchel, Karl Krolow (often), Günter Kunert, Horst Bienek. . . . And incidentally, I particularly regard Hubert Witt's postscript to the *Urban Ballads* as a genuine critical analysis.

I have long ceased to take any interest in the publication of my work, and that goes for broadcasts too. I should therefore not mind if you decided not to go ahead with the broadcast. I am naturally prepared to comply with your request and read my poems. But of course not if I am to be subjected to any indignities.

Yours sincerely

Stephan Hermlin

15 April 1976

Dear Herr Hermlin

I have received your letter of 12 February and regret that a great overload of work has prevented me from replying earlier.

I don't think there is much point in discussing your assessment of Herr Wallmann as a critic. But I certainly think I am obliged to enquire about the accusations you direct at Wallmann as a journalist. I do not regularly follow his articles either (any more than you do). In the few instances I am acquainted with I have to admit I was unable to discover Wallmann waging a 'Cold War' against GDR literature, unless, that is, you even call it cold war when someone calls a spade a spade and also publicises facts whose propagation is disagreeable to the leadership in the GDR. I don't know Herr Wallmann very well, but I don't believe he is capable of maliciously lying, either with regard to yourself or anyone else. You describe it as a malicious lie that Wallmann reports you did not take up a visiting professorship in the USA because your son was refused a visa. I have now asked Wallmann about the truth of this allegation, and whether his sources were reliable, and he tells me that the information came directly from the institution that invited you: they said you had telephoned the American university concerned and explained your non-acceptance as quoted by Wallmann. The most favourable interpretation I can now put on this is that either you or your hosts were misunderstood, and I would ask you to clarify the affair. I am aware that a number of GDR writers such as Reiner Kunze, Christa Wolf, Günter Kunert or Irmtraud Morgner have recently been allowed to visit the West with their *spouses* (please note, not with their families!), and I am sure Herr Wallmann was also apprised of the fact. But I don't think you are entitled to generalise from your personal experiences and assume that these GDR writers, and others not named above, had 'no difficulties of any kind' in travelling to the West. I know from a number of authors the quite extraordinary efforts, indeed the cost to their health required for them to be able to take up invitations to the Western hemisphere, to say nothing of the pressures they were subjected to in their own country both before and after their journeys. The media in this country which are conscious of their responsibility deal with all these things only with the utmost circumspection, or even not at all, because the repercussions in the GDR even now affect not the bureaucracy, but the author, who is suspected of having stripped off items of his ideological travelling gear in the presence of the 'class-enemy'. Please don't misunderstand me: I very much welcome the fact that more and more authors from the GDR have been visiting the Federal Republic in recent years, but I regret the circumstances that often enough still surround these visits. However, I most particularly deplore the fact that invitations are quite frequently not passed on by the Writers' Union to the addressee, and that visas must continue to be regarded as *privileges*. If the GDR dismisses references to such factors, which cry out to be changed, by reference to the CSCE as 'interference in internal affairs', as 'cold war', as 'deliberate lies', then we have reason to fear for détente and the development of cultural relations. And if I may apply the sharp end of this observation to your relations (or non-relations) with Herr Wallmann: I should be very interested to know whether you are accusing him of deliberately and maliciously lying. I very much hope you will feel able to withdraw that remark. And are you, furthermore, prepared to specify the errors in his article? For my part, I am confident that Wallmann will not hesitate to correct all genuine errata, regardless of where and in what context they appear.

I now await your answer; in the meantime I shall look more closely at what the literature has to say about you, and consider in what manner we can present your *Urban Ballads* to our listeners that would be acceptable to all parties.

Yours sincerely

Dr Carl Corino

6 May 1976

Dear Herr Corino

Let's keep it short. You are obviously upset that I called a hack-scribbler a liar. You adopt a threatening tone to ask whether I wouldn't be willing to state that he is not. I'm afraid I am not. And incidentally I never telephoned the university concerned. But I admit it is a lesser lie that is at issue here – I was recently shown another article by the same author in which it is announced that I received the National Prize 'as the price for silence'.

Just one remark concerning your disquisitions on the position of writers: the opponents that writers have in this country have always had their opposite numbers on the other side. You are a case in point.

As for your problem of 'finding a manner' in which I can 'be presented' and be made 'acceptable to all parties': it is surely you who are asking a favour of me, not the other way round – and the manner, indeed a manner acceptable to all parties, is simply not negotiable.

I should be glad if you would refrain from further correspondence.

Yours sincerely

Stephan Hermlin

28 May 1976

Dear Herr Hermlin

Dr Corino was kind enough to allow me sight of the correspondence he had with you. As my review of your *Urban Ballads* was discussed in that correspondence, I am taking the liberty of expressing my own views on the subject.

I will make no comment on the tone of your letter and the verbal abuse it contained, for which my review gave you no grounds. I have to admit I was somewhat put out by the way you use polemic in place of argument. I can only regard your irritation as an expression of the anger you felt at the literary criticism that I have at various times applied to your works. As a critic I am, of course, used to the authors under review not always reacting with pleasure. What no doubt makes the situation worse in your case is that you are unfamiliar with independent literary criticism, since you live in a country where 'literary criticism only exists in name' (as your colleague Rolf Schneider wrote in no. 12/1975 of the journal, *Europäische Ideen*), and where people have yet to demand the 'separation of art from administration' – as Franz Fühmann did in his paper delivered at the Seventh GDR Writers' Congress in November 1973. After all, in the social system in which you live – and this is something that is very hard for us to imagine here – every publication has to be officially approved; your volume *Urban Ballads*, for example, bears the licence number 360.340/17/75. We haven't had such licences here since the end of the Occupation. So I should think that it must be difficult for an author, whose books have thus appeared by official permission, as required for publication, to accept criticism of these books, to which the state has, so to speak, after all given a seal of approval. I therefore attribute your overreaction to the fact that you are unaccustomed to stormy weather in respect of literary criticism, and that you expect not to be 'subjected to any indignities' (as you put it). The idea that a book that the authorities have allowed to be printed should be 'subjected to indignities' and criticised, must indeed be unfamiliar to you.

In your letter of 12 February 1976, you refer to 'many inaccuracies' in my article. I cannot, of course, answer this charge since you do not specify the alleged inaccuracies. You merely refer to the 'lie' that higher authorities in the GDR had prevented you from taking up a visiting professorship in the USA. But I never made such a statement: what I actually wrote was rather that you had preferred to decline the professorship, as you were not allowed to take your son with you. You will hardly be able to dispute this account of events. Nor is it based on rumours, but on reliable information. In the autumn of 1974, Professor Jerry Glenn of the Department of Germanic Languages and Literatures at the University of Cincinnati had invited me to take up a visiting professorship in Cincinnati for the academic year 1975/76. In July 1975, Professor Helga Slessarev, who now chairs the Department in Cincinnati, then telephoned me and repeated the offer of a visiting professorship, explaining that they were interested in getting a German visiting lecturer as soon as possible, as Stephan Hermlin had cancelled his contract, because the authorities in the GDR had not allowed him to take his son with him on the journey.

This, my dear Herr Hermlin, is the truth. There are therefore no grounds for rejecting my account of events as a 'lie' and 'malicious'. Rather it is you who have moved some distance away from the truth.

Then you write that the authorities in your country have for several years placed 'no obstacles of any kind in the way of writers travelling to Western countries', and several of them had travelled with their families. I ask myself, my dear Herr Hermlin, whether – although I can hardly imagine it – you wrote this in ignorance of the facts, or whether you were deliberately misrepresenting the facts that were known to you. Your account is either irresponsible or cynically dishonest.

The fact is, of course, that – as Dr Corino did point out – it is still a privilege for an author from the GDR to be allowed to travel to the West on a visit. A number of writers whose names are known to me – I mustn't mention their names here for fear of getting them into bad odour with their authorities – have still never enjoyed this mark of favour from the state; indeed, they are already regarded with suspicion and have to explain themselves if they receive visitors from the West. Others, who were allowed to travel, were subjected to strong pressure both before and after the journey.

Even the examples you gave are incorrect. Thus Reiner Kunze has still never been allowed to travel to the West with his family, i.e. with his wife and daughter. And you will surely not seriously want to stick by your statement that 'no obstacles of any kind' are being placed in his way. I would just remind you that for years Kunze was forbidden to travel to Sweden in order personally to receive a literature prize the Swedes had awarded him in 1973; this journey to Sweden has not been approved to this day, so that the prize was eventually handed over to Kunze this spring in the Swedish embassy in Berlin (GDR).

And may I also remind you of your colleague Wolf Biermann who for ten years has been forbidden to perform or to publish in your country? Wolf Biermann was not even allowed to perform at a large anti-fascist rally against the Franco regime in October 1975 in Offenbach, and sing his 'Franco Song' and the 'Song of the Red Stone of the Wise'.

These facts are known to you, my dear Herr Hermlin, you know the sort of harassment being faced by a critical socialist and the son of an anti-fascist murdered by the Nazis – and you write that 'no obstacles of any kind' are placed in the way of your friends and colleagues by the authorities. Is Wolf Biermann not your colleague? Are the other authors who are being pressurised not your colleagues?

Let me remind you of the Charter of the International PEN Club, which you have signed just as I have; it says: 'PEN stands for the principle of unhampered transmission of thought within each nation and between all nations, and members pledge themselves to oppose any form of suppression of freedom of expression in the country and community to which they belong'. I now call on you, my dear Herr Hermlin, to comply with this obligation that you have undertaken, instead of falsely asserting that 'no obstacles of any kind' are placed in the way of GDR authors in your country. And incidentally it is not just writers who are affected: likewise, in accordance with the spirit of the Helsinki agreements, no one should face 'obstacles to travelling to Western countries'. We on our side are making every effort to combat reactionary tendencies and threatened restrictions on basic rights; your task is to work for the implementation of basic rights (such as freedom of expression, freedom of the press, and freedom of movement) in your country.

Finally, a word about the comment in your letter of 6 May 1976. It would indeed have been quite disgraceful if I had claimed you had been given the National Prize 'as the price for silence', in the sense that you had allowed yourself to be bribed into silence with money. What I actually wrote, in a review of your book, *Der Leutnant York von Wartenburg*, was that it was a long time since you had published any creative writing; and that was why in 1954, when you were given the National Prize, various derisive comments about 'the price for silence' were to be heard in the GDR. I was therefore merely quoting a witticism that was not of my invention and is no disparagement to you, but merely refers to the quantity of your literary production. And you can hardly have failed to understand the remark in the sense in which I intended it – I don't know why in your letter to Dr Corino you should make out that you took this passage in my review in any other way.

I have written to you in such detail and tried your patience at such excessive length, because I wanted to demonstrate to you point by point that the remarks you objected to in my review are correct. It will not only be of interest to Dr Corino that you have falsely accused me of lying, and yet have yourself, as I have shown you, knowingly departed from the truth.

Yours sincerely

Jürgen P. Wallmann

SOURCE: *Deutschland Archiv*, no. 8 (August 1976) pp. 843–7; no. 4 (April 1976) p. 418f.

10. WRITER JUREK BECKER ON THE POST-BIERMANN ERA IN THE GDR

SPIEGEL Herr Becker, at the 1973 Congress of GDR Writers you expressed the view that the increased interest West German critics were showing in GDR literature arose in part from an attempt to drive a wedge between GDR authors and the SED. Isn't it now the East German state party which has driven a wedge between itself and the writers over the Biermann affair?

BECKER Basically I still hold the opinion which you quoted.

Certainly, and I think one can say this without implying a value judgment, one motive of many reviewers in the Federal Republic for dealing with GDR literature, is to foment some kind of unrest. And the literature which these reviewers encourage is generally of a kind that causes and runs into difficulties in our country.

What has now happened is quite unconnected with this. In response to Wolf Biermann's expatriation a number of writers have done something which is very unusual in the GDR, but – in my view – appropriate, namely they have protested. The party in its turn has done something very usual, but – in my view – inappropriate, namely, taken reprisals. If writers are only allowed to state their opinion when they are proclaiming their agreement with some government policy, then writers are superfluous and they can be allocated to more useful forms of employment.

SPIEGEL So the SED has driven a wedge into the core of its own support. . . .

BECKER Yes. But this thing shouldn't be blown up out of proportion and turned into a sensation, because the number of writers who are, or think they are, on the other side of the split, is relatively small.

SPIEGEL But Jurek Becker, Stephan Hermlin, Christa Wolf, Volker Braun, Stefan Heym, Sarah Kirsch and Günter Kunert, to name just some of them, are among the most significant GDR authors.

BECKER That is also debatable. What makes a writer significant? The party doesn't necessarily feel that those writers are its most important and significant whom you or the West German publishers consider the most important and significant.

SPIEGEL Hermann Kant. . . .

BECKER Precisely, he is certainly not on our side of the split, and heaven knows, he isn't the only one. I must admit I'm also inclined to the view that the ones who have committed themselves here definitely do constitute a sizeable section of what I think of as worthwhile GDR literature. But when I say that, I have to remember that other people think differently.

SPIEGEL Up until the autumn of last year one might have believed that the SED had decided to allow writers considerable freedom – because it realised that if literature is too strictly censored it is bound to get bogged down in provincialism. You, Volker Braun and Ulrich Plenzdorf were able to publish books which certainly didn't kowtow to the party. Shortly before the Biermann row, you yourself optimistically stated that the GDR appeared to be consolidating itself and that the 'opportunities for free-ranging discussion' were increasing. Were you mistaken?

BECKER I suspect that the Biermann case is the result of a miscalculation. Those who instigated the expatriation haven't considered the consequences.

SPIEGEL Did you seriously think your petition would be successful?

BECKER Yes. But I must be more specific about that. I don't know whether I thought that just this letter to the government would result in the decision against Biermann being withdrawn. But I thought there was a good chance that, at the end of the process we had set going, it might be revised.

But regardless of whether the hope was realistic or not, I believed that I had no other choice than to do what I did. It seemed to me simply ridiculous to take such a decision lying down.

SPIEGEL Was it really so ridiculous to expel the trouble-maker Biermann from the GDR? Didn't the SED have to make an example, so as to maintain socialist discipline in society?

BECKER I can think of a lot of reasons why it perhaps wasn't necessary. For instance: the inhabitants of a country have to be told precisely what kind of remarks might result in them having their citizenship withdrawn. In other words, there must be a demarcation line which can be clearly seen. I regard that as a fundamental requirement of any state.

For instance: I consider the way this affair was set going

scandalous. It would be absurd to think that Biermann was expatriated because of that performance in Cologne, which until then no one in the GDR knew anything about. I suspect that they more or less planned to boot Biermann out, in a way that those responsible even thought was elegant; I suspect they thought it would save them the embarrassment of dragging him bodily to the frontier.

For instance: expatriation appears to me to be a political device that has nothing to do with Central Europe. Even if lawyers proved to me that it is allowed by some current law, such a law belongs to a world which can hold no attraction for me.

SPIEGEL What was it about Biermann that upset them exactly?

BECKER I'm not the person you should be asking, because I don't think there was anything upsetting about Biermann's public performances. And I think he could have lived in our country like anyone else. I think he ought to have. . . .

SPIEGEL . . . and of course he wanted to. . . .

BECKER Naturally I can try and read people's minds and repeat rumours about what made Biermann so unforgivably upsetting: a performance in a church; the fear that there might be more such performances, in bigger and bigger churches; disquiet that people were gradually seeing in Biermann a GDR version of Amnesty International. And you know – a singer who is not allowed to perform has got time on his hands. For some harassed people he really was someone they could turn to and set out their case.

You can understand a government getting uncomfortable if a fellow like that is starting to make a collection of embarrassing incidents, and on top of that he knows the channels to broadcast them loud and clear. The reasons why Biermann was thrown out must be hidden away in one of these areas.

SPIEGEL And Reiner Kunze?

BECKER The legal difference is that Kunze wasn't expatriated, but applied to leave.

SPIEGEL But Kunze didn't go voluntarily either, it was just that the means used to get rid of him were more subtle.

BECKER That is a problem of interpretation. The fact is, in my opinion, that Kunze had been living for a long time in an intolerable situation, a situation that he had brought upon himself simply and solely through writing and saying what he thought right.

However, Kunze is not the only one to have enjoyed this kind of treatment. You are right that an expatriation can be executed in an almost elegant fashion. One can also avoid expatriation in an inelegant fashion, by locking people up. . . .

SPIEGEL . . . such as other Biermann sympathisers, like the writer Jürgen Fuchs or the musicians Christian Kunert and Gerulf Pannach?

BECKER Those are basically variations on the Kunze case, only they are relatively unknown, relatively out of the public eye. You know, Fuchs, Kunert and Pannach and eight people from Jena are still in jail, six or seven months after they were put away for doing no more than I have done. We have taken note of what has happened, but life goes on. While we are sitting here, they are in their cells. It would seem dishonourable to me to behave as if those cells did not exist, as though one could just put them out of one's mind.

SPIEGEL Let us return to your former optimism. Do the Biermann and Kunze cases therefore mark the end of the liberalisation of art in the GDR, or was this liberalisation always spurious, and the Biermann affair, so to speak, just the logical outcome of a policy which artists had for too long mistakenly believed to be liberal?

BECKER I'm no soothsayer, nor can I pretend that I'm party to discussions like: shall we just give the appearance of liberalising cultural life, or shall we really do it?

SPIEGEL But you have had a taste of the SED's cultural policy yourself. So you can express an informed opinion.

BECKER My recent experiences make me think today that the extra freedom of movement for artists in recent years resulted primarily from not being able to prevent it any more, and less from the conviction that artists need freedom of movement. Or that a society needs freedom of movement. It is clear to me that this is a somewhat harsh conclusion to be drawn from what has happened.

SPIEGEL Can the damage done by the Biermann affair ever be repaired? Do you believe that the literary scene in the GDR will ever again be as it was before Biermann's expatriation?

BECKER You mustn't overdramatise the situation. There are certainly some writers who have excised from their minds the mechanism by which such things are repressed, once they had become aware of it. I count myself amongst them. In the case of many writers, this nifty action will sooner or later result in them acting and behaving as though nothing had happened – and that has already started. . . .

SPIEGEL . . . as though there hadn't been a break?

BECKER What do you mean by a break? I wouldn't call it a fundamental break, even in my case. It's just that I'm not prepared to keep silent any longer on certain matters out of what I now consider to be wrong-headed solidarity. Just because I once promised some woman I'd marry her, I can't be expected to go on ignoring her failings for ever. Keeping one's mouth shut only makes sense if one believes that the party basically wants what I want. And that belief has been somewhat shaken.

SPIEGEL Aren't you afraid you might end up like Biermann?

BECKER I'm not trying to evade the question by giving this answer: it is of no help to me, whether I have or might have such a fear. I can't prevent it happening, nor can I choose for it to happen.

SPIEGEL Yes, you can choose for it to happen, by adopting certain tactics.

BECKER That's just what I mean. I see myself as being at a stage when such tactics are beyond my powers. It would be pointless to try to hide from you that in the last seven or eight months my identity has changed in some way. One reason may be that I am now 39 and am suddenly afraid that at the age of 60 I shall still be playing a tactical game – for some purpose that has ceased to exist.

SPIEGEL How is the Jurek Becker of today different from the Jurek Becker of autumn 1976?

BECKER Until I was expelled from the party last December I belonged to the Socialist Unity Party of Germany. I believe I was what in my country they call a good comrade. I was always careful to observe the loyalty prescribed by the statute of the party. And often – if there were disputes or differences of opinion that I considered potentially explosive – I tried to sort them out, so to speak, through official channels, internally.

Just to give you one example: after the troops went into Czechoslovakia in 1968 quite a few people in the GDR, including myself, thought it should never have happened. I talked about it in the Writers' Union, and not with you in *Spiegel*, and there's a very considerable difference.

I don't have this sense of loyalty any more – after all, it wasn't implanted in me by God – because the party statute has ceased to apply to me. Now that I have been treated in a manner which I can no longer find acceptable, I can't for the life of me see any good reason for hiding my opinions, merely because they don't suit the line of my former party. . . .

SPIEGEL . . . and not telling them to *Spiegel* this time. . . .

BECKER Actually, it's appalling that I've got to talk to you about them. Would you believe how much happier I would be to give this interview to *Neues Deutschland*.

SPIEGEL Why don't you?

BECKER A very good question. I suspect that *Neues Deutschland* are not interviewing me now because it hasn't yet crossed their minds to do so.

SPIEGEL Joking apart, what in your view is then actually the task facing a writer who deserves the name in a communist country?

BECKER I believe that in a socialist country a writer has a function which he can never attain in the West. And that, basically, is what makes it fascinating to be here. Perhaps this sounds too grand: a writer is expected to be a guide for living.

SPIEGEL A function that in capitalist countries is fulfilled by the press and not by literature.

BECKER You said you wanted to be serious now. So: with the best will in the world one can't say that the press, radio and television in my country are free, as the West understands the word. Nor is there an uncensored literature. Yet the significance and explosive power of what goes on in literature are far greater than what the newspapers and television offer their long-suffering consumers.

SPIEGEL Isn't it logical to censor literature too, when the latter switches to trouble-making, as, in the SED's view, Biermann did?

BECKER I suspect that our censors originally started out by overestimating the power of literature, overestimating it both in a good and a bad sense. They thought, if we let people get at such and such a model television play, or model book, there will be certain specific consequences. Or they were afraid that if they let people get at this bad book or this bad film, there would be certain specific consequences. I don't think either of these things is the case. But having proceeded like that for twenty or thirty years, they now face what is known as a self-fulfilling prophecy. Because something of this kind now actually happens. The situation has thus gradually arisen where a literary person in our country has a power base that he can only dream about in the West. And that is also why the party keeps such a close watch on him.

SPIEGEL And what sort of a future does GDR literature seem to you to have? Will writers still be able to carry out the task of conveying information or exposing problems under the cloak of fiction at all?

BECKER You are not the only ones who would like to know that. I get an uncomfortable feeling looking at the culture sections in our papers in recent months. I fancy I detect a shift in what they consider worth disseminating. In other words, certain things are now being said pretty clearly which in a number of respects are different from before.

SPIEGEL Can you give some examples of what is worth saying and what isn't?

BECKER That would be like me giving marks.

SPIEGEL Well, what isn't said, then?

BECKER To put it over-crudely: the kind of literature that is given prominence is what our leading comrades would write if they were capable of it. And the kind of films that are praised are those that these same comrades would make if their time were not taken up with more important activities. What is far more important, i.e. encouraging critical producers, painters and writers, not just so that art can flourish, but to create happiness, that is neglected.

SPIEGEL Would you include Sarah Kirsch's volume of poems, *Rückenwind*, amongst those that are neglected?

BECKER Yes.

SPIEGEL But the book was allowed to come out, although Sarah Kirsch, like yourself, was kicked out of the party.

BECKER I said that I suspect that in the struggle for space to move in, the space that is granted is not what the party thinks appropriate but what it can't avoid giving. Perhaps the appearance of this book has something to do with that. There is a way of publishing books which is more like consigning them to the shredder than publishing. A book comes out in a very limited edition, it is never prominently displayed in the bookshops, it is nowhere reviewed, it is out of print in no time at all, there is no new edition. Then they say: what are you on about, we published it, didn't we?

SPIEGEL You have written a new book yourself. What is it about?

BECKER Amongst other things, about a man who is a teacher by profession, in his mid-thirties, and who feels like someone who all his life up till then has been able to draw on an inexhaustible bank account. Suddenly he feels that he has got to behave more responsibly than he has up to now with whatever he has left, however much it may be.

I describe how, as a result of this resolution, the man destroys more or less everything that he had, as they say, built for himself. He questions standards of behaviour that he had previously been subject to. His relations with acquaintances, friends and the authorities become more and more strained, because he now feels obliged to live up to his own insights. As a result he loses almost everything that had constituted his previous way of life. But it doesn't make him unhappy.

SPIEGEL A hero, then, who sets himself against the authorities, and wins the author's praise into the bargain. Have you any hope that this book will be published in the GDR?

BECKER Yes, I have, and I also have the hope that it won't just be a relapse on their part.

SPIEGEL Somewhere in the vaults there is a film with a script by Jurek Becker, in which a leading role is played by Manfred Krug, who went to the West at the end of June. Will this film get into the cinemas some time?

BECKER Whether this film will be shown or not, I'm not in a position to judge; as before, I hope so, but I'm afraid it won't.

SPIEGEL And why are you afraid it won't?

BECKER Oh lord, why? Because if you look at the way some

other things are normally dealt with in our country just now, I would think it would be most unusual for it to be shown.

SPIEGEL Not to mince words: because Krug is one of the performers?

BECKER And don't forget me. When Krug was in the West, a short newspaper report appeared in the East, the gist of which was that he had every opportunity to develop artistically, that he was being made offers and that he had turned them all down. That was just not true.

Why do they do that? The most likely answer: because the party is always right. That's why they do that sort of thing. But nowadays I think we may be allowed some serious doubts, the party is most certainly not always right. And it is providing so much evidence that it is not, that one can hardly keep up with it.

SPIEGEL After your experiences with the party, are you still the socialist that you once were?

BECKER I consider myself a socialist, yes. But I can't go along with your last four words, that I once was, because I still am what I once was, as far as my hopes are concerned, as far as my desires are concerned, as far as my intentions are concerned; but I am not what I once was, as far as my methods are concerned, nor as far as my friends are concerned, though I am not the only one responsible for that, nor as far as my comrades are concerned.

It is clear to me that whether someone is a socialist or not doesn't only depend on him and how he sees himself. But the strengths and weaknesses of a party that is called socialist don't only depend on the party either. And it's not only up to the party to award such stamps of quality.

SPIEGEL Your colleague Rolf Schneider recently told us he was afraid Jurek Becker would be the next to leave the GDR. Almost at the same time rumours cropped up in the GDR that you had already applied to emigrate. Do you want to leave the GDR?

BECKER Well I haven't applied to emigrate. I haven't spoken to Schneider for ages, and sometimes he says more than he knows.

You should have asked him from what direction this fear assailed him.

It is true that for some time I have been behaving in a manner that can't please the party. That raises the question: does someone who expresses opinions in our country that the party dislikes hearing, does such a person necessarily incur the suspicion of wanting to leave the country?

If so, that would be a bad sign. But I can't see that I have given any other indication than that to make anyone suppose I want to leave.

SPIEGEL Mightn't there be method in these rumours, to get rid of the awkward writer Jurek Becker in a more refined way than Biermann?

BECKER I watched from close by how it all started with Manfred Krug's emigration, as I am a close friend of his. Not with an application to emigrate but with rumours. Lies about him started simultaneously in Suhl and Rostock. They really became very bad, the sheer number of them became quite frightening. The number of people involved in circulating these rumours was terrifying. The variety of the rumours and the persistence of the people spreading them inevitably resulted in the situation gradually changing for Krug.

SPIEGEL Might your situation change in the same way too, until one day you are forced to go, although you want to stay?

BECKER It is not just empty talk if I say that despite many disputes I have always felt at ease in this country. This sense of well-being didn't come from enjoying nature here, or from the bread rolls tasting so good and the cars being so fast. I was happy because I always had the feeling of being able to get involved, of participating in something that I regard as important.

I want to stay in this country as someone who can publish what he writes; because in the long run, for a writer, that is the only practicable method of getting involved. But if I have to keep my mouth shut, then I'd rather keep my mouth shut in the Bahamas.

SOURCE: *Der Spiegel*, no. 30, 18 July 1977.

11. HARTMUT KÖNIG AT AN FDJ CONFERENCE ON CULTURE

Pseudoculture and self-styled 'modernism'

Dear friends and comrades!

Our country is, as everyone knows, not impervious to the outside world, and our young people are bombarded by a wealth of aesthetic impressions, which impinge on their consciousness, indeed even on their unconscious, from every sphere of reality, including the arts, from the past as well as the present, from close to home as well as from far afield. Our young people get to know not only contemporary works which are profoundly imbued with socialist ideas, but also works of contemporary art from our country which do not accord with their true interests or their expectations.

At the same time, young people are confronted by unsolicited imports 'over the ether' of a reactionary or trivial nature. Sometimes indeed by those that have been solicited, such as *Towering Inferno* which after all was presumably not purchased for the instruction of the fire brigade; films, in other words, which for all their occasional idealism or value as exposés, inevitably offer an idyllic picture of conditions in late capitalist society. Let me say at this juncture: we are in favour of high-quality excitement and entertainment, particularly as we are not exactly spoiled by our film industry and televison in this respect. But we are against unthinkingly taking over products of the capitalist 'dream factory', the romanticised Westerns à la Reagan. We want sunrays, not Rayguns; but not the sunrays emitted by a glittering pseudoculture masquerading as the solution to every problem. That is why we agree with those young people, who in our cultural discussions asked those who buy in foreign films to take more account of young people's need for entertainment in which human beings retain their humanity.

Interesting productions of *Faust*, such as those we have seen in Schwerin or put on by young drama students in Berlin, show how much interest the classics have for young people in particular. At the same time, their desire for modern, up-to-date treatment of this heritage is only natural.

But not everything that assumes this guise of being 'modern' or 'avant-garde' shares our socialist thinking, for instance, Heiner Müller's distasteful *Macbeth* at the *Volksbühne* Theatre. The press talked of a wilfully fatalistic 'insistence on the absolute discord and incompatibility between human attitudes and objective power structures', the esoteric 'celebration of a black mass', 'cheap exploitation of theatrical devices' and 'alienating the audience'.

And in fact it is not only the historical perspective that is lost here, but also the belief in humanity. Young people rightly object if the humanistic heritage is sacrificed to an anti-historical, indeed a pessimistic view of life. But many people even welcome it, saying that youth has no time for 'museum pieces'. To which we reply: the oldest museum piece we know of is the inability to recognise social progress. And true enough: we are against such museum pieces.

Portrayal of socialist development

It is remarkable that some literature specialists elevate to the status of true art works which reflect the revolutionary conflicts of our age inadequately or even not at all, by asserting that the main characteristic of the 'central literary and artistic development' since the Eighth Party Congress has been 'the shedding of illusions'. This was rightly attacked years ago. Expressions like 'a real hunger for the unvarnished', and the attempt to declare the seventies and early eighties to be a kind of 'age of majority for artistic sobering-up processes', result in new works of art not infrequently being measured by this mistaken yardstick. It is unreasonable and unacceptable for our continuing struggle for the victory of socialism to be divided into periods of 'illusion' and 'sobriety', 'varnish' and 'unvarnish'. The best works of our national art often demonstrate that at all stages in our evolution real revolutionaries were both soberly analytical and capable of passionate inspiration. They have always thrown themselves into the breach, learnt by their mistakes and never been afraid of taking new initiatives.

The crucial development in our literature and art today, and with our greater ability to understand society today, is the exploration and true-to-life portrayal of the dialectic of our socialist evolution. And not for its own sake either, but with the clear aim of advancing social consciousness and the thoughts, feelings and actions of people for socialism.

The political and social climate in our country favours this. Thus, at the Tenth Party Congress, Comrade Erich Honecker was able to describe it as one of the most remarkable achievements of socialist–realist art in the previous five years to have taken up and answered 'questions of our time concerning the value of man and his position in society, concerning freedom and responsibility, and concerning the desire for happiness and the possibilities of realising it under socialism'.

No room here for the unprincipled

Dear friends and comrades!

The loyalty to the principles of socialist–realistic artistic creation which characterises the great majority of our artists, is the only correct answer to the enemy's tactic of 'eroding' socialism. The enemy attacks our constructive portrayal of contradictions and conflicts, and encourages people who have a destructive approach to our development. The West has these 'critical chain-stores', as Hermann Kant once called them, 'pronouncing on the morality and decency or immorality and indecency of GDR authors, through their countrywide sales network'. Their aim is to injure and destroy socialism, and to this end they hire anyone who is ready to market his anti-socialist views, even in the absence of artistic merit. And so Poche gets a capitalist copyright for *Atemnot*, as Schneider does for *November*. And indubitably, not on account of any literary ability, but solely for denying and slandering the essential truths of socialism in the GDR. Have not such people in spirit already clearly overstepped the boundary between capitalism and socialism, across which our passport enables them to travel to the West? One remembers Mayakovski, who expressed his pride in the red Soviet passport in imperishable verses. And one then asks oneself how the attitude of those who commute between one world and another and pour out buckets of filth against us in front of Western cameras and in institutes of higher learning or even – as in the case of Jakobs – trot along to the 'House of the German East', can accord with the hammer and dividers on our GDR passport. Their love for our passport doubtless amounts solely to the fact that it also temporarily dispels a serious worry: namely, that the literary honours in the West may dry up if their dissident status lapses, which is the only thing of interest for imperialist strategy and is itself created by the West. Young people in our country stand firm in their opposition to such lack of principle and such continual betrayal of our homeland and our ideals. We show our love and respect to those artists who consciously place all their knowledge and ability on the side of socialism, who in the struggles of our time stand on the side of progress, whose opinions cannot be bought, who love our country and our people from the bottom of their hearts, and whose art is a signpost to us, the youthful builders and defenders of socialism.

Young artists aiming high

It is characteristic of the large majority of young artists growing up in our country that their socialist patriotism and proletarian internationalism, their attitudes and actions, their partisan search for truth and their ceaseless striving for greater artistic mastery are in full accord with each other.

But from some people we have heard a different tone: 'Literature is a form of opposition. . . . It means resistance, firstly to adults, to school, and later ideologically too.' That, and more, could be read in a GDR journal for literature, aesthetics and cultural theory, and came from the mouths of people whose uninformed, other-worldly statements about what they consider to be the daily life of the people, must appear more than strange to every young person whose existence is firmly rooted in our way of life.

Nurture the budding talents fighting for socialism

Whilst the Marxist–Leninist classics always referred to the need to grasp the relationship between individuals and society in concrete historical terms, some of these people prefer a general 'philosophy of man', indeed they represent society and our state as being in conflict with individuals, and the present also in conflict with the future.

What they are basically saying is this: the 'constraints of socialism' prevent the free development of the personality.

Developing one's individuality in the face of our society is regarded as the 'humanisation of socialism'. What a contradiction, totally divorced from our reality, in which socialist society gives all its members the best opportunities to achieve their right to happiness!

One thing must be made clear: one must always have patience with talent while it is still searching and developing. Pushing precipitately ahead in its desire for change, revolutionary impatience – these things are natural and not unnatural in youth.

Understanding is therefore always called for when early attempts at art come to grief, and our party has the greatest understanding. It has confidence in artists and confers considerable social responsibility on them while they are still young. But what cannot and will not be tolerated is a basic attitude towards existing socialism which takes a pessimistic view of history and ignores realities, whether such an attitude is adopted by young or experienced artists. The world in which we live and work cannot be intellectually illuminated in such a way. Those who cannot see the truths of life will thus find their soul shrivelling and their talent going to waste, because from the outset it does not even try to discover the processes and contradictions by which socialism progresses. To say nothing of artistic creation, for which discovery is essential.

False laurels of certain 'Friends of Art'

It is also instructive to observe what 'advisers' and 'friends of art' arrive on the scene, from far and near, to encourage this attitude of ignoring existing socialism. Let us look at those in our own country. Sometimes they bear famous names, and if young, inexperienced people hear words of flattery like 'behold: a poet', their chests at once swell at such praise. And the false laurels go to their heads, often enough tempting them into a form of creativity lacking any secure foundation. The unctuous attentions paid by certain Western publishers particularly towards first attempts at literature are misinterpreted by some young authors as high regard for their abilities, and then they complain about what they call the blinkered character of the 'socialist apparatus' when people who have their feet firmly on the ground are unable to accept other-worldly, shallow thinking as art. We would be happy if the

Writers' Union, together with the FDJ, would take a clearer stand against such false patrons. The youth league must, and certainly will, enter into discussion with young writers who are going astray. What they need, above all, is for social structures and processes to be clarified. But we also say, our chief concern is to nurture those budding talents who love and defend our country from the bottom of their hearts, also defending it intellectually against ignorance, stupidity, treachery and ideological diversion. It is beyond our comprehension that, in assessing a manuscript, some publishers' readers give higher priority to mastery of certain kinds of formal language than to content itself. A publisher's reader has only done his job, and a publisher has only succeeded in his promotion policy, if he has advanced the process of political and artistic maturation of the young writer to the point where publication is in the interests of society. The criteria for this cannot, and must not, vary from one publisher to another. Today in particular, when our opponents are attempting to misuse culture and art as a 'Trojan horse' for the purpose of ideological diversion against socialism, we would encourage all young artists to place their art at the service of socialism, the true humanism of our age. For it is, and will continue to be, a simple truth of the class struggle that the development of budding talent in our country requires close emotional ties with the life, the struggles, yearnings and feelings of our people. The youth league asks all artists to help, through their work and their personal example, to arouse and consolidate this attitude to life in every young person who is artistically active.

SOURCE: *Junge Welt*, 22 October 1982.

12. APPEAL BY THE WRITER JOACHIM SEYPPEL AND TATJANA RILSKY TO KURT HAGER, SECRETARY OF THE SED CENTRAL COMMITTEE FOR CULTURE AND SCIENCE

Dear Professor Hager,

What has happened to Robert Havemann cannot just be accepted in silence. We may wish to write to you on wider, more general issues at a later date, but with particular regard to Havemann, we feel obliged as citizens to say what we think, and whether we support or deplore the actions that have been taken. Or are we perhaps supposed to support his house-arrest, his isolation, the involvement of his family, in other words all the suffering inflicted on an honourable man? And the fact that his case is being kept secret from the population? And the fact that his house has been searched and that the materials he needs for his work carted away, and that an old man is being tormented? And the fact that we are not being told the reason for these repressive measures?

If the organs of state are so sure of themselves, why is it all being kept secret, why is he being kept incommunicado, why go outside the law? Is this state so weak that it has to fear a writer? Or can a writer be so powerful that he can make this state tremble? Now they are looking for evidence that Havemann has broken the law, so that they can prosecute him, and in particular, for contraventions of the 'Customs and Currency Regulations', so that they can present every tinpot capitalist with proof and say: Look, it's no different from your country, those who don't declare foreign currency earnings must naturally expect to suffer the consequences. With the plethora of laws that are to hand, it is easy to convict any citizen of violating them – if one wants to.

And now they do want to. It is as though they wanted to get even with him. The actions being taken against Havemann are dishonourable, indeed they deserve to be punished themselves. They pre-date 'McCarthyism', being a symptom of old-style Stalinism, which people believed was a thing of the past or at least they seemed to want to make it so. It will now be interesting to see what bureaucratic reprisals we shall ourselves have to face for expressing our opinions in an open letter – because public problems can only be discussed openly.

Incidentally, we can't for one moment imagine that someone like yourself, who is serving the cause of our culture, could be behind the actions taken against Havemann. . . . Dear Professor Hager: please exert your influence to ensure that Havemann is treated humanely. For our part, we feel a deep sense of shame.

Yours sincerely,

Tatjana Rilsky

Joachim Seyppel

Berlin, 25 April 1979

SOURCE: *Frankfurter Rundschau*, 3.5.79.

Hager replies to Seyppel

My dear Frau Rilsky, my dear Herr Seyppel,

In an open letter that appeared in the *Frankfurter Rundschau* on 3 May 1979 you appeal to me to exert my influence to ensure 'that Havemann is treated humanely'.

You would have done better to address yourself first to the competent organs of justice in the GDR to establish the facts; as it is, however, you have naïvely and uncritically based your letter on reports about Havemann in the Western media, without checking them first. You talk of 'repressive measures' and 'going outside the law', and repeat word for word other assertions made by these media which supposedly prove that Havemann has been inhumanely treated. But what are the facts?

1. From the beginning of the sixties Havemann has been stepping up his attacks on the socialist order of state and society in the GDR, publishing them chiefly in FRG journals. His hostile political views were publicly criticised for instance at the Fifth Conference of the SED's Central Committee in 1964, at conferences of party activists at the Humboldt University, and in my closing remarks at the social scientists' conference held in Berlin

on 25 and 26 November 1976. . . . We have as yet not changed this assessment of him in any way.

2. As Havemann continued to malign the socialist order of state and society in the GDR in articles and interviews published in conjunction with Western publishers and mass media, on 26.11.76 the local court in Fürstenwalde passed a legally binding judgment, in accordance with paragraphs 2 and 3 of the Decree on Residential Restrictions, by which Havemann is confined to his property in Grünheide. Thanks to the lenient attitude of the organs of justice, he was able to maintain contact with acquaintances and relatives in the GDR, visit members of his family in various parts of the GDR, and receive visits from them. He likewise regularly met his doctor, neighbours and the parish minister. The freedom of movement of his wife and child was at no time restricted.

3. Although Havemann constantly abused the leniency with which the judgment was enforced and recently made false allegations to the Western media to try to give the impression that he and his family were totally isolated, no further action was taken against him as a result of these gross violations of the law. The preliminary investigation into Havemann's affairs initiated by the customs authorities of the GDR on 17.4.79, on suspicion of offences against the GDR's currency law, was marked by similar restraint, inasmuch as the hearing took place at his own request in his home in the presence of a doctor.

It is therefore quite irresponsible of you to speak of 'going outside the law'. Or perhaps you believe that in a socialist state laws such as the currency laws may be flouted? (As everyone knows, currency offences are punishable in capitalist states too.) The laws of our state apply to Havemann as they do to every other citizen.

One also notices that Havemann enjoys making an exhibition of himself and getting himself talked about. The Western media would like to turn him into a martyr, although they have to admit he is an unpromising subject: without any help from him and despite all the slander, the socialist German Democratic Republic has made good progress in recent years. Or are you casting doubt on the successful implementation of the policies that were agreed at the Eighth and Ninth SED Party Congresses?

I have replied to you although it is not my custom to respond to 'open letters' or other publications of the Western media. Just think how much time one would waste if one were to deal with the rubbish that the Springer press, the so-called liberal bourgeois papers and FRG television are putting out, day in, day out, about the SED's cultural policy, for instance.

Herr Seyppel, you have obviously not yet grasped the fact that these media have been following an anti-communist line for thirty years, which includes constantly vilifying the first socialist state on German soil, and that Havemann has for years been actively participating in this anti-socialist campaign.

Yours sincerely

p.p. Kurt Hager

SOURCE: *Weltbühne* no. 20, 1979.

Havemann to Hager

Dear Kurt Hager,

Number 20,79 of *Weltbühne* carries your response to an open letter that the writer Seyppel and his wife published in the *Frankfurter Rundschau* on 3 May 1979. This letter was addressed to you and called upon you – I quote from your response – to exert your influence so 'that Havemann should be treated humanely'.

In fact the letter made a number of other points, the essential thing actually being the call for you to stop sending in the police to deal with people who criticise your policies, and instead to conduct an objective public debate.

To be quite honest, I am astonished that you reacted to these requests by saying: 'As Havemann continued to malign the socialist order of state and society in the GDR in articles and interviews he published . . .' (in the West, where else?) 'on 26.11.76 the local court in Fürstenwalde passed a legally binding judgment, by which Havemann is confined to his property in Grünheide.'

That is remarkably frank, franker than the local court in Fürstenwalde was allowed to be, at all events. It was obliged to base its – as I see it – unconstitutional judgment on just one publication of mine, namely my response in *Spiegel* to the expatriation of my friend Wolf Biermann. In its explanation of the judgment, it said that my publication endangered security and order in the GDR.

When one considers how many readers *Spiegel* has in the GDR, and the sort of people they are, one wonders what sort of simpleton thought up this explanation. Your explanation is of a quite different order. But though it makes things clearer, it certainly doesn't make them better: the local court's judgment blatantly contravenes Article 27 of the GDR constitution, which states:

> 1. Every citizen of the German Democratic Republic has the right, in accordance with the basic principles of this constitution, to express his opinions freely and in public. This right is not limited by any contract of service or employment. No one may suffer disadvantage from exercising this right.

Perhaps you will object that Article 27 restricts the freedom to express one's opinons to those opinions 'which are in accordance with the basic principles of this constitution'. But apart from the fact that I have a better opinion of the honest intentions of our constitution, I would ask you to point to just one line in the texts I have published which is not in accordance with the basic principles of this constitution. Or do you believe that only those opinions accord with the basic principles of this constitution which agree with the current opinions of the current Politburo? One might almost suppose that is what you think, when one reads what you wrote under point 1 in your reply to the Seyppels: 'His hostile political views were publicly criticised for instance at the Fifth Conference of the SED's Central Committee in 1964, at conferences of party activists at the Humboldt University (also 1964), and in my closing remarks at the social scientists' conference in Berlin on 26.11.76. (That was the day when I was placed under house arrest. Note R.H.) We have as yet not changed this assessment of him in any way.' Case proven!

But you are yourself perfectly well aware that in this 'assessment' of my political views you are flatly opposed by the large majority of communists in Europe and even in the GDR. That does not mean that all these comrades agree with everything I stand for. But the assertion that I am anti-communist and that my criticisms are an attack on socialism is something you could only permit yourself here in the GDR, because you mistakenly assume that no one here has any closer knowledge of what I have written, as you have declared it prohibited literature.

I never cease to be surprised at the low opinion you have of the persuasiveness of your own arguments. Are the positions you adopt really so weak that you think you have got to use the harshest methods of persecution to suppress all criticism, however tame? I believe the Seyppels are entirely right when they speak of 'going outside the law' in this connection. Even the judgment of the local court in Fürstenwalde was outside the law because it was unconstitutional. But what is one supposed to think when the lawyer who lodged an appeal against this judgment on my behalf, the internationally highly regarded Comrade Götz Berger, an old communist who fought in Spain, was thereupon disbarred without notice and without a word of explanation, by decree of the Minister of Justice?

And this whole business of setting dozens of policemen to keep watch over me in my house for two and a half years, and declaring the entire area round my house in Grünheide out of bounds, so that only local inhabitants and my closest relatives could enter, and having a procession of between three and six cars pursue me – at least while I was still allowed to leave my house and drive my car (over very short distances) – and when I used my small motor boat, setting two fast police boats to tail me, while my guards drove along the bank in cars: did I really owe all that, as you put it, to the 'leniency of the organs of justice', whose remarkable leniency furthermore eventually dwindled away until in the end they even prevented not just myself but my wife too from travelling to Berlin, and they ultimately also used force to prevent her and my six-year-old daughter from leaving our property?

It seems to me that when the Seyppels refer merely to 'reprisals' and 'going outside the law', their language was very much on the mild and restrained side, because they thought that would be more effective. And as far as the actual events during my two and a half years of isolation are concerned, they were at least better informed than you. You simply must appreciate the fact that the police guard outside our house also prevented my wife and daughter from leaving our property, and that they were not allowed to come and go freely again until I had protested about it in a public statement addressed to the West German broadcasting network, Amnesty International and the Italian comrade, Prof. Lucio Lombardo-Radice.

Under point 3 in your answer to Seyppel's open letter you even accuse me of constantly abusing 'the leniency with which the judgment was enforced' and making 'false allegations' to try to give the impression that I and my family were completely isolated by these actions. But what was the nature and purpose of the exercise, if not to try to isolate me from everyone around me, by intimidating my friends and acquaintances, and to prevent me by means of continual threats from expressing my critical opinions in public, and thus to suppress a right which the constitution guarantees to every citizen of the GDR? But in your view, to exercise this right appears to be one of the 'gross violations of the law' that you accuse me of, in which connection you remark that – generously – 'no further action was taken'.

You then begin discussing the preliminary investigation initiated against me on suspicion of violating the currency law, and you remark that here too the proceedings were 'marked by restraint, inasmuch as the hearing took place at his request at his home in the presence of a doctor'. But I think you are aware that the hearing had to be conducted at my home, not at my request, but on my doctor's instructions. I shall not express an opinion here as to how far the form and content of this whole preliminary investigation are still within the law: its purpose is quite obviously not to prosecute currency offences, but, as with all the other actions previously undertaken against me, simply and solely to suppress the freedom to express one's opinions.

And in case anyone should still harbour the slightest doubt about this, I should like to have explained to me why, when the house was searched, the only objects that were seized were those that have to do with my publishing activities: my typewriter, cameras, tape-recorder, cassette-recorder, all the manuscripts I was then working on, all my recent correspondence, all my tapes and cassettes, my whole photographic archives, over 190 journals and 177 books from my library, mainly modern Marxist literature, but also every copy of my own books, including foreign editions, and even two copies of James Joyce's *Ulysses*. I ask myself: how far can one actually go outside the law without covering oneself with shame before the whole civilised world?

I have appealed against the 10 000 mark fine imposed on me on 25 May 79 by the local court in Fürstenwalde for alleged currency offences, because I regard this prosecution as an act hostile to the state, which severely damages the national and international reputation of the GDR. In case the affair comes to court, I have contacted my comrades in the Eurocommunist parties to ask them to provide a defence lawyer. Ever since my friend, Götz Berger, lost the right to practise his profession because he enjoyed my confidence and was willing to defend me, I cannot – nor do I wish to – expose any lawyer to the risk of being treated like Götz Berger. But nor do I wish to expose any lawyer to the risk of not being treated like Götz Berger, as that would make people suspect he was not a lawyer whom one could trust at all. In these circumstances the only possible solution is therefore to have a foreign comrade as my lawyer.

But, my dear Kurt Hager, would it not be even better simply to abandon all these inappropriate methods, and instead to return to the method of open and fair debate, which once upon a time was so highly regarded among communists. Would it not be a good idea to recall how Rosa Luxemburg and Lenin once publicly debated with each other on matters of principle, and yet without any personal hostility! Release Rudolf Bahro and enter into debate with him! And then it will be possible in the communist world – as is already occurring in the world at large, but could then happen here too – to discuss not just Bahro's views, but to weigh up your counter-arguments as well. Repeal the unconstitutional Paragraph 106 in the GDR's Penal Code (agitation against the state), which is being used to turn every attempt to exercise the right of free speech into a criminal act. Release all the prisoners who were sentenced under Paragraph 106. Open the newspapers and publications of the GDR to the voices of your critics and conduct an uninhibited public debate without reprisals against anyone.

Do you still believe that our state would collapse and socialism would be betrayed if you adopt these proposals? In fact the opposite would happen. I am fully confident of this: wherever I go I hear people's unvarnished opinions about you, because people trust me. People say: they'll never do that. But if they do it, it would be absolutely, inconceivably magnificent. And presumably not even the most pusillanimous doubter among you can deny that the international resonance that would result would give a great boost to our comrades in the Euro-parties, because at a stroke it would deprive anti-communism of its most effective arguments.

This is what I am proposing as a way of preparing for the thirtieth anniversary of our Republic.

With socialist greetings

Robert Havemann

SOURCE: *Frankfurter Rundschau*, 22 June 1979.

13. SECRET SPEECH BY ERICH MIELKE, MINISTER OF STATE SECURITY, TO HIS PROPAGANDA OFFICERS, 16 OCTOBER 1978

The aggressive and subversive nature (of the enemy) is apparent . . . from the fact that

- — he is concentrating the ideological offensive much more specifically on inspiring and organising 'internal opposition' and underground political activity in the socialist states.
- — he is more and more openly aiming to mobilise hostile forces and groupings in all the socialist states, and to unite these forces, in other words to internationalise his anti-socialist activities, and
- — to a much greater extent than previously, he is passing specific guide-lines for action to the hostile and negative forces in our countries. . . .

Imperialism's strategic plans in the ideological struggle against socialism are reflected particularly clearly in the large-scale human rights campaign launched by imperialist circles, which has been raised to the status of official government policy, especially by the Carter administration.

In this context the leading imperialist forces continue to attach great importance to supporting and instigating so-called human and civil rights movements in our countries. . . .

The following are absolutely typical: in addition to a multiplicity of measures to raise the effectiveness of the imperialist secret services, the centres of political and ideological diversion, and research on the GDR and the Eastern bloc, there has been a reorientation of long established hostile bodies, and a host of new subversive organisations has sprung up. Let me by way of example just remind you of such as the so-called 'Committee for the Protection of Freedom and Socialism', the 'Committee for the Release of Rudolf Bahro', the 'Brüsewitz Centre', etc., which are becoming ever more numerous.

These and other subversive organisations are using a great variety of devices and methods as their part of imperialism's campaign to soften up and undermine our socialist system and create widespread opposition within our society. . . .

The enemy's subversive operations are increasingly also involving such hostile forces as Western writers, creative artists and people working for publishers. . . .

It is generally recognised that our considerable efforts and carefully targeted practical political work have succeeded in unmasking the true nature of a whole series of these new, or newly emerged, hubs of enemy activity or enemy forces. I will here mention by name only a few of these organisations known to this audience, such as the 'Society for Human Rights', the magazine programme 'Calls for Help from the Other Side' on Channel 2 of West German television, the 'League of Free Berliners in Distress', the officially registered 'Martyrs' Church Aid Force', and others. It is now our task to build on these successes and further intensify and sharpen up our practical political work, to unmask other similar organisations and bodies as organs dedicated to opposing the GDR and socialism. . . .

At the same time, in certain cases it will still be politically incorrect or ineffective to brand certain organisations, bodies or those who collaborate with them as hubs of enemy activity or enemy forces. I will just mention organisations such as Amnesty International and people like Böll, etc. But they are no less antisocialist for that. . . .

Correspondents accredited to the GDR, visiting correspondents, and journalists employed by organs of the imperialist press who enter the country in a private capacity have taken on a special role in the subversive operations directed against us. Instructed by imperialist secret services and other hubs of hostile activity, and abusing the facilities they have been granted for working here, they not infrequently attempt to influence events, in particular when it comes to organising political and ideological diversions and creating an 'internal opposition' in the GDR.

To this end, they gather relevant news items, fabricate carefully calculated canards for the purpose of anti-communist propaganda and the manipulation of public opinion, and provoke suitable incidents, happenings and pretexts, which the enemy can then highlight to malign the GDR and inspire and mobilise hostile and negative forces within our country.

The general public was left in no doubt as to how they are thus conspiring against us, when such elements as Mettke, Loewe and Schwarz were expelled from the country, the *Spiegel* office was closed and our Foreign Ministry intervened against the activities of the West German television correspondent Lehmann, which were designed to mobilise hostile and negative forces amongst writers. . . .

The enemy is continuing to use correspondents of organs of the imperialist press to inspire and mobilise ideological bases here. They work as couriers and intermediaries between enemy centres and suchlike forces, and make available to the latter the facilities they enjoy for their work and for communication, in order to smuggle anti-socialist material in and out of the country and to distribute it, as again demonstrated by the wide popularisation of Havemann's anti-socialist nonsense through Western mass media.

Furthermore, by maintaining extensive and carefully selected official contacts with citizens who have the relevant information, and by building up illegal networks of correspondents here, they attempt to find out about or obtain military, economic and state secrets, classified information, documents and material evidence, and to exploit all available sources of information for their subversive activity.

Every collective must devote renewed and intensive efforts to our ideological and practical political work – and that is the reason why I am addressing the subject before this audience – to uncover the subversive secret-service activity both of correspondents and of hostile forces in diplomatic missions, the offices of capitalist firms and banks and other institutions within our frontiers, and their hostile operations. In this way, we can further limit their opportunities for abusing the facilities afforded by their work for subversive purposes, and prevent these forces from engaging in hostile and negative operations.

We must use the facilities and powers specifically available to us to further increase our effectiveness in raising the vigilance of our citizens towards each and every activity of such forces, in ensuring that our people never forget their duty to the state and vigorously advocate our party's policies at all times, and that the provisions of the law are even more strictly observed in necessary contacts with these forces on the part of the responsible leaders in every sector of society.

We must not underestimate the dangers that may arise from the wide propagation of such theses as the alleged new class divisions in the GDR, the so-called underprivileged position of the working class and alleged injustices in distribution, and from the arousal of envy and resentment in connection with Intershop, Exquisit and Delikat stores, and with regard to imminent price increases, and the like. Their purpose is to prepare the ground for antagonising even some workers, stirring them up against the leadership of the party and the state, discouraging initiatives, inciting people to work slowly, provoking discussion of mistakes and ultimately inspiring people to 'struggle for their rights'.

SOURCE: *Der Spiegel*, no. 9, 26 February 1979.

14. RUDOLF BAHRO

(The party) ought to be the social institution which develops society's processes of understanding, a kind of cerebral cortex for society's nervous system, an organ with which all thinking sections of the population can involve themselves (certainly not a great deal to ask!). Instead, it interposes itself between society's thought processes and reality, like a discoloured distorting lens which has blind spots systematically built into it. The working people can have no knowledge of how this lens evolved and is designed, how it is focused and angled, what it tones down, and what systematic errors it produces; all they can do is refuse to use the instrument, which is indeed what happens: they 'switch off', even before the official mouthpieces have gabbled out their first sentence. But the tragedy is that, because society lacks any alternative channel, they have to do without any kind of subtler understanding at all. Worse still: revolutionary Marxism, the only theory capable of penetrating the jungle of bureaucratic centralism and its inner sanctum, the Politburo, is still being so effectively usurped by the party bureaucracy, whose apparatus totally controls the media and education system, that to the masses it seems tarred with the same brush. In whatever guise it appears, people suspect it has been specially created to justify the present rule of the party.

The near total vacuum which has thus arisen is bombarded by the mass-produced ideology of the West, wherever the latter's communications technology reaches. And the contradictions within our system have burgeoned to such a degree that, at least in part, the bourgeois propaganda apparatus acts rather as a useful corrective: where it has no influence, as is presently still the case in large parts of the Soviet Union, the working people are intellectually and politically worse off *vis-à-vis* the Politburo's regime than they are here, in the peripheral countries of the bloc.

SOURCE: *Die Alternative*, p. 204f.

15. LETTER FROM JÜRGEN KUCZYNSKI TO HERMANN KANT ABOUT ERWIN STRITTMATTER'S NEW NOVEL *DER WUNDERTÄTER*

As you perhaps know, I've often said, and written, that it will be much more important for future historians to read our contemporary novels than most of the social science articles that we publish these days – our novels portray developing socialism here as it really is, with all its contradictions and aggravations, against the grand backcloth of a newly emerging world; whilst our social scientists on the other hand, though they may talk of existing socialism, tend so often to show things through rose-tinted spectacles in their concrete descriptions of reality. Perhaps it has also struck you that I have just used the term developing socialism – as I have done elsewhere too – and not, as it is so often called, developed socialism. I'm not one to have any illusions about our level of development. I only need to think of the thousand aggravations of daily life, whether it is when going shopping, using services, encounters with bureaucracy, and I am bound to ask myself: is that what they call developed socialism?

Strittmatter makes us look particularly at the aggravations of party life, journalism, the film industry, etc. Let no one say that I object to Strittmatter's realistic portrayal of existing socialism. Quite the reverse. I regard it as an extremely important task for our writers to portray such things, and it has always given me pleasure. And why? Think how often Lenin wrote about criticism, criticism of those above from below, criticism of those below from above, and self-criticism! As when he said: 'We are not afraid to admit our mistakes, and we shall judge them without emotion, so that we may learn to correct them.'

Lenin particularly condemned that fear, which is so widespread here too, that, if people criticise, the enemy might allegedly or actually take advantage of criticism of conditions here: 'We must not cover up our mistakes for fear the enemy might exploit them. Those who are afraid of that are no revolutionaries.'

And that is why many of us are so dissatisfied with our press, which normally only reports successes, and avoids criticism, and hence the educative effect of the latter.

And that is why many of us so enjoy our novels, which often criticise conditions here so constructively and intelligently, and raise genuine problems of everyday life under existing socialism.

But what of Strittmatter's criticism? Here I come to my first main objection to your discussion, as well as to the third volume of *Der Wundertäter*. An old comrade was saying, 'It's all so "petty".' Of course, particularly at that time, in the fifties, a great deal was 'petty'. The petty ambition, the petty cowardice, the petty conceit that one knew better, that was typical of a lot of comrades in the party apparatus – right up to the 'Top Bureau', with many people fancying they could decide that Einstein's theory was wrong and Käthe Kollwitz's art decadent and pessimistic. We of the older generation did live through it all. And the consequences were often not in the least 'petty'. In all too many areas they seriously obstructed our development, and were even counterproductive. And there are still all too many after-effects today. We need only think how hard we still find it today to encourage argument. Nor is it ever 'petty' if people are treated as badly as they were then – inside and outside the party! Why, Marx and Engels pointed out as long ago as the Communist Manifesto that society exists to make individuals happy, it is not the individual's duty to make society happy.

Or doesn't that yet apply? I sometimes get that impression. In a transitional society like ours, I suppose it isn't yet possible. In your discussion you hint at how this whole set of problems is reflected in the novel, indeed they basically dominate it.

> Certainly, the group and the individual, that has always been a basic motif in literature – because it is so in real life. But it is also thought self-evident (at least in our country) that the individual's happiness essentially derives from being in harmony with the community. And it seems to be thought self-evident that this harmony is only attainable if the part submits to the whole. But what seems to be so unquestionably self-evident positively cries out to be reconsidered. *Der Wundertäter* is such a reconsideration.

Yes indeed, we must pursue that idea, so that we may eventually jerk the pitifully large number of our social scientists out of what Engels called the 'dung-heap' they are wallowing in, proclaiming: 'In our country the interests of the individual coincide with those of society, and that is why only idiots and enemies can be unhappy here.'

But are you right that *Der Wundertäter* is such a reconsideration? If I say that in many respects society today cannot yet exist for the happiness of individuals, what I am saying is that there are two reasons for this. Firstly, because capitalism is still so strong that in the world class struggle very often we can't take account, as we ought to, of the happiness of individuals, and then also because, partly as a result of this, our socialism has not yet developed to the point where the happiness of the individual necessarily always coincides with that of society.

SOURCE: *Neue Deutsche Literatur*, no. 10 (October 1980) pp. 158–60.

16. STEFAN HEYM ON THE WESTERN CONNECTION

How many people actually suffer by a sense of being hemmed in is hard to say. The GDR is a small place; you drive from one end to the other in a few hours; and though it is a beautiful country and not as spoiled as most of the industrialised West by the uncontrolled mushrooming of cities and by pollution, it offers little of the 'Aroma of the Wide World' that is being advertised on Western television to sell a certain brand of cigarettes.

Since the best-guarded wall is not an obstacle to the electron, and since most of the GDR is easily covered by West German and West Berlin television stations, its citizens get glimpses of the attractions of that Wide World without being able to enter it and catch a whiff of its real odours. That makes for a certain frustration – and for illusions. . . .

The government's figures on the number of television viewers are kept a deep secret. I can only report my experience: whenever I was on West German television, a variety of GDR people, from border guards to street-car conductors to barbers and store clerks, have told me they saw and heard me; when I appeared on GDR television with a statement on Vietnam, one person, an old party comrade, called up to say how happy she was that finally I had graduated to a spot before our own cameras.

The influence of Western television and radio on the minds of people here is considerable: it shapes their tastes in fashions, music and film; it creates consumer demands that GDR industry and trade make belated efforts to fill.

SOURCE: *New York Times*, 23 March 1975.

17. STATEMENT BY STEFAN HEYM

At the end of Clara-Zetkin-Straße in Berlin, a few hundred yards away from the Reichstag, but on the GDR side of the frontier fortifications, the so-called Copyright Office has its premises in a few modest rooms on the second floor of a restored ruin. It has some fifteen employees, peaceable and in some cases even quite pleasant people – and it is the knife at the throat of the Republic's writers.

Originally established to administer currency exchanges arising from buying and selling authors' rights, it resembles in this respect very similar institutions in other socialist countries – for instance, the Soviet VAAP, the DILIA in Prague, the Bureau Hongrois pour les droits des Auteurs in Budapest – but only in this respect.

In fact, besides dealing with these technical matters, the GDR Copyright Office also has the right and duty to approve or prohibit the contracts that GDR authors or their publishers wish to sign with their foreign partners regarding publication abroad of their books or other works. The office was given this right by a decree with the proud title 'For the Protection of Copyrights', which was signed by the then Minister of Culture and present GDR ambassador in Rome, Klaus Gysi, to the accompaniment, no doubt, of some inner amusement. The reason being that none of the people who work at the office is employed, or even entitled, actually to assess the books on whose fate, for good or ill, they have to decide. The question of which books receive the office's imprimatur is decided by other authorities altogether, and they do not apply literary criteria. However, if a writer violates this decree of Gysi's and signs a contract with a foreign publisher without the approval or even despite explicit prohibition by the office, then the decree allows him to be fined 300 marks, and there is no possibility of appeal.

This fine is, however, not, as one might expect, imposed by the office itself, but, surprise surprise, by the Deputy Minister of Culture, and the author doesn't get the 300 marks back even if the prohibited book that has been published abroad in defiance of the Copyright Office – as for instance with my novel about the workers' leader, Lassalle – is finally allowed to appear in our country, the GDR, too, after the Chairman of the Council of State has died, or something else has made the authorities change their minds.

This idyllic state of affairs, where one could buy oneself a little bit of freedom for 300 marks, lasted quite a number of years, until the literature of the GDR became such a source of aggravation that influential comrades in elevated positions in the party began to cry out for the situation to be remedied. Some ingenious fellow – in what niche of the Prussian bureaucracy he had his desk can no longer be determined – had the idea of linking Gysi's decree 'For the Protection of Copyrights' with the Currency Law;

the reason being that if the Copyright, or rather now the anti-Copyright, Office doesn't approve the contract with the foreign publisher, and the author gets his book printed abroad without official blessing, then the office doesn't register the foreign currency payments arising from the contract, and the result is technically – I stress the word technically – a violation of the Currency Law, which requires such registration.

Violations of the Currency Law, however, don't simply entail prosecution for a minor offence, with a 300 mark fine; no indeed – the author is now dragged before the courts and receives a fine of up to 10 000 marks and/or a prison sentence of up to two years, or in serious cases up to ten years. The extended arm of the censor, for that is what the office in the Zetkin-Straße in effect is, has thus now been provided with substantial muscle, and the head of that institution, a Herr Adolph, warned several authors back in late 1978 that they might face proceedings as they were knowingly and deliberately violating the Currency Law. Adolph's threat was followed by an announcement by the present Deputy Minister of Culture, Klaus Höpcke, to the party group of the Writers' Union, that it was now the Ministry of Finance that would be dealing with the writers who were publishing abroad without official approval.

We may therefore expect that in the near future a dismal drama will unfold before the courts of the GDR – the conviction and punishment of writers, simply because they refused voluntarily to let themselves be gagged. That the Public Prosecutor will refer to the Currency Law, and only to the Currency Law, is only to be expected. All the talk will be about currency, but in reality it is freedom of speech at stake. To force someone to break the law, by a legalistic trick, when he wants to exercise his democratic rights as guaranteed in the constitution, has been a well-tried device from time immemorial. In America too, in the days of the notorious Senator McCarthy, writers were after all not put away for their books or films, God forbid, but for bringing Congress into contempt. That the judiciary of the GDR is planning to follow the example, of all things, of the methods of US justice of the fifties, is regrettable, but it may perhaps serve at last to bring the whole question of censorship in the GDR out into the open for discussion.

SOURCE: *Frankfurter Allgemeine Zeitung*, 26 April 1979.

Dissident Intellectuals

18. STEFAN HEYM: STATEMENT ON POLAND (14.1.82)

My first point is that neither the East nor West Germans should be giving advice to the Poles, let alone actually intervening. As we know, the Germans were involved in four partitions of Poland, the most recent in 1939, and whatever happens, it is incumbent upon them to exercise the maximum restraint.

My second point is that I hope the reports are not well founded about the bad conditions in the camps and prisons where the detainees and internees in Poland are held. But if they should be, then everyone, in both East and West, ought to speak out against them. It is not so very long ago that Poland in particular saw quite enough such cruel camps, and that sort of thing must never, never happen again.

Furthermore, we ought to be clear that the trade union that calls itself Solidarity is not the cause of the present troubles; on the contrary, it is itself a consequence of shortcomings in the social and political system. If one wants to discuss the reluctance of the Polish workers to work, then one has to start by asking: why don't they want to work, and whom don't they want to work for?

And indeed one ought to give some thought to the question of what kind of socialism that might be, where the army and other security forces are deployed gun in hand against the working class; because a trade union that has 9½ million members out of a total population of 36 million really is the working class. What has happened there, and where its roots lie, surely deserve serious examination, especially as the problem has arisen before elsewhere, in a somewhat different form. And as there is no rational alternative to socialism – unless one wants a return to capitalism, and all that that entails – we should consider what changes need to be made in the structures of this socialism, so that, from the one that exists in reality now, a genuine socialism can at last emerge with which the workers can identify.

But we also have to beware of an illusion which is cherished in certain quarters, namely that in the prevailing circumstances it might be possible to detach Poland from the ranks of the Warsaw Pact countries. There are geographical facts which can't be simply ignored and which, if not treated with due respect, could plunge this world into a catastrophe.

And finally, I very much hope that the martial law, which has now applied for far too long in Poland, might be lifted: no doubt you can suppress social questions by force, but you can't use force to solve them.

SOURCE: W. Büscher *et al.*, *Friedensbewegung in der DDR*, pp. 235–7.

19. THE BIERMANN PETITION

Wolf Biermann was not, nor is he, a comfortable poet – and that is something he shares with many poets of the past.

Our socialist state, mindful of what Marx said in *Eighteenth Brumaire* to the effect that the proletarian revolution never ceases to criticise itself, should be unlike anachronistic forms of society and be able to tolerate such discomfort in calm reflection.

We do not agree with Biermann's every word or action, and we dissociate ourselves from attempts to use the events surrounding Biermann to discredit the GDR. For all his criticism, Biermann himself has never left any doubt about which of the two German states he supports, nor did he in Cologne.

We protest against his expatriation and ask for the action that has been decided upon to be reconsidered.

Sarah Kirsch, Christa Wolf, Volker Braun, Franz Fühmann, Stephan Hermlin, Stefan Heym, Günter Kunert, Heiner Müller, Rolf Schneider, Gerhard Wolf, Jurek Becker, Erich Arendt, Fritz Cremer.

20. WOLF BIERMANN

Rosa Luxemburg's political testament has now been published in the GDR: late, but not *too* late. The fourth volume of her collected works contains the piece, 'The Russian Revolution'. No one has ever more passionately celebrated and paid historical tribute to the October Revolution – and no one has more passionately warned against making it a model for all later proletarian revolutions. Rosa Luxemburg wrote at that time:

> Without general elections, untrammelled freedom of the press and of association, and the free contending of opinions, life will drain from every public institution, it will become a mere semblance of life, with bureaucracy alone remaining an active force. Public life will gradually become somnolent, a few dozen party leaders with inexhaustible energy and boundless idealism will direct and govern, and amongst them it will in reality be a dozen leaders of outstanding ability who will lead, and a working-class elite will be occasionally drummed up to meetings to applaud the leaders' speeches, unanimously support the resolutions they are presented with, in other words at bottom rule by a clique – a dictatorship, it is true, but not the dictatorship of the proletariat, rather of a handful of politicians, in other words dictatorship in the bourgeois sense!

SOURCE: *Nachlaß I*, p. 467f.

21. RUDOLF BAHRO, 'A CRITIQUE OF SOCIALISM AS IT ACTUALLY EXISTS'

The revolutionary process since 1917 has given rise to a *totally different* social order from what those who originally fought for it had hoped for. And in fact everyone who lives in this new order now knows that. If conditions here are officially described in terms of the old Marxist categories, this has long been no more than deliberate hypocrisy and the conscious inculcation of false consciousness. My critique of socialism as it actually exists aims to lay the theoretical foundations for a *radical* (in other words one that goes to the economic roots) *communist alternative* to the dictatorship of the Politburo which holds our social processes of working and living in thrall. My proposals are items for the programme of that new Communist League, which in my view needs to be established everywhere, to prepare for and lead to the breakthrough from socialism 'as it actually exists' to real socialism. As I analyse the situation, only socialism and communism offer prospects for the future. As such an alternative is concerned not just with a few details, but with overturning the whole social order, in other words replacing one form of society with another, it must at least be outlined in its full complexity, even if not immediately expounded in its entirety.

That socialism which Marx and Engels foresaw and which Lenin and his comrades no doubt hoped for in Russia too, *will one day come*. It must be *fought for* because more than ever it is the only alternative to a worldwide collapse of civilisation. But nowhere on earth has it yet got beyond the first stage. Such a first stage exists, it seems to me, in Yugoslavia for instance. It hardly exists in the other countries of Eastern Europe.

Today's communists, even those who really are communists, are none too familiar with what Marx *actually* understood by socialism and communism. But it is at least clear that Soviet and East European society is incompatible with the future as envisaged by Marx. A number of achievements notwithstanding, socialism as it actually exists is characterised:

— by the continuance of wage-labour, the production of goods, and money;
— by the rationalisation of the old division of labour;
— by the encouragement of social inequalities far in excess of the range of money-incomes;
— by official institutions that keep the population in its place and spontaneous expression on a tight rein;
— by the elimination rather than the preservation and realisation of the liberties won by the masses in the bourgeois era (I will just mention the all-embracing censorship and the purely formal and theoretical nature of what is called socialist democracy).

It is further characterised:

— by full-time cadre-functionaries, a standing army and police, *all* of whom are responsible only to those in higher authority;
— by the duplication of the ponderous machine of state, with a state *and* a party apparatus;
— by its isolation from other countries.

We will for the moment content ourselves with this description – its individual features are well enough *known*. What is not well enough *understood* is how, by their very nature, they all fit together. But more of that later.

Particularly in the more developed countries, a system with such characteristics gives the masses *insufficient real progress towards freedom*. It makes them subject *first and foremost, not to capital, but to something else*. The conditions of alienation and subordination have merely lost a surface layer; they continue to exist on a new level. And inasmuch as positive achievements from the preceding epoch are also lost in the process, this new subjection is in *many respects that much more oppressive than the old one*. As this political system is at present constituted, it offers not the slightest prospect of winning anyone over. In view of the total concentration of social power, the insignificance of the individual is more visibly and generally apparent here than on the scintillating surface of the process of capitalist reproduction with its interplay of chance and probability.

The colossus that goes by the name of 'party-and-government' here, and which of course includes the trades unions, etc., 'represents' that free association which the classic thinkers of socialism conceived of, in exactly the same way as in all earlier civilisations, but especially in the oldest, the state represented society. Ours is a state-machine the like of which Marx and Engels wanted the proletarian revolution to smash, so that it could not be resurrected in any form or under any pretext. This is clear beyond all question, especially from what they wrote about the Paris Commune. In their eyes the state is – and all the following expressions are in the original – a parasitic excrescence, a monster, a boa constrictor crushing the living society, a supernatural miscarriage, a repulsive machine of class rule. All that. 'The proletarians must destroy the state, so that their personalities may find expression.' And they were saying that back in 1845–6, in their book *The German Ideology*.

But Marx's description also anticipated what has become the model for everyday life here. 'Every individual interest, however small, that arose from the relations between social groups . . . [is] separated from and set in opposition to society as such . . . which assumes the form of the interests of the state', and then 'administered by priests of the state with precisely defined hierarchical functions'. This was therefore certainly not how the classic thinkers imagined socialism. Particularly in Yugoslavia, where the League of Communists refused to accept this phenomenon, they coined the expression 'etatism' (from *l'état*, French for 'the state'), as a shorthand expression for the principle of bureaucratic–centralist dictatorship.

For me the term 'socialism' was thus totally ruled out for describing present conditions. On the other hand, although the term etatism is most apposite with regard to one particular aspect, I nevertheless felt it was too narrow. So it took me a long time to decide what to call it. However, although it was distasteful to me to echo the system's self-appellation as 'socialism as it actually exists', it does at least by implication concede one thing: that there is a difference between the traditional socialist ideal which they claim still to cherish, and the reality of the new society. So I eventually settled for this designation after all, and without quotations marks too, but I have made up for it by highlighting that difference quite unmistakably.

In no way is it an accusation that any hallowed principles have been departed from. If I indulge in polemics, it is for the sole purpose of demolishing misleading facades. It is my firm belief that, in discussions with revolutionary Marxists, it is high time to abandon 'deformation theories', to stop getting indignant about the distortion and 'betrayal' of socialism, understandable though it once was. If one reduces the drama of history to a problem of bad implementation, one is starting from unreal premises and leading political theory up the garden path. Certainly, one can bring the practice of socialism as it actually exists face to face with the classical theory, indeed one must do so, in order to preserve, by way of contrast, the substance of the socialist ideal intact. But that practice must be explained in terms of its own inner laws. For to say that it arose arbitrarily, or was 'allowed' to occur by default, could not be further from the truth. Its foundations are quite unlike what was originally conceived. One should not attempt to justify it, or make excuses for it, or gloss over it, but truthfully to describe and analyse it.

Let me briefly describe the basic approach by which I was guided in this respect. There can be no question but that revolution has by and large brought nations considerable progress in terms of material and cultural benefits for the masses. In many cases it has preserved or restored their national existence and individuality from dissolution and destruction by industrial capitalism. One can say with certainty that a fundamental historical necessity is expressed through this process, which is today continuing in Africa and Asia, where it is much more suited to the conditions. But communists need to appreciate that what they are involved in there does not offer *a socialist, or communist, or any kind of prospect for general emancipation*. The new system may be called *proto*socialist, in other words, it may be the *larval stage* of socialism, the *preparation* for socialism, but in the same sense, if not with the same overtones, as late capitalism too has long been regarded as protosocialist, as the larval stage of socialism, as the preparation for socialism. And inasmuch as the influence exerted by communists in this society serves the interests of the state and they do not struggle to overcome existing conditions, they must be made aware that they are participating in another form of *domination* of man over man, which is another system of oppression and exploitation – for exploitation is indeed also what it is. The 'actually existing socialist' functionary, the superior, the 'nachalnik', and that means not just high-ranking Politburo dignitaries, but all the run-of-the-mill functionaries in the party, state or economy too: all these represent – often despite themselves – the latest manifestation of the *boss*. I played the part long enough myself, and know it from experience.

The established ruling apparatus, seemingly sanctioned by history, identifies itself with the Marxian ideal, the concept of the Commune. In so doing it has made all the old socialist hopes appear ridiculous in the eyes of the masses. From the Elbe to the Amur it is now daily encouraging people to seek the restoration of some earlier form of society. It is characteristic of the process of rapid ideological decay in the countries of Eastern Europe ever since the militarised police action of August 1968, that the bulk of the opposition forces in the first instance see themselves forced back into making straight liberal, democratic demands, and campaigning for human rights, that is, into a position which is at the same time the broadest, and the most insipid, and, in any constructive sense, most vacuous. The crudities that are rightly being attacked can only disappear with the political superstructure that has need of them. The regime has, of course, inflicted a deep and continuing shame on our whole society by the fact that the most prominent section of the internal opposition has turned for advice and help to the President of the USA, of all people. Human rights, political democracy – certainly! But what the countries of Eastern Europe lack, and the Soviet Union itself not least among them, is an *organised long-term struggle for a change in overall policy*. It requires thorough preparation, initially above all by a broad campaign of education, which would spread understanding of the context in which present conditions arose, and their inner logic, so that they can be overcome. . . .

When we analyse the structure of actually existing socialism, we come to see the need for a new social and political upheaval, a cultural revolution against the predominance both of the old division of labour and of the state. The essential thing, however, is to uncover within present conditions themselves the *seeds of the movement* which will put an end to the existing state of affairs. So where are these forces that will undertake the task? Do they even exist? It is true that they do not exactly force themselves on our attention just now. The great exception was Czechoslovakia in 1968. . . . At that time it was not only shown that the potential is there. The reason why it is usually blocked also became apparent. It became apparent precisely because for a few months it failed to operate: it being the rule of that party whose programme formerly espoused universal emancipation, but which today represents the nucleus of all oppression in our society. That party, and its apparatus, now occupy the very position which should be taken by the vanguard of emancipatory interests. As soon as the Czech Communist Party dropped the first slight hint that it was about to resume the original emancipatory role of the Communist Party, every compass-needle of hope in society at once began to swing round and point towards it.

And this is our empirical evidence of the extent to which the *problem of revolutionary potential* in actually existing socialism is bound up with *the problem of the party*. Both problems have to be considered in our analysis of the present relations of production, indeed they concern the dynamic aspect of these relations, which is crucial for the prospect of change. . . . First, let us define the two problems more exactly. To begin with there is the *massive generation of surplus consciousness* by the overall process of reproduction in actually existing socialism. Secondly, there is the *leading role of the party* as a sociological fact. Both factors are central to our relations of production. The first factor has hitherto scarcely even been recognised as a politico-economic fact, and the second has rarely been as consistently integrated into the theory as it has been put into practice in the exercise of political power. The two factors, let me at once make clear, are *at present in conflict with each other*. And in the face of this dilemma, actually existing socialism is stagnating, after an initial period of accumulation, when little surplus consciousness was generated.

If, in asking who is to be the agent of change, I look towards surplus consciousness, seeing it as the potential, the reservoir from which this agent will emerge, I am departing from an ancient theoretical custom, which is all too easily, but wrongly, identified with historical materialism itself. For normally one would first have to look around for the particular class or stratum of society that stands ready to play the historical role in question. One might, for instance, be tempted to think of the intelligentsia. That would at least have a rational basis, but it would nevertheless be the wrong point to start from. The social structure of our class society which is in an advanced stage of dissolution can only be described in such terms with regard to the past.

The concept of the working class has become particularly inappropriate. In post-capitalist society it serves only to disguise and give a veneer of legitimacy to the realities of power. There can be absolutely no question of the workers as a ruling class, least of all in the future. Nor does the apparatus rule vicariously *on their behalf*; it rules *over them*. The workers have just as much say in the state which bears their name as do private soldiers in a regular army.

However, the contradiction revealed by our analysis, between people and functionaries, or, more exactly, between the masses and the apparatus, does not yet give any grounds for hope. This contradiction is as normal a part of the functioning of actually existing socialism as the contradiction between wage-labour and capital in classical bourgeois society – and it *by no means* necessarily spells its destruction. Certainly things sometimes get critical and come to a head, but the result is usually a compromise to patch things up, as in Poland in 1970, where Edward Gierek encapsulated the outcome, as far as its effect on the workers was concerned, in this revealing formula: 'you will work well, and we shall govern well.' Which means no more than that the built-in dilemma will now start a new cycle. The contradiction between the masses and the apparatus cannot, by its nature, take us beyond the existing system.

The reason, when we look at it more closely, is that this contradiction reflects the global situation of society in too narrow, too one-sided a way, i.e. *from the viewpoint of the apparatus*. In contrast to the apparatus, and defined in its terms, the masses primarily represent a *mass of subservience*, which is the consequence and obverse of the concentration of all officially recognised knowledge and all power of decision-making in the hands of the bureaucratic hierarchy. One party to this, the most important contradiction which is the motive force behind our political development, the rule of the apparatus, is amply and fully represented in this confrontation. The concept of the apparatus, as the target for attack, is precise enough for strategic purposes. The historic task is to break its *rule* – which, by the way, is not synonymous with abolishing it. But 'the masses' will not be the agent for such a deed. Unless, of course, one were again to expand the concept of the masses, as Marx in his day expanded the concept of the proletariat by giving it a world–historical mission. I think it is clear today that there was a kind of sleight of hand involved here, though it had some justification and was not without useful effect. It reflected the role of the revolutionary intelligentsia, whose task was to bring 'consciousness' to that class which after all in itself really was subservient, in other words to assume leadership of it. And by that very fact, incidentally, the seeds of the post-capitalist or non-capitalist rule of the apparatus were already sown in the pre-revolutionary workers' organisations.

The inadequacy of this model of apparatus and masses (the latter seen as they really are, devoid of any mission) lies particularly in the fact that it is confined totally to the sphere of 'alienated' consciousness, which is *absorbed* by the necessity of labour and its regulation, and takes no account at all of *surplus* consciousness.

In this way the theory is partly shaped by the *apparatus's own viewpoint*, which has no use for this surplus, and indeed fears it. By *absorbed consciousness* I mean that quantity of psycho-social energy which is consumed on the one hand within the hierarchy of leadership functions, and on the other hand within the routine activities of the process of reproduction. It thus consists in the confrontation between: on the one side, the knowledge possessed by the bureaucracy, organised to command the processes of labour and living, and expressed politically as the interests of the apparatus, as the inevitably provocative arrogance of those who exercise power – and on the other side, the abstract, alienated labour of production, services, administration, which takes the form of *subservient reactions and behaviour*, refusal to exert oneself or stand up and be counted, lack of interest and indifference to questions of public concern. In short, these are two sides of one and the same coin; in the last analysis, and for as long as the forces involved adhere to this model, it will always be an unproductive configuration. The *bureaucratic* apparatus and the *subservient* masses are truly worthy of each other.

But it is precisely what is excluded from this equation, in other words *surplus consciousness*, which represents the crucial potential for changing society. Surplus consciousness is the growing quantity of free psycho-social energy which is no longer tied down in necessary labour and hierarchical knowledge.

To a certain extent this has always existed. It is part of human nature never to be entirely confined by the restrictive circumstances which the unavoidable, official context of any given society imposes. In earlier times it was predominantly religion whose motive force was derived from this essential human drive toward transcendency. As long as society produces only a low level of skill and only a small elite, the apparatus absorbs most of the mental energy and capacity released from actual production. The form taken by the economic despotism of old was also dependent on the size, or rather the small size, the skills and the laws of reproduction of the available elite. In those days these social skills were produced merely as required for the simple reproduction of the relevant power structure. For material production there was after all scarcely any need for intellectual labour!

Today we are faced with a thoroughgoing intellectualisation of the subjective forces of production. Although the apparatus is holding down the rate of development, society is producing such a quantity of ability of *every kind*, of sheer *human* skills, that the apparatus cannot possibly make direct use of it all. We therefore witness its ceaseless efforts partly to cut down this unused surplus consciousness by means of unproductive activities, partly to paralyse it by means of terror, but above all to fob it off with some alternative source of satisfaction. The latter is, incidentally, the real power-political purpose behind the much vaunted 'unity of economic and social policy'.

In socialism as it actually exists the explosive potential of this surplus consciousness is further increased by the fact that it comes up against barriers that have been specially erected against it, the restrictive jealousy, which the bureaucratic monopoly of power simply cannot resist showing. Its genuine high quality, its potential as a productive force, its capacity to understand society and take decisions affecting it, all these are systematically denied. The apparatus acts on the typically arrogant assumption that in any given situation it itself already represents the sum total of significant consciousness. Where should we all be, if any Tom, Dick or Harry knew more and knew better than the politbureaucracy? Everybody must at least keep their own insights in check, they must wait patiently and modestly to see whether their proposals are 'feasible', that is to say, whether the machinery can assimilate them or not. Everybody has to fit in with the ultimate goal of bureaucratic stability. The arts and sciences have primarily to serve as organs for this preservation of power. Everything that goes beyond the confines of the official universe, and that is the essence of surplus consciousness, is either blocked or relegated to the sphere and isolation of private affairs.

Alienated labour and pressure from the apparatus initially result in the *mass* of surplus consciousness seeking easy alternative sources of satisfaction, and as far as possible these are provided. Circumstances restrict and prevent the blossoming, development and fulfilment of countless individuals from their earliest years onwards. They have consequently no choice but to seek compensation in material consumption, passive entertainment and those postures which are associated with prestige and power. That is what *compensatory interests* are based on. I regard this concept as most important; I will come back to the question of how the cultural revolution should react to them. But the true character, the innermost instinct, of surplus consciousness finds expression not in compensatory, but *emanicipatory interests*. They are concerned with the growth of human personality, the differentiation and self-fulfilment of individuals in every dimension of human activity. They demand above all the potentially all-embracing *acquisition of culture*, which admittedly has to do with material things that can be consumed, but is fundamentally aiming at something else: essential human drives, which are realised in other individuals, in objects, patterns of behaviour, relationships, as well as in institutions. The supreme goal of this acquisition is liberation from all narrowness and above all subservience of thought, feeling and behaviour, uplifting the individual to the plane of the collective life of society.

> And whate'er may be the lot of humankind,
> That would I savour, in mine inward self,

as Goethe put it. In their conscious form, emancipatory interests are revolutionary, and the political programme that embodies them will then become the struggle for the *conditions* of general emancipation. So as to reveal the potential for future transformation, I have proceeded via a *structural analysis of social consciousness*, which I take to be actual material, socio-economic reality. The apparatus, the state itself, is, as we all know, the 'ideological superstructure', it is, in its substance, alienated consciousness operating in the form of a ruling class. The whole intellectual life of society will be the battlefield for the coming cultural revolution; however, this intellectual life will not be in conflict with material existence, but will be based on facts and decisions about the reproductive process and its goals. At its heart is a new type of control over the whole life of society, a new order and institutional framework for the labour of *establishing scientific facts*.

A revolutionary strategy must therefore focus on a quite specific pattern of forces within the consciousness of society, or, as one might also put it, on a pattern of forces within the array of accumulated skills and subjective productive power, on how the turnover and investment of mental energy in society are distributed.

I accordingly distinguished four categories of social consciousness, as briefly described above, two of them within the absorbed consciousness and two within the surplus consciousness.

Within the absorbed consciousness, as we saw, there is a confrontation between the bureaucratic interests of the apparatus and the subservient reactions of the masses, while within the surplus consciousness it is between the compensatory and emancipatory interests of individuals.

These four categories, which evolve ineluctably from people's responses to the contradictions of the system of production in actually existing socialism, represent the constellation of political forces that is characteristic of conditions in our country.

Yet it is not a matter of linking particular individuals, for instance, with any particular one of these categories of consciousness, or at least it is so only in exceptional cases. In general we may take it that *every individual to a greater or lesser extent features in all four of these categories*. The question is simply, which is the dominant alignment of interests in their motivational structure and thus in their behaviour. *This* is where minds will differ. There are, of course, people whose subjective being is so imbued with the spirit of bureaucracy and who are so closely identified with the apparatus, that they scarcely exist outside their official role. This minority constitutes the *party of the apparatus* in the narrow sense, the party of *politbureaucratic reaction*, on whom the attack must be concentrated.

This attack can only be launched by *emancipatory interests*. Between these two poles will be fought the ideological battle for influence over the mass of psycho-social potential that is bound in by necessary labour and compensatory satisfactions. For as long as the apparatus is dominant, the emancipatory interests, which sociologically will largely consist of individuals, will find themselves confronting all the other categories of consciousness, which in these circumstances tend to behave in a predominantly *subservient* fashion, in other words, the apparatus subordinates every other form of consciousness to its political power. In the cultural revolution, on the other hand, for which the conditions are becoming ever riper, it is the ruling apparatus itself which will be isolated, and individuals will learn, even in their necessary labour and in their free activities and pleasures, how to behave *integrally*, in other words, how to act as intelligent parts within a whole.

The emancipatory interests represent the *substance* which has to be concentrated together and organised as the *agent* of the coming transformations. In purely empirical terms, this agent will consist of the dynamic, creative elements in every stratum and area of society, of all the people in whose individual character the emancipatory interests are dominant and at least play a major part in influencing their behaviour. It is the task of a truly *Communist* Party in actually existing socialism to shape this force, to give it the convergent political organisation that it needs in order to fight against the rule of the apparatus and to assert its identity against every influence of merely subservient or compensatory behaviour.

The ruling parties in actually existing socialism quite obviously do not provide a basis for this. Their 'leading role' has a completely different and totally repressive meaning. After all, they have entirely sold out to the interests of the apparatus. More than that, they explicitly form the militant spear-head of the latter. They are the most jealous guardians of the authority of the state. They have thus left a place vacant for a new League of Communists which will offer support and solidarity to emancipatory needs and guarantee a higher moral and political authority than any apparatus can. *The communist movement must be created afresh*, as a movement which will once again clearly inscribe human emancipation on its banner and then proceed to transform people's lives. . . .

Marxism does not complain when it finds people clinging to their comforts and enjoying their subservience, and apparently, or sometimes even really, having no desire for freedom. Its plea is for active, Promethean solidarity with those who are most oppressed, and for energies to be concentrated on enabling the less developed, the disadvantaged, the underprivileged classes and groups to catch up. For one thing is clear: if the conditions enabling individuals to develop freely – and these are concrete manifestations of the economic and social process which can be observed with considerable precision – are not met for *everyone*, emancipation can only be halfway achieved, and will rapidly lose all meaning once more.

What is therefore implied is a kind of two-stage programme. Before considering the ultimate goal, in other words the question of how to organise a society to ensure the free development of every one of its members, in practical politics one has primarily to concern oneself with the *prerequisite* for a move in that direction, and develop the whole strategy as a map of the *path to be taken*. The first problem is then this: how can *the compensatory interests* which bind people to the existing form of civilisation *be neutralised*?

How you answer naturally depends on the ultimate goal; the two stages of the cultural revolution cannot simply follow on mechanically, one from the other. Our target must be a new form of macroeconomic reproduction, not only, as we have said, because of the crisis of the environment and resources, but significantly also to remove the incentive for people to seek alternative sources of satisfaction. The race for growth inevitably promotes inequality of material standards of living between individuals and nations, and thereby their compensatory needs. The more people produce, the more they have to hunt, own and consume, and the more mental energy is tied up in abstract labour and compensatory pleasures, and is therefore denied to the forces of emancipation. Our insatiable appetite for material things deprives us of the freedom for higher development, subjects us to regulations whose sanction is compulsion, and creates an uncaring society. If the explosion of material needs cannot be contained, communism will be psychologically as well as economically impossible. When Marx said it would require an abundance of goods, he primarily meant the actual means of subsistence, the absolute necessities of life. In the industrialised countries, the driving dialectic of production and needs has shifted to the field of those goods that provide pleasure and permit development. The compensatory desire and compulsion to own, use up and consume necessarily means continuing a production war which even after a hundred years will still leave us too poor for communism. The vicious circle of the capitalist growth-dynamic must be broken. . . .

The apparatus is still having some success with its well-tried tactic of preventing any fundamental criticism being expressed within our society, and at the same time claiming that, when it is voiced outside their domain, this proves it is external. The opposition may choose either to say nothing – and that would mean not to exist, politically – or to 'serve the enemy'. It is easy to see that this impression is created by the dictatorship itself, because it must be a matter of some urgency to them to make the contradictions that are expressed internally appear foreign. What we here observe is the last ideological defence of politbureaucratic control of opinion in our society. Let us deal with that by ignoring it, let us, regardless of the consequences, draw a dividing line between our loyalty to the non-capitalist base and loyalty to its outdated superstructure! It is of the utmost importance to make use of every opportunity for communication in our own country, and as far as possible build up a new network for this purpose. Yet we must not shy away from exploiting the techniques of the other power bloc in our political struggle either. Whose sealed carriage conveyed Lenin from Switzerland to Russia, and who gave the all-clear for the journey? The crucial question was what the 'German spy', as his slanderers consequently called him, pulled out of his pocket in Petrograd. On that occasion it was the famous April theses, the strategic guide-lines for the road to October.

Furthermore, in recent years the subjective internal conditions for a more effective mobilisation of opposition forces have improved. The first generation that has not been marked by the war is reaching political maturity. Clearly people are more ready to risk their secure position in society and more eager to show their true face to the world. Those who harbour feelings of opposition so long that the party's central organ can devote an obituary to them, praising their faithful service, will, of course, prove not to have been what they for so long thought they were.

What is still lacking is the initiative to come together and join in a conscious, purposeful fight. Prevailing conditions directly point the way. As those of us who belong to the party must expect to be effectively expelled as soon as we unite around our own programme, we shall have to have recourse to our general civil rights, as far as organisation is concerned. The wording of the constitution guarantees freedom of assembly and – something that is particularly important since we can't consider public premises for the present anyway – inviolability of the home. The time is ripe for bringing together those who are willing to commit themselves, without being too conspiratorial about it, but rather with the knowledge and under the protection of certain interested sections of the public. To begin with, of course our activities will be predominantly concerned with theory, ideology and propaganda, and not yet with a mass movement. But a start must be made.

We can no longer pin all our hopes for a shift of power within the party, though there are plenty of historical precedents for this, on the painfully slow and inarticulate process of replacing the old guard within the institutions. The new organisation must have its nucleus outside existing structures. The expected expulsions aside, the foci of a new, changed awareness will be objectively located outside the control zone of the official party know-alls and the apparatus's idea of what is 'realistic'. We must get the apparatus used to looking open opposition in the face. Doubtless it will try out more than one method of suppression, but circumstances will prevent it from resorting to extreme measures. As soon as it encounters the determination of even a small group of people to sacrifice family life, prosperity and popularity rather than a higher order of objectives, the whole machinery of deterrence will suffer the most abject defeat. The 'organs' will not, for instance, be able for much longer to continue exiling communists whom revolutionary and progressive forces elsewhere in the world clearly regard as responsible people, who have their feet firmly on the ground of concrete socialist conditions. Indeed, reprisals will now tend to accelerate the process, and not just because they will mobilise international solidarity. Taking a somewhat longer view, we shall achieve legality and a public presence as a communist opposition.

There are signs that the train of history is about to leave for the next station. *When that will happen will depend partly on subjective decisions. Indeed, the key factor will be a critical mass of individual impulses*. If there are today in every Eastern European country many people who, despite the certainty of years of unpleasantness, are applying to leave, then it is high time for the communist minority to stick out their necks, and say that *here, in* the countries of actually existing socialism, life is going to undergo a fundamental change.

SOURCE: *Ich werde meinen Weg fortsetzen*, pp. 9–55.

22. ROBERT HAVEMANN, 'FREEDOM AS NECESSITY'

The depth of mistrust between the state and its citizens could not be greater, on either side. And it is well-founded. In the so-called elections over 99 per cent vote for the United List. There are no opposition candidates. If the state believed this expression of confidence from its citizens, it could have the Wall torn down tomorrow. But the state knows that this figure of 99 per cent only arises because the citizens do *not* trust the state. And so the Wall stays put, and indeed improvements are for ever being made to it. It is the concrete manifestation of the state's mistrust, and thus also the irrefutable argument for the continuation of the citizens' general mistrust of their state. Which is a vicious circle. As Bertolt Brecht put it after 17 June 1953: 'The people has lost the government's trust. The government must elect itself a new people.'

Unfreedom as necessity! This new people now exists that the government has elected for itself. It perfectly realises the necessity for its unfreedom. And the outcome is a new, higher form of freedom. It is based on the consciousness that the consciousness of the masses, in other words of every individual, is irredeemably feeble. The new men and women have realised that they would be easy prey for the siren songs of the capitalist West and that, if they heard them, their socialist consciousness would melt away like wax in the sun. So they decide to stay here voluntarily. They read only newspapers from the East, magazines from the East, books from the East. They don't listen to radio-west nor watch tele-west. They don't allow the class enemy into their homes, and are deaf to his lies. They are the ones who read the leading articles in the newspapers and take them to heart. They are absolutely clean, totally, aseptically sterile. They are the socialist German nation in the socialist German state. Ninety-nine per cent of them vote for the candidates of the National Front which the state apparatus in its wisdom has selected for them; for they know that they would certainly not make the right choice if they had to select them for themselves.

That the Central Committee has selected the right popular representatives and the right government is at once evident from the fact that whenever a vote is taken, the government's suggestions are always passed unanimously – after they have previously been decided by the Central Committee, naturally. Can anything match this socialist democracy for sheer perfection? . . .

Today, more than half a century after the October Revolution, we know that it was by no means the terminal phase of capitalism that was then being ushered in, as the Bolsheviks hoped. Instead, another, further period of enormous growth followed, in which scientific and technical progress permitted such a huge growth of productive forces that the long-drawn-out initial phase of capitalism appears, when measured by economic and technical criteria, as a relatively short stride along the road in comparison. The two great World Wars did not hold up but if anything further accelerated the pace of development of the productive forces, and it has continued to increase right up to the present day. When, over a hundred years ago, Marx analysed the laws of the capitalist economy, not even the boldest imagination could suspect what unimaginable technical progress was to be made in a comparatively short time. . . .

In fact Marx was analysing capitalism in an age when it had just begun to develop freely. Since then its economic growth has progressed geometrically through time.

The Club of Rome's famous Meadows Report shows that such exponential growth cannot be continued without limit. Earth's resources of energy and raw materials are not inexhaustible and they set limits to this unbridled growth which just cannot be exceeded. However, since capitalism cannot survive without growth, there is a great economic crisis ahead of us, which may easily end in the universal catastrophe of a nuclear war.

It is, of course, the never-ceasing advances of technology which have so far made possible the existence and success of the capitalist economy. Every new invention, every new technology creates new opportunities for profit and acts against the general tendency for the rate of profit to fall. By re-equipping itself technically every ten years – the old equipment is 'morally' obsolete, as the jargon has it, long before it is on purely technical grounds – the capitalist economy is forever putting off its ultimate fate, only experiencing minor recessions, and postponing the great, life-threatening crisis. The signs of the latter's approach are already unmistakable: breakdown of the currency system, progressive inflation, incipient mass unemployment. How long it will take before the great collapse comes is hard to say. But that it will imperil the whole of mankind, and not just the inhabitants of capitalist countries, is beyond question.

Although the great industrial countries of West and East have armed themselves to a level that defies imagination, and have weapons of annihilation at their disposal with which they could make our planet uninhabitable in a few weeks, the third great war has not occurred so far, and, apart from small-scale local wars, we have been living in 'peace' for almost thirty years. We owe this remarkable peace to nuclear weapons. Because under the present conditions of technology there can be no victor in an all-out nuclear war, but only universal nuclear death, war is impossible. But if one of the two sides were able, through some invention, to secure a technical advantage which would enable it to annihilate the other side before the latter could prepare itself to retaliate, the danger of war would be right back with us again. The survival of mankind hangs by a slender thread. Only a major and profound transformation of political and economic conditions can avert this threat to our very existence.

It is true that the Meadows Report on the limits to growth does not say that only the elimination of capitalism can save us from the danger that threatens our existence. It merely indicates that the essential condition for economic catastrophe consists in the consequences of the economic and technical policies, which will be its cause, not ensuing directly from these causes, but with a delay of several decades. People only ever think about short-term advantages and are blind to the catastrophic future consequences of these – or so it is said, in an attempt to attribute the shameless, ruthless capitalist lust for profit to human nature. Whilst in vast areas of the world there is desperate famine, in the highly industrialised countries enormous efforts are being made to reduce food production – to keep prices up. Compared with the vast expenditure on private luxuries and the generally high standard of living, or even compared with the expenditure on what are basically quite nonsensical armaments, what falls from the tables of the rich to the starving of the world is less than crumbs. Do people really believe, in the lands of the rich, that they can go on like that for ever with impunity? When one considers that it takes decades for the effects to follow from the causes, one has to ask: when will it finally be too late? Or is it perhaps already too late?

The warning voices are becoming more numerous in the capitalist countries of the West. After all, that is where the Club of Rome report came from too. But everyone knows that what ought actually to be suggested to avert the danger that threatens, is not remotely possible under the conditions of capitalism. To carry *that* out, we would have to give up our freedom and democracy, and put an interventionist dictatorship in its place – or so a good friend from the West recently told me. You mean a regime similar to ours? I asked. His reply was in the affirmative.

This answer reveals just how nonsensical has been the development of socialism in the socialist countries. Because this answer did not in fact mean that the friend I was talking to accepted this kind of solution to the problem. Quite the contrary: not merely could he only regard this 'socialist' solution with horror, but he also considered it quite impossible and impracticable under present conditions. And in this he was unquestionably right. The answer given by my friend, who is a Social Democrat, also expressed the deep disappointment felt by socialists in the West about how the socialist countries had developed. The system of 'unfreedom as necessity' for the peoples who have lost the confidence of their governments, this 'socialism', offered no prospects for the future, even where it was in control.

You can see that straight away, just by looking at its economic goals. The 'qualities of life' for which it is striving are those that capitalism is already providing. But while capitalism is already beginning to suffer surfeits from the effects of its consumer-explosion, the socialist economy, with its thoroughly backward technology, is permanently engaged in a desperate attempt to follow the capitalist economy on its ever more senseless path, and if at all possible, catch it up. Instead of socialism having liberated the productive forces from their capitalist chains, as Marx prophesied, so that they could then forge ahead unfettered, in practically every field it has become a technological lame duck, which has to spend good money buying know-how from the capitalists. The example which most clearly illuminates this situation is surely the motor car. It is a high-quality item of technical merchandise, which, with an average life-span of not many years, is by no means worn out by being used, but actually by not being used, because for more than 95 per cent of its life it stands around unused, blocking the streets, totally exposed to wind and weather – and as such it is only perceived as a nuisance. It is supposed to provide local transport, and is built for four to five people. But it is nearly always used by a single individual. A car can reach enormous speeds. Top speeds of 90 mph are perfectly normal. But as there is only very rarely an opportunity to drive so fast, its owner is sorely tempted to make the maximum use of the few opportunities that do arise. Because not everyone is an experienced racing driver, there are frightful accidents. But thousands also die in traffic accidents every year in the blocked streets of the cities, drivers and pedestrians alike, small children and especially old people. In 1973 in West Germany 20 000 died, in 1974 rather fewer, but presumably largely because of the oil crisis and the stagnant economy. The car is far and away the most dangerous means of transport that has ever existed. Plane crashes only claim a few hundred or a thousand lives each year, despite the huge number of flights throughout the world – and the miles flown per person are many times greater than the 'passenger miles' covered by car in West Germany. In fact, the cost in lives alone ought to lead to cars being banned. But the economic objections are no less weighty. Enormous quantities of valuable raw materials end up in the wreckage of cars, in effect lost for ever. The weight/load ratio is so poor that their engines need a power of 50–200 hp, instead of 1–2 hp, which is what is required to transport a person at speed (as on a moped, or by bus or suburban train). The sheer waste of energy is just as great. To this must be added the enormous expenditure by the state on road-building and for the whole road and motorway system. Finally, the car is one of the most prolific polluters of the environment. Simply looked at from the technical angle, it is clear that to meet the transport needs for which it is supposed to exist, the car is fundamentally misconceived. And it is not as if, at the present level of technology, we lacked a better solution to the problem. A team of experts could design an automated transport system in the twinkling of an eye, by which all local destinations could be reached more quickly by everyone – and virtually without any danger, and which at the same time would only require a fraction of the materials and energy that cars currently swallow up, in all branches of the economy. This would, however, mean that the car industry, which is today one of the pillars of capitalist industry, would have reached the end of the line. Car buyers, who have hitherto been private individuals, would be replaced by a small number of customers who would presumably be mostly representatives of the state.

Not merely roads and motorways, but all the traffic using them, would become part of the infrastructure. Private consumption of 'passenger miles' would have been replaced by their social consumption. The free-market economy would have lost its largest and most powerful partner.

I am not claiming that this major transformation, with the enormous advantages it would have for people, would be absolutely impossible in capitalism. But it could certainly only be achieved with great difficulty and in the face of fierce opposition. Under socialism, one would have thought, its implementation would merely have been a technological and scientific problem.

But what is actually happening in the socialist countries? With the aim of at last reaching 'world standards', vast car factories are built under licence from Western car firms, and in direct technical co-operation with them. If in the near future the flood of motorised armchairs produced in these factories pours out on to the road systems of these countries, which in comparison with those in Western Europe are mostly very primitive, then even sooner than in the West we shall be faced with the absurd and chaotic traffic conditions we see under capitalism. It is entirely in keeping with the class structure of capitalism, which lives off the constant incitement to individual consumption, that it should have bred the car as its key social status symbol. But how to explain, or indeed justify, the same process being repeated, in a most frightening manner, in the socialist countries? One might perhaps excuse it by saying that the masses in the socialist countries, whose standard of living is still considerably lower than that of the masses in the capitalist countries, would not understand it if they continued to be denied cars, and expensive experiments with new forms of public transport were being made instead. But that is only an excuse: long before the mass production of cars was even considered, medium and luxury cars were being produced for state and party officials.

And one should not imagine that the economic costs of producing the large luxury Chaika cars are insignificant. But even if they were, why not make do with basic cars? Why are we copying capitalism by reflecting the social hierarchy in a corresponding range of car models? The reason is simply this: the fundamental fact has obviously not yet been grasped, that, to ensure its historic survival, socialism must be different from capitalism, and that means in its economic objectives too.

What I have here demonstrated by taking the car as an example, could be shown by detailed reference to the whole sphere of economic activity in the socialist countries. One must conclude that the economic goals of capitalism can, of course, be achieved with much greater success in a capitalist than in a socialist society. For as long as this mistaken policy is pursued in the socialist countries, socialism will limp along in capitalism's footsteps, with no prospect of ever catching it up, let alone of overtaking it. And socialism would be struck by the full force of a profound and catastrophic crisis of capitalism. . . .

The abolition of democratic rights and liberties, which even the capitalist state is obliged to grant its citizens in order to be able to develop, indeed otherwise the enormous economic and technical development of late capitalism would be unthinkable: that is the underlying cause both of the economic failure of socialism hitherto, and of the progressive erosion of its international standing and the consequent morbid fragmentation of all the left-wing and revolutionary forces in the world. And how badly we need them to unite – especially now! The time is approaching with giant strides when socialism in the literal sense will be the last salvation of mankind. If, by then, the decisive major transformation of socialism has not been achieved, it will be mercilessly dragged into the conflagration of the capitalist inferno too.

'Unfreedom as necessity' is Stalinist pseudo-socialism's motto, which could only emerge and consolidate itself in the special and to some extent tragic historical circumstances which accompanied the first successful socialist revolution in world history. However, despite its great internal weakness, the victorious October Revolution was nevertheless able to assert itself even against the barbaric attack of the German fascists. Whether in the course of this contradictory process unfreedom has ever constituted a historical necessity is hard to decide today. Questions such as 'What would have happened if . . .' rightly enjoy scant regard even among pure historians. Politically it has no relevance whatsoever.

But after everything that has happened, we are that much more entitled to say, and can do so with that much greater certainty, that the principle of 'unfreedom as necessity' not only has no social and political justification whatsoever today, but that – for as long as it still applies in any socialist country – it is the decisive brake on development within these countries and at the same time a blot on the reputation and credibility of socialism internationally. The popular masses in the capitalist countries can only fight their class struggles with some prospect of success, if they are at the same time struggling to preserve and secure bourgeois democratic rights and liberties. They cannot identify with a socialism whose first act when in power would be to remove these rights and liberties. At the same time one must bear in mind that bourgeois, capitalist society is by no means indulging in democratic rights and liberties for its citizens merely as a kind of luxury either, but requires them as an indispensable precondition for its existence and growth. Only when that society is shaken to its foundations, and threatened by revolutionary upheaval, does it throw overboard the achievements which it itself once brought into the world, and seek refuge in fascism. But where capitalism is still firmly in the saddle, as it is in the great centres of capitalism to the present day, democratic rights and liberties, and the institutions that defend them, are the fundamental conditions of its existence; and that in two respects: on the one hand, they are the indispensable precondition for the effectiveness of bourgeois ideology, which attempts to give the impression that all power emanates from the people and is subject to its control, whilst those who really possess power are neither elected by the people nor are they under its control. On the other hand, however, the capitalist economy operates, despite its basically chaotic character, by means of rapid democratic self-correction, like an ingenious cybernetic feedback system, which can to some degree rapidly compensate for any signs of imbalance that occur. The public's right to unrestricted information blurs the bounds of secrecy, even when the interests of the state are involved, including the military sphere.

In socialist countries on the other hand, even what is common knowledge, and especially what is commonly thought, is a carefully guarded state secret. An opinion poll conducted by the SED's Institute for Public Opinion Research recently established that 90 per cent of young people answered 'yes' to the question whether they could imagine living in the West – a result that is naturally treated as top secret.

Whilst the bourgeois state permits an extremely free flow of information, both horizontally and vertically, the socialist state keeps its hatches battened down like a warship on battle-stations. And at every hatch where information might try to seep through, there is not merely an inspector who carefully checks all the accompanying paperwork, but also an official from the Orwellian Ministry of Truth who deletes everything from the report that doesn't precisely correspond to the picture of reality desired by the immediately superior authorities. What becomes of the information after it has been several times through this process, before eventually arriving at the top, is often positively mind-boggling. Thus a member of the Politburo, with whom I was travelling to India in the year of the great compulsory collectivisation of agriculture in the GDR, believed that the difficulties the party was facing with collectivisation in the countryside arose from the rural population having rushed into the process too enthusiastically, with the party struggling to restrain them in their headlong haste. This mind-boggling misinformation did, however, contain a grain of truth, albeit mutilated beyond recognition: the excessive zeal with which our worthy comrades in the countryside had pressurised the rural population into the Agricultural Co-operatives had led to a competition between districts and regions, with those party organisations naturally winning the laurels who were able to report whole villages at a time voluntarily joining. The party then subsequently excused the catastrophic decline in agricultural production in the first years of collectivisation by reference to the excessive zeal of the rural population. Leaders of a party and state who are so badly misinformed are totally incapacitated. The management of economic processes becomes a matter of pure self-deception.

The system of totally blocking the free flow of information, of sealing oneself off at home and abroad, of painting everything in rosy colours, of the state's boundless mistrust for its citizens, this whole massive diversion into unfreedom as necessity: all this must be blown apart and overcome, if socialism in the socialist countries is still to have any chance of becoming true socialism. Superstructure and base have entered into a contradiction which threatens political and economic development as a whole. For economic reasons alone, therefore, the Stalinist vicious circle must be blown apart. When one considers to what degree the old structures have already calcified, and how fiercely those who represent them will defend their positions, then one can appreciate how complicated and difficult this process will be. But it is necessary, indeed it will scarcely brook delay. It will not endanger or weaken socialism, any more than that first hopeful attempt in Czechoslovakia in 1968, which succumbed then to those who saw it as threatening their personal power.

So what has become a necessity under socialism, as never before, is freedom. It is true it will not be a carbon copy of bourgeois freedom, nor can it possibly be so. For socialism can create freedoms which in bourgeois society were merely hopes and dreams: the freedom of the individual from all material dependence on others. Under capitalism people can only free themselves from material dependence on others by making others yet more dependent on them. Under socialism the material freedom and independence of the individual are based upon only being dependent on the socialist community as a whole, on its culture and maturity.

SOURCE: *Berliner Schriften*, pp. 62–77.

23. ROBERT HAVEMANN

I am also very much in favour of dissolving the SED as it has existed up to now, and us founding a League of Communists; whether this name is the most appropriate is another question. What Bahro has in mind is, of course, correct, but really these are pipe-dreams – when set beside present realities. There is an enormous amount to be done before this demand can be put on the agenda. What we need now is a policy of 'small steps'.

Firstly, we have to ensure that discussion is less inhibited in the existing institutions and organisations: in the SED, in the Free German Federation of Trade Unions, in the factories, in the League of Culture, in the Writers' and Artists' Associations. *Secondly*, it must be possible for articles to appear in the press conveying views about the central issues of the day, not from the standpoint of any particular Politburo resolution, but giving expression to the author's own opinions. *Thirdly*, the publication of an autonomous and independent literary journal, for instance, would be a gigantic step forward: a journal which is edited and run by people who have not been selected by the party's Central Committee, but are perhaps picked by the associations themselves and whose qualifications are already demonstrably proven by their own initiatives; for example, writers such as those who protested against Biermann's expatriation. People whom the public *can* regard as independent, and who can then show it in their journal. *Fourthly*, it would be a good thing if a newspaper were perhaps allowed that was independent of the party. Such a thing is after all not beyond the bounds of the imagination. A newspaper based on named individuals, who have some standing and qualifications in politics, and whose articles and opinions the party would be obliged to take seriously and discuss. And it would, *fifthly*, be a good thing if a different style of proceedings were introduced into the *Volkskammer* – this was even tried once under Dieckmann – whereby Representatives would no longer read everything out from prepared manuscripts that had previously been vetted and approved, but could make speeches freely and really speak their minds, openly and uninhibitedly, without suffering for it. After all, one need have no fear that any of the Representatives at present in the *Volkskammer* would say anything untoward or hostile. But they should at least be allowed to take some small steps in the direction of independent thinking, something which would enhance the dignity and reputation of Parliament.

And all this would require from the rulers is a bit of courage. I believe they might cover themselves with glory, they might even become popular, if they took such a line. They would not need to fear for their positions, as they now undoubtedly do, and rightly so. Never have our rulers' positions been so insecure and so much in conflict with general public opinion as today.

The state, even the modern socialist state ruled by communists, the state for which they bear a share of the responsibility, does not force everyone to accept an official ideology, and leaves people completely free as regards what they think, what they find beautiful, what they believe in and what they don't believe in. It encourages the free evolution of all ideas and ways of thinking, for one thing so that they can compete with each other, contend with each other, a friendly, productive, creative form of contention, through which human culture develops and always has developed throughout the ages. Even when the contention was not friendly, and the state always sided with reaction, the ensuing grand conflict gave rise to something new, something interesting, new ideas – and what's more, it resulted in their acceptance, from Giordano Bruno and Galilei, to Einstein and Heisenberg.

I also think it important for us to be clear about the aims and the kind of life that socialism offers, as opposed to the terminal phase of capitalism, what it is striving for, and what its striving truly amounts to.

1. Is a quite specific level of material existence, a specific standard of living for everyone – in other words a specific technical and economic stage of development an absolute precondition for communism? What does communism mean anyway? I don't believe that we can define communism, or whatever we want to call the future social system we are aiming at, by saying: every man must have an electric shaver, every woman an electric hair-curler, or everyone a television set, a car or a motorbike or a motorboat, or a cabin in the forest, etc., etc.

I don't believe that such technical and economic definitions of wealth get us very far: they are all only relative and they still represent poverty, compared with the wealth that the rich amass even today, all over the world. You can never define communism by such definitions based on wealth. As I see it, the essential preconditions for communism are, firstly, that there must be no privileged people. There must not be people who enjoy ten or a hundred times more resources, material and other, including intellectual, than anyone else. There must be no privileged people, classes or groups of any description, but everybody, every person must have exactly the same opportunities, the same chances, and be equal with regard to each other. That is communism. 'Communis' after all means being equal.

2. It is essential that this should not be a communism of hardship and poverty. Every person's life must be secure: food, life, dwelling, sleep, clothing, health-care. No one must be allowed to fall on hard times, illness must entail no more suffering than is inherent in the disease itself. There must be complete social security for every individual, for every member of society. That is the second crucial precondition.

3. All individuals must be equally free to make their own decisions.

They must be free to go where they want, to move from one place or country to another, to travel, to seek out the job or area of interest that suits their tastes and preferences, and they cannot therefore be directed by any higher, more powerful authority, which forces something on them that they don't want.

4. The thing I regard as quite crucial is that every person should be given access to the supreme cultural values of mankind, and take an interest in the fact that there are groups in society who are actively engaged in encouraging and stimulating interest in painting, architecture and music, and liberating people from their enslavement to all this cheap, kitschy music, kitschy art, and the banal world of detective stories; so that finally they discover the enormous wealth of superb literature and intellectual beauty, as well as profound wisdom, and get to know the great philosophers of the past from all countries; all that must increasingly become the centre of social life, and something that people are interested in; and that in itself simultaneously also implies the chief function of a communist society that is developing in forever increasing freedom: the upbringing of children, the education of young people, and the concern that their lives should not be doomed from the outset, but that all their great talents should be able to blossom freely. I believe that if one envisages a world without armaments, without the senseless waste of capitalism, then such a communism could long ago have been feasible for all mankind. From the purely material point of view, these simple basic principles could be put into practice throughout the world. We would rapidly come to regard the luxury of the exploiters as an absurd burden, and ultimately despise those who were weighed down by it.

I believe that it is a major task of our time to define such a communist Utopia. It is a question I have been working on for a long time. I believe a new set of objectives must be developed before we can agree on the way to reach them. Socialism is a path to the goal, which by its very nature is fantastic, inspiring, Utopian. And like all Utopias, it is the form in which we imagine all the inhumanity that we are forced to endure today being overcome. And our Utopia is consequently bound to be one-sided, and marked by the miseries of our present lives. Enormous dangers lie along the road to this goal, because naturally the powerful of this world will not willingly or so easily yield their positions of power, but are ultimately insane enough to threaten the lives of all mankind, merely to ensure the continuation of what they regard as its only true path. And it is insane that modern capitalism can only exist by the uninterrupted growth of production, by ceaselessly squandering human labour and human intelligence on senseless projects. And it really is senseless, when one considers that the consumption and production of energy is multiplying a thousand times over in the space of a hundred years. It is something which just won't work, in the long run it cannot be done like this, it is simply bound to lead to a catastrophe.

The greatest insanity of all, of course, is armaments, the atom bombs, the hydrogen bombs, the many fearful weapons of mass destruction, undergoing ceaseless further development, with which the great powers lie in wait for each other, sincerely believing that the other will launch an attack if, through any advance of a technical kind, he could see some gain in doing so. And then the question arises: does one have to respond with a pre-emptive strike now, to stop the other side exploiting a momentary advantage? We, and the whole of mankind, live in this terrible state of total uncertainty as to the decisions of a small number of very limited people who are incapable of seeing far into the future. Never throughout history has there been a remotely similar situation, where the inhabitants of this planet have made the most utterly foolproof preparations for completely wiping themselves out.

SOURCE: *Ein deutscher Kommunist*, pp. 98–103.

Rejection of the GDR

24. HELSINKI CONFERENCE ON SECURITY AND CO-OPERATION IN EUROPE, FINAL ACT, AUGUST 1975

VI. Non-Intervention in Internal Affairs

The participating States will refrain from any intervention, direct or indirect, individual or collective, in the internal or external affairs falling within the domestic jurisdiction of another participating State, regardless of their mutual relations.

They will accordingly refrain from any form of armed intervention or threat of such intervention against another participating State.

They will likewise in all circumstances refrain from any other act of military, or of political, economic or other coercion designed to subordinate to their own interest the exercise by another participating State of the rights inherent in its sovereignty, and thus to secure advantages of any kind . . .

VII. Respect for Human Rights and Fundamental Freedoms, Including the Freedom of Thought, Conscience, Religion or Belief

The participating States will respect human rights and fundamental freedoms, including the freedom of thought, conscience, religion or belief, for all, without distinction as to race, sex, language or religion.

They will promote and encourage the effective exercise of civil, political, economic, social, cultural and other rights and freedoms, all of which derive from the inherent dignity of the human person and are essential for his free and full development.

Within this framework the participating States will recognise and respect the freedom of the individual to profess and practise, alone or in community with others, religion or belief acting in accordance with the dictates of his own conscience . . .

The participating States recognise the universal significance of human rights and fundamental freedoms, respect for which is an essential factor for the peace, justice and well-being necessary to ensure the development of friendly relations and co-operation among themselves as among all States.

They will constantly respect these rights and freedoms in their mutual relations and will endeavour jointly and separately, including in co-operation with the United Nations, to promote universal and effective respect for them.

They confirm the right of the individual to know and act upon his rights and duties in this field.

In the field of human rights and fundamental freedoms, the participating States will act in conformity with the purposes and principles of the Charter of the United Nations and with the Universal Declaration of Human Rights. They will also fulfil their obligations as set forth in the international declarations and agreements in this field, including inter alia the International Covenants on Human Rights, by which they may be bound . . .

Reunification of Families

The participating States will deal in a positive and humanitarian spirit with the applications of persons who wish to be reunited with members of their family, with special attention being given to requests of an urgent character – such as requests submitted by persons who are ill or old.

They will deal with applications in this field as expeditiously as possible.

They will lower where necessary the fees charged in connection with these applications to ensure that they are at a moderate level.

Applications for the purpose of family reunification which are not granted may be renewed at the appropriate level and will be reconsidered at reasonably short intervals by the authorities of the country of residence or destination, whichever is concerned; under such circumstances fees will be charged only when applications are granted.

Persons whose applications for family reunification are granted may bring with them or ship their household and personal effects; to this end the participating States will use all possibilities provided by existing regulations.

Until members of the same family are reunited, meetings and contacts between them may take place in accordance with the modalities for contacts on the basis of family ties.

The participating States will support the efforts of Red Cross and Red Crescent Societies concerned with the problems of family reunification.

They confirm that the presentation of an application concerning family reunification will not modify the rights and obligations of the applicant or of members of his family . . .

25. PETITION FOR ASYLUM IN WASHINGTON'S EAST BERLIN EMBASSY

To the President of the United States

Dear Mr Reagan

We are requesting political asylum in the embassy of the United States of America in Berlin. We are asking you for protection from persecution by the security organs of the GDR. We are threatened with internment. We have informed the authorities of the GDR that we are undertaking a hunger-strike of unlimited duration because we are being refused permission to leave the GDR. A hunger-strike is our last, desperate opportunity to make known our desire to emigrate to a democratic country. For attempting to leave the GDR two of us have already had to endure prison sentences. Action has been taken against us because we wished to exercise rights which the statutes of the United Nations say all men are entitled to and which every American takes for granted.

One of us is an Italian citizen, but he too is being refused permission to leave. Despite efforts over many years, personal privations and prison sentences, there is still no prospect of our being released from the GDR. Because of our inner convictions it has become impossible for us to live in the GDR.

It is intolerable to us that people in the GDR are denied all rights of self-expression and freedom. The Western democracies guarantee the personal dignity and freedom of every individual. The United States of America, with its tradition of freedom and long practice of democracy, is for us the guarantor of human rights and now inspires us to hope for freedom. We address you with confidence, Mr President, and in our plight ask you to grant us political asylum.

Bernd Apel, René Faccin, Jörg Hejkal, Petra and Daniel Klingberg, Bernd Macke.

SOURCE: *Frankfurter Allgemeine Zeitung*, 23 January 1984.

26. CHRISTIAN SOLIDARITY (BROTHERLY LOVE) VERSUS THE SOLIDARITY OF HATRED (THE CLENCHED FIST)

Without Christian solidarity from outside, we who are victims of oppression in the East are totally at the communists' mercy, though in present circumstances no doubt we can only be helped on an individual basis. It is a dangerous error to believe that communism will take on a human face if it is allowed free rein.

The very opposite is the case: if the West knuckles under, the communists will be intoxicated with victory and certainly raise the stakes, even to the point of launching a surprise attack.

From time immemorial, starry-eyed idealists have inflicted unspeakable suffering on the world – but none of them, in their zeal to impose happiness, has yet violated nations to the degree that the communists have.

Ordinary people have scarcely any chance of escaping to the West by their own unaided efforts.

I am addressing my general request to the Federal Republic because, in terms of social policy, suppport for emigration – which I like to call Christian solidarity – must surely be just as important for a state where justice prevails as it is for the petitioner.

Through Christian solidarity, the free democratic basic order in Western Europe will remain a benchmark for humanity, because Christian solidarity has its origin in brotherly love.

The solidarity of the clenched fist, by contrast, is the solidarity of hatred in a dubious and bloody guerilla struggle.

Even Hitler could afford to allow general freedom of movement. (I am referring to the pre-war years.)

The brutality required on the zonal frontier with the West proves that all censored reports of the mood among the population in the GDR are only a calculated lie.

The communists are obsessed with the idea that they have to 'domesticate' mankind to live in a Communist Party animal-house. The communists themselves state quite openly that this is the new type of man they want to breed.

Ostensibly the new man is to be more virtuous – but virtue is relative. The kind they want is a mental degenerate, who will apathetically let himself be harnessed, abused and forced to be happy, and simply isn't allowed to know that such things as basic freedoms, self-determination and dignity exist.

And we know how they 'domesticate' people: by coercive detention.

In fact what I am saying ought to be pretty well known; so why do I keep hearing from the Federal Republic about people being fed up with the state, although this is demoralising for a free welfare state? The mere sight of the unique and horrific security devices on the GDR frontier surely really ought to rouse any normal person from his sleep and demonstrate the truth about the alternative system of state which the Marxists have to offer.

Has there ever previously been a situation where people are permanently forbidden, on principle, to leave their own country, and anyone who cannot accept such restriction is shot down like a rabbit?

Anyone who wants to live in a socialist state probably need never fear unemployment, it is true, but he must be willing to be a slave to the Communist Party.

The party propagandists stifle questions about human rights by cunningly claiming that only fascists demand and require the basic bourgeois freedoms – so that they can carry on with their sabotage undisturbed. As no one can afford to be branded a fascist only people writing letters of farewell or appealing for help refuse to knuckle under.

Communists and Human Rights

The communists boast that basic human rights are guaranteed under socialism, since the basic human rights are said to be the right to employment, education and medical care. Not to mince words, what this attitude of mind implies is: the citizens of the GDR may not be free, but they do have the duty to work – and the most important human rights are thereby guaranteed in the GDR!

Such a philosophy of state makes me wild. Man faces the difficult and very urgent task of giving all the inhabitants of the globe a job and food – but not under the conditions of a forced labour camp, as under Hitler and Honecker! When communists sound off about their 'full employment', they are being characteristically cynical. What informed West German without a job would take one that meant accepting socialist living conditions? Who would want to be remorselessly controlled and harried from pillar to post in every sphere of life by a party they disapprove of?

Remorselessly means: there's no ducking out of it; anyone who can't stand the humiliating lack of freedom and the enforced involvement in the communist ritual is eradicated as a 'class enemy'. Work without the basic civil freedoms is a demoralising form of forced labour.

Under socialism you can in practice no more take your own decisions than cannon fodder can in wartime.

Is it not unparallelled impudence for a head of government to declare to the whole world: 'Our citizens can travel; for instance, 1.2 million travel to the FRG each year.' Is it not a sign of extreme terror, if such announcements are silently accepted by the population?

Compare that piece of communist provocation with the following sleight of hand by the SED: 'humanitarian concessions for the population of the GDR would require certain political demands to be met by the West'. Are any cases actually recorded in world history, where an administration has taken its own people hostage, and appealed to the world: 'Take pity on our people . . . whom we shall keep gagged and bound until you agree to the following conditions?' And every Western step in their direction immediately gives rise to yet another demand.

I consider Eurocommunism only as a ploy in the struggle, but it is difficult to philosophise about it.

The right thing, in my view, is to make the Eurocommunists face up to the inhumanities of their brother-parties in power.

The Eurocommunists should allow their attitude to communist terror to be used as a touchstone for their credibility.

Dissidents Penetrate the Iron Curtain

Fundamental to the East–West dispute must be the voice and tragic fate of the dissidents.

I don't mean to say by this that these individuals represent their peoples; but I do compare them with the noble-minded antifascists of Hitler's Germany – they were few and far between too . . .!

From the outset the communists have feared those honest and courageous dissidents who penetrate the Iron Curtain with the gravity of their testimony.

Not for nothing do they react hypersensitively to all those who lend an ear to the 'criminals' (naturally) calling for help in the East.

The most momentous violation of human rights in the GDR is the drastic limitation on freedom of movement. This restriction must not continue to claim victims for all eternity.

It is an essential part of the SED's strategy for governing to create a sense of complete hopelessness among the population; this is indispensable if a subject people is to be made totally submissive . . .

Socialism Means Ceasing to be Human

The question of human rights is none other than the question of being human, and for that reason it should be at the centre of the ideological struggle with communism.

In a totalitarian state any decent and intellectually alert person feels so oppressed that he can neither realise his potential nor relax. Any normal person with a traditional view of civilisation has become an outcast in the GDR. Virtually everything that one is confronted by is alien, incomprehensible, revolting. . . .

Yearning for Germany

I unreservedly declare my allegiance to the Federal Republic of Germany, which I regard as my fatherland, now that the territory of the GDR has obviously been lost to Germany.

This is not a confession of nationalism on my part, but a commitment to the values of the Basic Law and the manner in which that constitution, in which human rights have priority over the state, is applied in practice.

I am tormented by this yearning for the Federal Republic, because this free, pluralistic welfare state is my intellectual and political home, and because for me the Federal Republic of Germany most definitely provides all the conditions for enjoying that minimum of happiness and relaxation which is important in life.

SOURCE: Rainer Bäurich, *Manifest eines Christen im Sozialismus* (Bad Oeynhausen) pp. 16–26.

27. PETITION TO SECURE FULL HUMAN RIGHTS

This petition has been drawn up in free self-determination and signed by responsible citizens. We have submitted

(a) requests to move residence to the Federal Republic of Germany
(b) requests to be released from GDR citizenship.
Over a period of months and years the organs of state in the GDR have either not answered our requests at all, or not given a final answer to them, or have rejected them.

We, the signatories of this petition have submitted our requests to the GDR authorities for religious, political, humanitarian or for one of these reasons. We base our requests on the following international documents to which the GDR has given its signature:

(I) Universal Declaration of Human Rights, Arts. 13(2), 14(1), 15(2).
(II) International Covenant on Civil and Political Rights, Arts. 2, 12(2).
(III) Final Act of the Helsinki CSCE, co-operation in humanitarian and other spheres.

and
(1) Constitution of the GDR, Article 8,
(2) GDR Citizenship Law, Paras. 9, 10, 11.
(3) Basic Treaty between the two German states, Art. 2.

The conduct of the GDR authorities contravenes these international documents to which the GDR has given its signature; as responsible citizens we are therefore left with no alternative but to submit this petition, which we are signing in free self-determination. We are submitting it

to the United Nations – Division of Human Rights,
to the accredited representatives of the states party to the CSCE, to the national organisations for Human Rights
and to world public opinion

with the plea that effective support be given to the undersigned citizens and their families in their efforts to secure full human rights, including that of free choice of domicile and place of work, as guaranteed in the above international documents.

Riesa/GDR 10.7.76.

SOURCE: *Freiheit heißt die heiße Ware,* p. 65.

28. EXTRACT FROM A LETTER BY HORST GUNDERMANN, A DOCTOR WHO APPLIED TO LEAVE THE GDR WITH HIS FAMILY IN JUNE 1975, AND WAS PERMITTED TO DO SO ONE YEAR LATER

Neuruppin, 20.12.75

Outwardly the situation hasn't changed since that Wednesday evening, when our civil rights struggle was broadcast on Channel 2 of West German television: no official reaction, either to the television broadcast, or to my third application, which I submitted six weeks ago now. Of course, the television story went round the town like wildfire. Everybody here knows about it. And that's why it seems paradoxical that everything has remained absolutely quiet in our vicinity. That's the spooky thing about it. All the same, without being overconfident, I have to say that I'm not afraid. I'm arming myself against fears and uncertainties – though no doubt it is a very old-fashioned way of doing it – by praying and reading the psalms every day. Yesterday I came across verse 30 of the 119th Psalm: 'I have chosen the way of truth; thy judgments I have laid before me.'

Naturally I am extremely anxious for my family's sake. I can't stop imagining the sanctions that might, or will, be used against us by the powers that be. But for the moment, I am convinced that for tactical, sentimental reasons they won't embark on anything spectacular between Christmas and the New Year. We were expecting to be arrested immediately after the television broadcast on 10 December, on Human Rights Day. Occasionally I also thought we might suddenly be forcibly expelled from the country. But on thinking it over more calmly now, I feel that they will probably not resort to such measures, which would create a great stir; of course, authoritarian regimes are unpredictable, and that's why we can't rule out *anything* on this 'great journey' in the coming year either. So as not to give the public the impression they are giving way, they may keep me, or us, waiting for quite a while – three months or six or a whole year – and then allow us to leave, or expel us.

I'm particularly worried by what is for us the most dangerous ploy: they continue to act as if nothing at all had happened, they let me keep my job, and public status, and don't harass the family either. Then in the course of time, the mood in the country will quieten down, in fact people might even interpret such *non*-intervention as a sign of tolerance on the part of this state. And not just here, either, but in the West too, where as far as I can judge from the television news, people are increasingly anxious to obtain a 'subtler understanding' of the GDR!

Of course, we should not deceive ourselves: once someone has stuck his neck out as far as I have, and kicked against the ideological pricks, and not shown the slightest remorse about it either, he won't automatically be crossed off the register of class enemies. He'll still be struck down with ideological excommunication long after he thought he'd wiped his 'sin' from his own recollection. Political puritans have a long memory when it comes to renegades and dissidents. I thought I should put that in writing to you sometime. Of course, in their own transparent way, people here count on time, forgetfulness and the lack of democratic solidarity.

Let me waste a few more words on this: few people shake me warmly by the hand, most people press it shamefacedly, but one senses their fellow-feeling. But there are some who appear indignant at what I have openly gone and done. They fancy they are showing a special sense of responsibility by asking: 'Hasn't he thought of his children then? How could he do such a foolhardy thing!' My God, it was precisely because I was thinking of my children that I had to take this path, and could no longer stand as a liar before them!

Finally there are some, often enough they come from the same social level, who shake their heads and say: how can he be so stupid! Isn't he well enough off as he is? As a Christian who knows his Bible he should take to heart the saying that there are circumstances in which one must also be as cunning as the serpent! I must confess that this is just what I expected from intellectuals of this kind. But it is disappointing how awkwardly some West German colleagues express their support for what I am trying to do. I'll give you one example: a few days ago I was telephoned by Herr C, a specialist, for whom one must have a great deal of respect. He began the telephone conversation with the following words: 'I've been told to ring you!!' At first he couldn't think of anything else to say. Initially I was confused, because I didn't know what this colleague wanted of me. He then went on: 'I've been told to ring you by Herr D.', he gave the full name, as well as the home town. You've apparently got into trouble because of a television broadcast! He then hurriedly added, he was ringing from work and didn't have much time, but would write to me some time at length. I'm sorry for Herr C. There is absolutely nothing I can hold against him. He behaved correctly, and helpfully too. But has he got enough imagination to conceive of the risk we are taking? Or is there at the back of his mind – though that is the last thing I would suspect him of – the thought: he did after all bring it all on himself, by insisting on his 'I can do no other' principles.

I can only repeat the words Solzhenitsyn is reported to have spoken before an audience of American trade unionists, and which were picked up in a Western radio broadcast: 'Unless you stay awake, you are all doomed!' What indeed can one add to that? A different point: a few days after the Gerhard Löwenthal Magazine broadcast, a journalist from West Berlin rang me up. He was interested in our case. From what he told me, something has meanwhile appeared in the Berlin press about it too. Of course, Western newspapers are only read here by official departments that have been specially selected for the purpose. So I can't judge how serious the articles were. I don't even know whether you are aware of them. I am only anxious that it should continue to be the 'Gundermann case', and that the press should not reduce it to avidly sensationalised tittle-tattle. There is a law in this country which was previously entitled 'Incitement to Boycotting', but is now 'Agitation against the State'. Like many things in the new Penal Code, this law is open to a variety of interpretations. I'm saying this so that you realise that for as long as at all possible I would like to stick to campaigning for civil rights, in other words I am fighting for something, for basic human rights and basic values, for my family, and not against anything. Obviously that doesn't prevent the slightest ill-considered remark being used as a noose to hang me with.

The next step I am planning is to submit a fourth, very tersely worded application just before Christmas Eve. Then I shall wait until the New Year, in the expectation that something will happen. I almost suspect that the party has decided on the ploy of 'psychological starvation'. In the hospital there was a Trade Union Group meeting, at which the District Medical Officer was also present. It is astonishing that at this meeting someone had the courage to ask whether it was true that Dr Gundermann had applied to emigrate from the GDR with his family. The District Medical Officer, with whom I have had two longish talks, is said to have answered: 'Really? That's the first I've heard of it.' And the man who said that was someone who a few weeks earlier had been sounding off to me as to why he had chosen communism. . . .

It is a shame it is so hard to shake off these anxieties and share the children's excitement about Christmas – the journalist from West Berlin, who incidentally is from the Springer press which stands in such evil repute here, is now ringing me up every day. It is hard to decide – constant manipulation by the press makes one suspicious – whether it is a gesture of sympathy or just the normal professional interest of a reporter. However that may be, this not unpleasant voice over the telephone is now our only lifeline to the outside world. But the crucial thing is still that the Lord will help us.

SOURCE: *Entlassung aus der Staatsbürgerschaft* (Frankfurt a.M.; Vienna, 1978) pp. 88–93.

29. BERND JANUSZEWSKI, AN ENGINEER, AND HIS WIFE BÄRBEL, A SWIMMING INSTRUCTRESS, BOTH NOW LIVING IN THE FRG, ON THEIR EFFORTS TO OBTAIN PERMISSION TO EMIGRATE

Our reasons for wanting to emigrate were numerous: among other things, the restrictions on information, restrictions on travel, the order to shoot escapers at the frontier, the fact that children are educated to hate and the hypocrisy in the system – for example, the fact that members of the SED have special access to Western goods.

We submitted our first application to emigrate to the Ministry of the Interior and to the Department of Internal Affairs in our home town of Rostock on 15 August 1976. In our applications we quoted the relevant provisions of the Final Act of the Conference on Security and Co-operation in Europe. Shortly afterwards we were summoned to attend an interview by local government officials who told us that our application would not be granted. They also told us that the Final Act of Helsinki was only a 'declaration of intent' – it was not binding in international law. I quoted a speech by Erich Honecker, Chairman of the Council of State, in which he had said that 'not only the letter but also the spirit' of the Helsinki agreement 'was realised in the GDR'. We told them that we would write to Erich Honecker, to the Human Rights Commission in Geneva and to the GDR Committee for Human Rights. They shrugged their shoulders in response.

We did as we had said, first sending a petition to Erich Honecker. We never got a reply despite the fact that under GDR law petitions from GDR citizens to elected representatives should be answered within four weeks. We also wrote to the GDR Committee for Human Rights. When this petition had not been answered after some months, I rang up and enquired about it. They asked what the letter was about. I explained it concerned our application to emigrate. They replied, 'We do not answer letters on this subject.' I asked if they could confirm in writing that they did not answer such letters, but they replied that they could not. I also wrote a letter to Willi Stoph, Chairman of the Council of Ministers, in which I said 'a life in the GDR for my family and me does not seem to be worth living in conditions where human rights are violated'. This sentence was taken as blackmail, almost equivalent to a suicide threat, and was later used as evidence to convict me.

I lost my job because of my applications to emigrate – I was transferred to another department and to a less well paid job for 'security reasons', although in my original job I did not have access to confidential material. After that we were earning only 650 marks a month between us, which meant that we were only subsisting. We bought essential goods like food and clothing but no extras like furniture. We lived like this for the next two years, submitting applications to emigrate at three-monthly intervals, but without success.

We were finally arrested on 24 September 1979 and charged with 'obstructing the activity of organs of state by force or threats' under Article 214 of the Penal Code. They read the text of the article out to me. I asked to see it, but they refused. I then asked if they could read it out to me again, but this they also refused. In my case the charge was based on the statement I had made in the letter to Willi Stoph. In the case of my wife the charge was brought because she had once said to local government officials, after repeated refusal on their part to grant our applications to emigrate, 'You are sending us to our deaths.' We realised that our interviews with these officials must have been recorded.

Later charges were brought for 'treasonable activity as an agent' (Article 100 of the Penal Code). (This article proscribes contact with organisations abroad or their helpers or representatives 'in order to damage the interests of the German Democratic Republic'.) This was because we had written to some cousins in the FRG asking for help, and they in turn had contacted FRG television about the possibility of publicising our case.

The preliminary investigations involved detailed questioning about friends and relatives. I was interrogated at length about a collection I had made of references to human rights in the GDR press, which they had found while searching the house at the time of our arrest. This included an article by a history professor in the magazine *Horizont*, in which he argued that the right to emigrate was only necessary in countries where other rights were denied, and this clearly did not apply to the GDR. They seemed very suspicious about this collection and questioned me on my motives for making it. My wife was interrogated at length because she had noted down the address of the *Gesellschaft für Menschenrechte* (Society for Human Rights) from a television programme. However, they were unable to prove contact with this organisation. We were also questioned to see how much we knew about the 'buying out' scheme. This was difficult for them because they could not admit its existence. It took the form, 'Have you heard these rumours . . . do you believe them?'

We were tried on 15 February 1980 by the regional court in Rostock and found guilty of 'obstructing the activity of organs of state' and 'treasonable activity as an agent'. I was sentenced to two years nine months' and my wife to two years three months' imprisonment.

SOURCE: *Amnesty International Briefing EUR 22/01/82*, p. 18f.

The Unofficial Peace Movement

30. LETTER FROM THE CONFERENCE OF GOVERNING BODIES OF THE EVANGELICAL CHURCHES TO THE PARISHES (14.6.78) WITH AN INFORMATION SHEET ON MILITARY INSTRUCTION

Christians and churches alike have increasingly recognised that it is their duty to help our world achieve peace. Conciliation, with which God opposes all hostility between men, is the foundation of our lives. We owe it to all mankind to bear witness to this fact. As a community in Jesus Christ, we are working with others towards this end, wherever tensions can be reduced, trust increased and security between the nations reinforced.

Many anxious voices have spoken out in our churches about the introduction of military instruction in our schools. The Executive of the Conference of Governing Bodies of the Evangelical Churches has in its turn taken up these anxieties and asked the government not to introduce military instruction as a subject. It has received detailed verbal information concerning the introduction of this subject for pupils in the 9th and 10th classes. The conference regrets that account was not taken of the churches' concern, and it has again asked the government to reconsider the matter. The conference fears that the introduction of compulsory military instruction will work to the serious detriment of education for peace, particularly in the minds of young people, and the credibility of the GDR's peace policies will be called in question.

In view of this situation, education for peace in our parishes and families acquires particular importance. It must be our task

— to create room for the spirit of peace and conciliation,

— to demonstrate trust and openness by our example
— to prevent force being used as the final answer in resolving conflicts.

Parents and helpers in our parishes bear a special responsibility for education for peace. Together we must learn how to put that into practice, and help each other to do so. We are now sending some first guide-lines out to the parishes.

Many people will find their consciences sorely tried by the decisions they will have to take. To those who are thus troubled, we would say that our prayers are with them, as is such help as we can give.

Enclosure with the 'Letter to the Parishes'

For some months increasing concern had spread through our parishes about a government measure which we initially only learned of through hearsay: the introduction of military instruction to the ninth class of our general education schools. Parishioners have approached office-holders of the church, urgently asking for information and advice, and fervently requesting them to take action to prevent such a plan from being implemented. A number of petitions to this effect were also submitted to the Conference of Governing Bodies of the Evangelical Churches in the GDR.

I. In these circumstances the Conference of Governing Bodies of the Evangelical Churches approached the government of the GDR, asking for precise information on this matter, voicing reservations and objections and requesting the state authorities that, if there should in fact be any such intention, they should desist from it.

In response, the Secretary of State for Church Affairs made a detailed verbal statement on 1 June 1978 to the Chairman of the Conference and his deputies, together with the secretariat, about present planning in respect of the introduction of military instruction. The plans include:

— introduction of military instruction as a subject in the ninth class of general education schools from 1 September 1978. Four double lessons a year in addition to the present timetable. The course is compulsory for boys and girls; no assessment is envisaged.

— continuation of theoretical study with the same number of hours in the tenth class.

— a set course in civil defence for the ninth class from 1 September 1978, also compulsory for girls and boys, duration two weeks, five hours per day, at the end of the school year. No weapons training.

— parallel to these CD-courses, pre-military camp, two weeks' duration, on a voluntary basis. For boys only. Training includes use of weapons (small calibre).

— for the tenth class, from 1979, compulsory three-day exercise to conclude the course in the winter holidays.

The Secretary of State for Church Affairs commented on and clarified these plans in detail. The arguments which were used in further discussion with the church representatives included the following:

— the measures that were envisaged were not to be considered and judged in isolation, but must be seen in the overall context of the peace policies of the government of the German Democratic Republic.

— military instruction and the credibility of peace policies went hand in hand. The GDR's stability and readiness to defend itself had contributed decisively to preserving and securing peace in Central Europe.

— the introduction of military instruction was perfectly in accordance with the laws of the GDR: Article 23 of the Constitution, – Law for the Protection of Peace, – Law on the Uniform Socialist Education System, – Youth Law, – Law on Civil Defence.

— the introduction of military instruction did not mark a fundamental change of policy (cf. Hans Beimler Competitions – GST – pre-military training).

— the military instruction that was planned would enable Christians to provide a practical demonstration of loving one's neighbour in times of disaster, and to give effective aid to others through civil defence – survival techniques – first aid.

— all the other socialist countries already had compulsory military instruction as part of the school curriculum and had had very positive experiences with it.

The educational aims were: discipline – sense of responsibility – activity – promotion of physical fitness.

— the voluntary principle was respected in the case of weapons training. But 100 per cent participation was the aim.

Having heard this account, the church representatives set out their anxieties and objections in detail.

— they questioned whether a clear emphasis on peace education can still have priority, when the increased stress on military education is influencing attitudes in one particular direction.

— grave concern regarding the age at which military education is to begin. Danger of implanting a friend–foe mentality at an early age, and accustoming people to the use of force to resolve conflicts.

— fear that introduction of compulsory military instruction in the schools at this juncture (measures to create trust, détente, increased efforts for disarmament) would inevitably be interpreted abroad as a signal, and the credibility of the GDR's peace policies would suffer in consequence.

— the effectiveness of the witness for peace borne by Evangelical Christians from the GDR in the Oecumenical Movement would be impaired.

The church representatives declared that if military instruction was introduced as envisaged, they would support those parents and guardians who for reasons of conscience did not feel able to allow their children to receive this instruction. They expressed their concern that non-participation in the courses on grounds of conscience would be interpreted as a sign of political unreliability.

The representatives of the state listened attentively to the views presented by the representatives of the League of Evangelical Churches on the basis of common responsibility for peace and for mankind. It appeared that the government would continue with its plan to introduce the courses. Following a special session on 14 June the conference again requested the government to reconsider the proposed measures.

II. The conference's reservations about the introduction of a compulsory school subject, 'Socialist Military Education', were not removed by the discussion on 1 June. Since this subject is about to be introduced on 1 September 1978, and following our dialogue with the parishes, parents and young adults, who expressed these reservations to us, and as the result of discussions in advisory and policy-making committees, we wish to remind ourselves clearly once again of what these reservations are:

(1) The task of working for peace as prescribed by the gospel requires every church and every individual Christian soberly to examine how to reduce tensions in the present world situation, promote trust and serve peace. We recognise that the state has an obligation to protect the security of its citizens, and that is why we must ask ourselves what will give us true security today. If our preoccupation with security is the result of fear and threats, it will not in our view represent a step in the direction of greater peace, because it will lead to actions which will equally create fear on the opposing side and lead only to counter-threats. The proposed instruction threatens to become part of this dangerous mechanism, and for this reason it seems to us an inappropriate means for ensuring peace.

(2) Disarmament is what is urgently needed today. In our view the worldwide efforts by politicians to end the arms race must go hand in hand with educating people in society to an informed awareness of the question of disarmament. Disarmament will only be possible if we really want it and if it is deeply rooted in the thinking of every society. We see a danger that the compulsory military education of young people will lead to them becoming accustomed to the idea of conflicts being resolved by military means, and that might in the long term prove to be an obstacle to a real awareness of the question of disarmament. For the sake of disarmament we need an education which will enable people to settle disagreements without the use of force.

(3) Young people who have not experienced the horrors of war and are not capable of a sophisticated appreciation of the risks of securing peace by military means in the nuclear age, will have their capacity for peace seriously undermined by the proposed instruction, which presupposes as something perfectly natural the possibility of armed conflict between East and West, and which is essentially concerned with preparation for it. Educating the young at school to think in military terms, and to adopt military attitudes and patterns of conduct may mean that opportunities for peacefully resolving conflict are no longer exploited in years to come.

(4) The GDR consistently proclaims its commitment to a policy of peace and détente. We fear that the credibility of this policy abroad will suffer from the introduction of military instruction. The worldwide efforts being made to set up non-military security systems cannot succeed as long as within individual states people are being educated and trained only in terms of military security. The aim of a world without weapons, to which socialism knows it is committed, should in our view play a more prominent part particularly in shaping young people's minds in the schools. On this point the Oecumenical Movement is looking for specific help and guidance from representatives of the churches in socialist countries.

We know that the reservations and arguments that we have again summarised here cannot resolve the conflict in which many Christian parents will find themselves, whose children are due to receive military instruction from the autumn of 1978, and who are now asking themselves how they can responsibly fulfil the duty the gospel imposes on them of serving peace. However, it is our hope that this paper may offer some initial guide-lines to all those who are affected and worried by this development and help them to act responsibly.

III. The introduction of the subject, 'military education', makes concrete demands on the readiness and ability of all of us to educate our children for peace and for overcoming conflict in their personal and social lives, as well as between the nations. Many parents and educators, who are aware that our survival depends on practising and preserving peace, will be distressed at the contradiction between such education for peace and the practice of preparing for military defence, with all its associated emotions. As they stand by their children, they should try to ensure that the new instruction does not exclude education for peace, and exert their influence to achieve this.

There will be parents who after responsible reflection decide not to allow their children to take part in the new schedule of instruction. Such a decision should be seen as a pointer towards a future development of peaceful co-existence, which we must all be working towards today. It will only have this effect if it is convincingly accompanied by consistent and practical education for peace in the sphere of private responsibility. In these matters, so distressful for all parishioners, the congregation must now be a place of discussion, encouragement and support in a very special way.

Everything that disturbs and concerns Christian parents, educators and children about military education in the schools can ultimately only remind us how urgent it is to take specific steps to make peace more secure and more humane in the community of mankind, nations and blocs. As we consider such steps, we know we are united with all those who in earlier times committed themselves to peace and advocated trust and co-operation between the nations. We therefore regard it as our special task to continue with our efforts to achieve a true education for peace in the parishes and to support them even more than before. Education for peace must impart the knowledge, values and convictions which will enable the individual to form a balanced opinion about what will promote peace at the present time or what will militate against it. We ask the parishes to consider the following points in particular:

— force as a means of resolving conflicts in a world full of weapons is suicidal. We must start practising non-violent ways of settling disputes.

— preoccupation with security generates mistrust and further insecurity where there is no trust or co-operation. We must start pursuing paths to security which make others more secure as well as ourselves.

— thinking in friend-and-foe clichés prevents us exercising the common responsibility we all have for the world of tomorrow. We must start placing what unites us above what divides us, so that we may survive together.

All of us have the task of translating these ideas into action. Concrete steps in that direction might be:

— parents should bring up their children in an atmosphere of trust and not use force. They should instil in their children a distaste for the use of physical force.

— children's imagination and inventiveness should be applied to promote peaceful co-existence and not possible military conflict. Military life should never be romanticised, nor the unimaginable consequences of war understated. This has implications, for instance, when adults choose toys and reading matter to buy or give as presents.

— travel to countries beyond our borders should be used even more than it is at present to get to know and understand the people better, and it should be prepared accordingly and lessons drawn from it afterwards. Comprehensive information about the life, history and traditions of other nations is important for mutual understanding. This might include examining each other's schoolbooks: what image of other people do schoolbooks convey, and what image of our country do people receive in other countries.

— Christian communities should teach how much more desirable it is to resolve conflicts in peace than by force and without love. Christ's gift of peace should also be the object of explicit celebration in the parish.

Trusting in Jesus Christ, who is our peace (Ephesians 2, 14), we ask one on behalf of another for prayer to go with us and intercede for us, and for the strength to take the necessary steps, large and small, that peace may be realised in this world.

SOURCE: W. Büscher *et al., Friedensbewegung in der DDR*, pp. 69–77.

31. APPEAL FROM THE INITIATIVE-GROUP 'SOCIAL SERVICE FOR PEACE' (9.5.81).

Dear Friends,

We are continuing our search for ways to promote peace. 'Reverence for life' demands that we make peace without weapons, and that we act to ward off the threat to life.

We are deeply concerned about the ever rising level of armaments in both the West and the East.

We are deeply concerned about the ever increasing importance attached to military matters in our society. But we are equally deeply concerned about the shortcomings in the social services, affecting the sick, the physically and mentally disabled, the elderly in old people's and nursing homes, those at risk from addiction, as well as the rehabilitation of released offenders. In these areas there is a serious shortage of staff.

This shortage could be partially remedied even with ancillary staff offering good will and humanity. The specialist staff could devote themselves entirely to their proper duties.

We came together on 25.4. and 9.5.81 in Dresden, and have continued to work at our 'Social Service for Peace' Initiative (SSfP) which has been under discussion for six months. We here present the re-edited text. Our initiative is intended as a positive step towards maintaining peace, at the same time benefiting those in our society who most urgently need help.

Social Service for Peace

We call upon the *Volkskammer* of the GDR:

1. To establish a Social Service for Peace (SSfP) as an alternative to Military Service and Substitute Service, with which it shall have equal status. Registration, medical examination and entry shall be the same as for Military Service. The law of 24.1.62 on compulsory military service, with the relevant ensuing decrees, shall be amended accordingly.

2. Those undertaking SSfP shall be liable for twenty-four months' service

— to indicate their desire for peace by this additional commitment.

— to deter 'shirkers'.

3. Those undertaking SSfP shall enjoy the same rights as those undertaking Military Service (for example, insurance, pay, leave, right of return to former employment).

4. Those undertaking SSfP may be quartered in residential hostels, to avoid any unfair advantage from sleeping at home.

5. There shall be basic training in First Aid and Disaster Control.

6. Those undertaking SSfP shall receive regular political instruction, with particular emphasis on: maintaining peace, disarmament, non-violent resolution of conflict.

7.1 Those undertaking SSfP shall be employed primarily in the following social services:

— residential care (children's homes, old people's homes, nursing homes, homes for the physically or mentally handicapped)
— ancillary staff in hospitals
— social welfare (drug addicts, youth service, social rehabilitation)
— social work among the old and infirm
— the field of environmental protection shall be examined as a possible area of service.

7.2 The purpose shall be to
— release specialist staff for their proper duties
— release parents from work at night and away from home during the week.

If you agree with this initiative, discuss it with your friends – and write by 1 September 1981 (World Peace Day) to the synod of the church in whose area you live.

Every individual is vital, including you!

SOURCE: W. Büscher *et al.*, *Friedensbewegung in der DDR*, pp. 169–71.

32. THE BERLIN APPEAL – MAKE PEACE WITHOUT WEAPONS (25.1.82)

1

There is only one kind of war now possible in Europe, a nuclear war. The weapons piled up in East and West will not protect us, but annihilate us. While the soldiers in their tanks and rocket-bases and the generals and politicians in their bunkers, whom we trusted to protect us, are still alive and continuing to annihilate whatever is left, we shall all long be dead.

2

So: if we want to live, get rid of the weapons! And the first step: get rid of nuclear weapons. The whole of Europe must become a nuclear-free zone. We propose: negotiations between the governments of the two German states on the removal of all nuclear weapons from Germany.

3

Divided Germany has become the mobilisation point for the two great nuclear powers. We propose an end to this deadly confrontation. The victors of the Second World War must at last conclude peace treaties with the two German states, as was resolved in the Potsdam Agreement of 1945. After that the former allies should withdraw their occupation troops from Germany and agree on guarantees for non-intervention in the internal affairs of both German states.

4

We propose holding a great debate on the questions of peace, in an atmosphere of tolerance and recognition of the right of free speech, and to permit and encourage every spontaneous public expression of the desire for peace. We declare before the public and before our government that the following questions should be discussed and answered:

(a) Oughtn't we to stop producing, selling and importing so-called war toys?
(b) Oughtn't we to introduce peace studies in our schools in place of military instruction?
(c) Oughtn't we to allow social work for peace instead of the present alternative military service for conscientious objectors?
(d) Oughtn't we to stop all public displays of military might and instead use our ceremonies of state to give expression to the nation's desire for peace?
(e) Oughtn't we to stop so-called civil defence exercises? As no worthwhile civil defence is possible in nuclear war, these exercises merely make nuclear war seem less serious. Does it not perhaps amount to a kind of psychological preparation for war?

5

Make peace without weapons – this does not just mean ensuring our own survival. It also means stopping senselessly wasting our people's labour and wealth on producing the engines of war and equipping enormous armies of young men, who are thereby taken out of productive work. Oughtn't we rather to be helping the starving throughout the world, instead of continuing to prepare our own deaths?

Blessed are the meek:
For they shall inherit the earth
(Jesus of Nazareth in the Sermon on the Mount)

The balance of terror has up to now prevented nuclear war only by constantly putting it off till tomorrow. The nations are fearful of this coming morrow of terror. They are searching for new and better ways of securing peace. The 'Berlin Appeal' is one expression of this search. Think about it, put your ideas to our politicians and everywhere discuss the question: what is conducive to peace, what is conducive to war?
Let your signature lend strength to your agreement with the 'Berlin Appeal'.

Berlin, 25 January 1982

Names of the first signatories (GDR citizens from various towns): Reiner Eppelmann, Minister of the Samaritan Church, Friedrichshain, and Minister with responsibility for youth in the District; Manfred Altmann, craftsman; Axel Bayer, worker; Evelyn Bayer, worker; Eva-Maria Eppelmann, housewife; Volker Elste, deacon-in-training; Stefan Preyer, machinist; Lorenz Göring, deacon-in-training; Katja Havemann, housewife; Robert Havemann, scientist; Eberhard Henke, manager; Ralf Hirsch, mechanic; Michael Heinisch, deacon-in-training; Christfried Heinke, deacon-in-training; Gerd Jäger, deacon; Daniela Karschewsky, office worker; Rosemarie Keßler, worker; Günter Keßler, worker; Olaf Kraensel, office worker; Detlef Kucharzewski, worker; Regine Maywald, office worker; Johannes Maywald, office worker; Lothar Niederohe, worker; Rudi Pahnke, Parish Minister and Minister with responsibility for youth in the District; Jürgen Pagel, deacon-in-training; Lutz Rathenow, writer; Thomas Schulz, worker; Ralph Syrowatka, deacon; Friedhart Steinert, worker; Bernd Schulz, worker; Winfried Weu, machinist; Andrea Weu, nurse; Günter Weu, District teacher of religion; Bernd Weu, engineer; Hans-Jochen Tschiche, minister and Director of the Evangelical Academy Magdeburg.

SOURCE: W. Büscher *et al., Friedensbewegung in der DDR*, pp. 242–4.

33. OPEN LETTER TO ERICH HONECKER

Dear Chairman of the Council of State

In this letter we would like to put some ideas to you which have been preoccupying us since the new Military Service Law of 25.3.82 was passed, relating to military service for women. Some of us have children, others do not, some of us are Catholic, others are from the Evangelical Church, others have no church affiliations, some of us have been through a war, while others have been spared this grim experience; but we are united by one thing: that we are concerned and do not want to give our tacit consent to a law imposing quite new obligations on women which cannot be reconciled with the way we see ourselves.

— We women wish to break the circle of violence and refuse to participate in any use of violence for the resolution of conflict.

— We women see army service for women not as an expression of their equal rights, but as inherently contrary to their nature as women. We see our equal rights with men not in standing side by side with *those* men who take up arms, but with *those* who like ourselves have recognised that the concepts of 'enemy' and 'opponent' in fact imply the destruction of human beings, which we reject.

— We women see willingness to perform military service as a threatening act which conflicts with the striving for moral and military disarmament and allows military discipline to drown the voice of human reason.

– We women feel a particular vocation to defend life, and to support the old, the sick, and the weak. We must work against war and for peace in the social and educational sphere, if we are not to fail in our duty to the next generation.

– We women protest against one day having to join the ranks of the National People's Army and defend a country which will be uninhabitable, even after a conventional war, which in Europe would probably end in a nuclear catastrophe.

– We women believe that mankind is today on the brink of an abyss, and that piling up further weapons can only lead to an insane catastrophe. This terrible fate can perhaps be averted if all the questions implied by this fact are publicly discussed. According to Art. 65, para. 3 of the GDR constitution, the draft of any law that is of fundamental importance is to be put to the public for discussion before being enacted, so that the outcome of this popular debate can be taken into account in the final version. In our opinion this is a law of fundamental importance, because of its subject matter, and not least because half the population of the GDR is *directly* affected by it.

– We women declare we are not willing to submit to this compulsory military service, and we demand that the possibility of refusal should be enshrined in the law. The right of refusal is necessary because our freedom of conscience is infringed by the promulgation of this law which extends the duty of military service to women.

As it was not originally possible to have public discussions on this law, some of us have submitted a formal request that they should be held, and others are hoping to be able to take part in the ensuing talks. Unfortunately these expectations have been disappointed, since no one was prepared to initiate talks on this subject which so pressingly concerns us.

The speech made by Academician Prof. Arbatov at the Peace Congress of World Religions in Moscow encouraged us to address our questions to you once more. We are requesting that those who are responsible for this Military Service Law should also be prepared to talk openly. No doubt you are familiar with the speech, but we would like to quote several sentences from it nevertheless.

Amongst other things Prof. Arbatov deals with the psychological and moral allies of the arms race, and refers to the myth that constantly building up weapons and armed forces contributes to security.

> All these myths encourage the arms race. Nowadays people try and wrap them up in the form of complicated analyses and paradoxes, using terminology that is incomprehensible to the layman. I would not rule out the possibility that this is done deliberately to keep the 'uninitiated', the 'man in the street' at arm's length. It is sometimes even said that he should not be allowed to involve himself in questions of nuclear weapons and problems of war and peace, as he would only do harm and create confusion. But in my opinion that is the biggest, most dangerous and most harmful myth of all! . . . This problem should be resolved by everybody getting actively involved . . . if they wish to serve mankind and not armaments.

The need for this request of ours could not have been better advocated.

We ask you to give us the opportunity of an open discussion.

SOURCE: *Der Spiegel*, no. 49, 6 December 1982, p. 117.

34 STEPHAN HERMLIN AT THE SECOND BERLIN MEETING OF WRITERS, APRIL 1983

I am firmly convinced that, in whatever imperfect form socialism manifests itself, and it can only manifest itself in an imperfect form, since it is only at the very beginning of its development, it has ultimately a great deal more to do with peace than capitalism has. Of that I am convinced. But I do believe, even if I tell myself that I support a government – I support the government of my country, voluntarily, and both intellectually and emotionally; I support it, because I support a cause that I have long fought for, before this government appeared on the scene, before the GDR came into being – I do believe that as a socialist writer I must act in accordance with Brecht's dictum: 'Let others speak of *their* shame, I shall speak of mine.'

It is very important to see and describe precisely what is happening. We must first recognise that not everything that goes by the name of an independent peace movement in the socialist countries is concerned with peace; for the most part it is also concerned with quite different things. But there are many people, especially young people, who passionately want to make their own personal contribution to peace, but are regarded with suspicion. That is something I regret. We know that in December a number of young people were detained in Jena. They have all long since been released. I have to tell you in this connection that those papers which gave an inordinate amount of space to reporting about the detentions and the detainees, did not report anything about their release shortly after. Then there was a demonstration in Jena in February. According to my information no one was arrested on that occasion. But I regret that at this demonstration – I believe Rolf Schneider reported about it – placards or notices were destroyed whose message was unquestionably that of any genuine peace movement. If young people proclaim on a notice 'The future depends on peace', they are absolutely right. For what are we all doing here anyway, if we don't share that view?

There are a lot of things wrong in the letter in today's press from three writers, who cried off at short notice after being previously very keen to take part in this event of ours and agreeing to attend. One of the things wrong – and I'm not talking about personal things now – one of the things that is wrong is that it contains a quotation from a speech by the GDR Defence Minister, Heinz Hoffmann, with which the writers of the GDR are en bloc, so to speak, associated. It is a sentence from Heinz Hoffmann, denying . . . that nuclear war would mean total destruction, as the pacifists claim, and that there can be no just wars in the age of atomic weapons, and arguing that one can survive a nuclear war, a just nuclear war. And incidentally, there is no doubt in my mind that if the Americans begin a war – this would be my own view – that such a war would be a just war, as far as the side I'm on is concerned, whatever the circumstances. The only thing is, this just war is of as little use to us, would be of as little use to us as the unjust war that was being waged by the other side. We are in the same position.

But one can't simply associate writers in this demagogic fashion with the words of a Defence Minister – and incidentally, there are many reasons why I have great respect for him, as he was one of the best commanders in the war for Spanish freedom – one can't simply associate writers with this sentence, even if politically they agree with the Defence Minister. That's demagogy. And for my own part . . . I can't agree with him.

SOURCE: *Zweite Berliner Begegnung*, pp. 65–7.

35. CHRISTA WOLF

The supreme commands of NATO and the Warsaw Pact countries are conferring about a fresh arms race, on both sides, to counter the enemy's presumed weapons-technology superiority with something equally effective. The realisation that the physical existence of us all depends on shifts in the delusional thinking of very small groups – that is, on chance, to be sure unhinges the classical aesthetic once and for all, slips it from its mountings which, in the final analysis, are fastened to the laws of reason. Fastened to the faith that such laws exist because they must exist. Literature: a valiant, if groundless, effort to create a shelter at the same time for free-floating reason and for oneself. Because to compose words presupposes conditions which appear to lie outside literature. It also presupposes a measure, for aesthetics is also rooted in the question of what can be ascribed to man . . .

The Swedish Peace Research Institute declares in its annual report that the danger of an atomic war in Europe has never been as great as it is today. Sixty thousand atomic explosive devices have been stored throughout the world, the institute says. In the last few years, the time of détente, the two superpowers have vastly escalated armaments in their race to outbid each other . . .

Do we have a chance? How can I rely on the experts who have led us to this desperate pass? Armed with nothing but the intractable desire to allow my children and grandchildren to live, I conclude that the sensible course may be the one for which there is absolutely no hope: unilateral disarmament. (I hesitate: in spite of the Reagan Administration? Yes, since I see no other way out: in spite of it!) By choosing this course, we place the other side under the moral pressure of the world public; we render superfluous the extortionary policy of making the USSR arm itself to death; we renounce the atomic first-strike capability, and we devote all our efforts to the most effective defence measures. Assuming this involves some risk, how much greater is the risk of further atomic arms, which every day increase the risk of atomic annihilation, by accident if nothing else?

This is wishful thinking, you say? So, is it completely misguided to want to think and have a say about the life and death of many, perhaps all future generations?

The atomic threat, if it has brought us to the brink of annihilation, must then have brought us to the brink of silence too, to the brink of endurance, to the brink of reserve about our fear and anxiety, and our true opinions . . .

In the news, both sides bombard us with the need to make preparations for war, which both sides call preparations for self-defence. Emotionally it is unbearable to see the state of the world as it really is. The motivation to write, any hope of 'having some effect', is decaying at a breakneck pace that may parallel the speed of missile production on both sides. To whom should one say that modern industrial society itself, idol and fetish of all governments, stamped with absurdity, is turning against those who built, exploit, and defend it? Who could alter that? At night the madness goes for my throat . . .

Worth pondering even today: how the criticism of one-sided male rationalism runs the risk of being wrongly interpreted as irrationalism, hostility to science, and also put to wrong use. This is particularly so in restorational eras, when the way to the Mothers becomes a relapse into emotion, an escape route from the analysis of circumstances, an idealisation of more primitive social conditions, perhaps a lead-up to the blood-and-soil myth. This in turn raises the question of what today could possibly still represent 'progress' (given the postulates of our civilisation), now that the masculine way has almost run its course – that is, the way of carrying all inventions, circumstances, and conflicts to extremes until they have reached their maximum negative point: the point at which no alternatives are left . . .

In Priam's day, when kings ruled smaller realms (and enjoyed the additional protection of being considered divine), perhaps they were not screened off from normal everyday life as totally as today's politicians, who arrive at their decisions not on the grounds of personal observation and sensory experiences but in obedience to reports, charts, statistics, secret intelligence, films, consultations with men as isolated as themselves, political calculation, and the demands of staying in power . . .

Meteln, 1 May 1981 To prevent wars, people must criticise, in their own country, the abuses that occur in their own country. The role taboos play in the preparation for war. The number of shameful secrets keeps growing incessantly, boundlessly. How meaningless all censorship taboos become, and how meaningless the consequences for overstepping them, when your life is in danger.

About reality. The insane fact that in all the 'civilised' industrialised nations, literature, if it is realistic, speaks a completely different language from any and all public disclosures. As if every country existed twice over. As if every resident existed twice over: once as himself and as the potential subject of an artistic presentation; second, as an object of statistics, publicity, agitation, advertisement, political propaganda . . .

I am reading some writings of Hans Henny Jahnn, who stated on 6 May 1949, when the first cracks appeared in the Allies' Anti-Hitler Coalition: The programme has been laid down for World War III. He recognised immediately the devastating significance of the atomic bomb. He declared: There is no such thing as an armed peace. Peace is unarmed or it is not peace – regardless of what one thinks one has to defend. Twice in this century, war has arisen out of 'armed peace', each war is crueller than its predecessor. Brecht said exactly the same thing in the fifties: If we do not arm ourselves, we will have peace. If we arm ourselves, we shall have war. I do not see how anyone could think differently about this.

SOURCE: *Cassandra: A novel and four essays* (London, 1984) pp. 224–68 (extracts).

36. CONTRIBUTION FROM THE UNOFFICIAL PEACE MOVEMENT IN THE GDR AT THE EUROPEAN NUCLEAR DISARMAMENT CONFERENCE HELD IN PERUGIA, JULY 1984

On Questions of the Autonomy and 'Ideological Independence' of the Peace Movement in East and West

1.

Though there are fundamental structural differences between the two great blocs (differences which are, however, becoming increasingly overlaid by the inner dynamic of the military–economic complexes and the particular interests of their leadership élites), their existence and their power–political, economic and military development are responsible for the escalation of armaments, the misery in the countries of the Third World and the destruction of substantial parts of our natural environment.

The peace movement, by contrast, if it wants to have any impact, must become a movement for emancipation in the broadest sense. It must therefore enjoy autonomy from the established political systems and must not be susceptible to being taken over by them. It must also enjoy autonomy from the two superpowers, and from those who represent their interests, and this is in itself a reason why the movement must transcend the two blocs.

Autonomy must not mean cutting oneself off from social movements or regarding oneself as independent of them. The peace movement must become a social movement itself, must not confine itself to questions of disarmament, but must regard the many different forces of emancipation (Third World, environmental, women's, human rights movements) all as coming within the movement. At the same time it must remain a decentralised, grass-roots movement.

But nor must the peace movement overlook the problems arising from the structure of society and the various patterns of property ownership and power. In this context there are a number of fundamental differences between East and West, and one consequence of this is that the peace movement on one side cannot simply take over the forms of activity and organisation of the peace movement on the other. That does not mean that we have to give up trying to develop common strategies for peace.

2.

The aim of the ruling ideologies in East and West is at best to maintain the status quo.

They are marked, particularly in the USA, by their aggressive and irrational nature (Reagan's 'good' and 'evil', for instance). But we also observe how the ideology of the leadership in the countries of existing socialism is increasingly acquiring irrational features (though its dominant characteristic is rather an exaggerated desire for external security and consolidation of internal power). One example: the intentions of their own independent peace movement are equated with those of the political enemy. Instead of aiming at human emancipation, ideology here has been increasingly reduced to apologetics. The further development of the industrial system (including its increasing entanglement with the capitalist economy) is without a second thought proclaimed as a desirable goal, and an unthinking preoccupation with consumption and prosperity is the result. The poor countries of the South only count in so far as they are regarded as allies. Problems of the environment, energy and resources are trivialised and covered up by the centralist practice of secrecy.

The population is to be disciplined by attempting to extend military forms of organisation to every aspect of life (education of children, vocational training, civil defence exercises for working people) and by the doctrinaire, repressive behaviour of the organs of state (in particular the security apparatus and the judiciary) towards all citizens who publicly espouse opinions that deviate from the dogma, or even alternative projects. All this is intended to prevent a public dialogue on questions of the future of human existence, which would call into question the exclusive prerogative and decision-making authority of a small leadership élite. The military significance of this militarisation on the other hand is by comparison infinitesimal.

The trend towards militarisation in the GDR was one of the chief reasons why an independent GDR peace movement arose, to which both church and autonomous peace groups belong. The two have a lot in common, not least the fact that the ecclesiastical setting provides the only possible public arena for peace work independent of the state. Even though the church is subject to restrictions as an institution, and church leaders are concerned to achieve a *modus vivendi* with the state, there are scarcely any problems in arriving at a consensus between the different grass-roots groups. Nor can the other movements for emancipation (ecology, Third World, women's groups, alternative projects, etc) be divorced from the anti-military one, which was at the same time always an anti-missile movement too. The reason for this is not so much that the groups have a uniform strategy, as that the state overreacts and tries to strangle at birth any initiative it has not called for itself. Because of this inflexibility of the system it is, on the other hand, also possible for a few people, sometimes a single person, to make quite a significant impact with limited resources. The chief problems of the autonomous groups are lack of information and co-ordination, but never a lack of solidarity or ability to achieve a consensus.

The peace movement in Western Europe is of great significance for the autonomous grass-roots groups, especially the contacts with representatives of the Western peace movement since the second conference on European nuclear disarmament, and with West German Members of Parliament from the Greens' party, as well as the impressive demonstrations against NATO rearmament. What strikes us as problematic, on the other hand, is that the minimal consensus achieved has resulted in a narrowing of aims, which has left part of the movement disoriented, now that the missiles are in place. There appear to be similar tendencies now too. The split between so-called anti-imperialist and anti-militarist groups seems absurd and is more than likely to confuse people's thinking. The peace movement must unquestionably be both anti-imperialist and anti-militarist.

4.

The peace movement in both East and West must set itself the aim of transforming the status quo, not preserving it. And that is why it must keep its distance from the prevailing ideologies. On the other hand, if it wishes effectively to counter the threat to human existence, it will be dependent on a broad pluralism of views which will prevent it developing a uniform ideology. The concept of 'ideological independence' is therefore irrelevant to the peace movement. It must have concrete Utopias with which to replace the ideologies, it must make the future thinkable again, it must develop new values or resurrect old ones that have been forgotten. It must build on the statement, 'We want to live', which is part of the present minimal consensus, by adding answers to the question, '*How* do we want to live *tomorrow*?' It can oppose the 'objective constraints' of the politicians with moral categories, which it can introduce into political thinking, without turning them into political dogmas of its own (as has begun to happen over the questions of dismantling stereotypes of the enemy, and of non-violence).

5.

Joint activities by the peace movement in Eastern and Western Europe are at present made more difficult by the tense political situation, but we must keep trying to develop new initiatives of this kind in the future.

We regard it as necessary and possible to set up a reliable system of communication. Informal exchanges and, if possible, co-ordination should take place above all through personal contacts between grass-roots groups or through individuals. The problem that East Europeans are denied freedom of movement must be borne in mind.

Meetings should be used for formulating common aims and ideas for the European peace movement. They should include demands arising from the existing situation, as well as concrete Utopias and corresponding long-term strategies to put them into effect.

The following problem areas might be regarded as fundamental:

I. *Disarmament*
- stopping the further stationing, production and testing of weapons of mass destruction, as well as research on them
- dismantling existing missiles, including unilateral measures
- nuclear-free zones
- dismantling 'conventional' weapons-systems
- withdrawal of foreign powers

II. *A System of Peace in Europe*
- treaties concerning peace and economic matters
- a Europe free of nuclear weapons
- armaments clearly designed for defence
- non-alignment

III. *Democratisation in East and West*
- opposition to state-surveillance and to militarisation
- democracy at the work-place
- decentralisation in all fields
- public ownership

IV. *Emancipation, Human Rights, Value Systems*
- the North–South issue
- ecology, resources, problems of industrial society
- women's movement
- marginal groups in society and national minorities
- education and culture for peace

The list could be extended, the problem areas overlap, and they can't be 'gone through' in chronological order.

But peace cannot be achieved with a more modest agenda, unless it is a very limited peace.

At the same time the peace movement must have an educative role, countering the fatalism and hopelessness felt by large numbers of people, and display solidarity in the face of all forms of repression.

37. PEACE ACTIVISTS' APPEAL TO WESTERN PEACE ACTIVISTS

To everyone who is demonstrating against the latest American missiles

We are members of various independent peace groups in the GDR. We, too, say *No* to the latest American missiles. We are also demanding the dismantling of Soviet missiles. But we do not forget: peace is not just a question of missiles. Above all it is about the people who operate them, it is about those who carry out the deed and those who are the victims. It is about the indifferent or eager carrying out of orders. It is about a society which produces two types of people – those who give orders and those who execute them. Even without the latest American missiles, the world can be destroyed a hundred times over.

We know why certain people in the West will always have an interest in armament. Meticulous research has been carried out into the economic interests of the arms industry. We do not play these down, and they are a threat to us too. We are also threatened by developments that have hardly been researched yet, developments in socialist states.

To what extent can a neurotic need for security constitute a danger to peace? To what extent should the state, as owner of the arms industry, make money out of it – even it it is only from selling to developing countries? A connection is often made, in an abstract way, between the peace question and human rights. This sometimes sounds like someone fulfilling a moral obligation. If you take peace as an isolated issue it seems to be so much more important than the right to free travel, for example.

However, we think this is the wrong way to put the question. We ask: how closely is the right to refuse to obey an order linked with endangering or maintaining peace? To what extent does the right publicly to criticise increasing militarisation constitute a significant element in the securing of peace?

For there are certain paragraphs in the GDR's criminal law which endanger the peaceful exchange of opinions and information. 'Ganging up' outside an army base, considered by the state to be extremeley dangerous for its own military strike-force, can lead to a death sentence in our country. If you do not face these facts then you are not living in the real world.

How can you achieve real peace if you are not fully aware of the actual conditions? The Soviet Union does not want war – the USA probably does not either – but one country might anticipate an attack from the other and start a war by wanting to beat the other to it. It is hard for us in the GDR to treat the matter as an abstract problem. We cannot talk about humanity without looking at individual people and what opportunity they have to live peacefully and to demand it of their society.

We come across big differences here between what our government says and what it does. The GDR is becoming a more militarised society every year. That endangers peace. Rochau, Funke and Kathrin Eigenfeld are in prison in Halle because they wrote a paper on the peace issue. The paper is based on information from public sources, there are no state secrets involved. But the boundary of so-called 'state secrets' is much more quickly reached here.

The three from Halle were offering advice on how to become a *Bausoldat* ('construction soldier') or a conscientious objector – entirely within the law. But giving advice on how to make use of laws is regarded as punishable. It is called 'prevention of state-controlled measures'. We call it a threat to peace.

And the registration of women for military service has now begun. Hundreds of women in several towns of the GDR are now being subjected to 'suitability tests', after which a military registration card is issued. They are told to consider themselves part of the army.

In the interest of peace we object to such measures and demand the demilitarisation of public life. This is an area where the GDR could carry out unilateral disarmament without suddenly being defenceless.

We ask you: notice what goes on here. Comment on it, as we comment on the American threat to peace. Apart from protests, it is perhaps even more important to take a genuine interest in what goes on in the East.

It takes some effort to understand what is happening here. It is no use taking a dogmatically pro-communist or anti-communist viewpoint. One must try to see things as they are. Our peace activities stem from various sources: religious and socialist, liberal-democratic and radical. Poetry, songs, plays, art, photographs and political books have an important role to play, and especially literature, whose critical awareness helped the peace movement onto its feet.

Forgive us for not signing our names on this letter. We do not want to put ourselves as individuals into the forefront, we want to express an opinion which is widespread in this country.

In solidarity, best wishes,
Peace friends of the GDR

SOURCE: *Labour Focus on Eastern Europe*, no. 7 (Winter 1984).

38. SWORDS TO PLOUGHSHARES – A SIGNPOST

The Conference of Governing Bodies of the Evangelical Churches in the GDR has issued a statement on Christian responsibility for peace. The conference asks parishes to consider publicity in the parish. The statement reads as follows:

The Conference of Governing Bodies of the Evangelical Churches in the GDR met in Buckow from 12 to 14 March 1982 and once more discussed the question of the church's responsibility for peace and Christian initiatives for peace in our country. Since many of our younger and older members are wrestling with these questions, the Conference of Governing Bodies of the Evangelical Churches would like to say the following:

It is a consequence of our faith in Jesus Christ, the Lord of Peace, that Christians should, now and in the future, involve themselves in helping to preserve peace. Jesus Christ also died and rose again for mankind, for whom both inward and outward peace are so hard to find, and He desires us to use peaceful means to encourage world peace. We are convinced that we are thereby acting to support the worldwide efforts being made for peace in the political sphere, including those of our own government.

The Bible says 'and they shall beat their swords into ploughshares' (Micah, 4, 3), and in recent months these words have taken on a particular significance for various Christian peace initiatives in our country. The Conference of Governing Bodies of the Evangelical Churches adopted them for the 1981 Peace Week. These words of the prophet have given rise to misunderstandings, and even disputes with the organs of state.

They are the expression of our Christian hope that God will one day create a world in which man will no longer need weapons for his defence. At the same time, arising from this hope, it is the expression of our Christian responsibility for doing what is in our power today to ensure that human beings and nations settle their differences without weapons. If the nuclear weapons of our day are ever used, no one will emerge victorious. We are convinced that we are working for the same goal that our government for example has set itself.

Working for peace in the spirit of the image of 'swords into ploughshares' means, in particular, advocating disarmament. The words 'swords into ploughshares' can only mean turning weapons of war into implements of peace, and that means disarming. We are aware that we Christians are – thank God – not the first nor the only ones working for disarmament amidst the present threats of war. We also know that the struggle for peace is long and arduous and can only advance from one partial success to the next. We shall only make progress if the fear that each side has of the other can be reduced and mutual trust can grow. Nor do we Christians have any ready-made, politically practicable solutions. But for the sake of our faith we wish to become involved in our country's struggle for disarmament, indeed we must do so.

For us Christians the Bible's words 'swords into ploughshares' have the significance of a figuratively expressed precept. We are not recommending it as an instruction for everyday political application, nor as a simplistic prescription against nuclear weapons. It is a signpost pointing the direction in which those who seek disarmament must go. It is not an emblem that will conjure up everlasting peace, but a symbol of encouragement for working towards it. Christians must relearn that obeying the implications of faith in this way may entail suffering.

Young men in our parishes are struggling for an answer before God to the question whether they should embark on their military service in the armed units of the National People's Army, or opt for service in the construction units, or whether they should refuse to undertake military service altogether. It remains our view that even in our present era, and despite the greater danger, Christians may risk serving in the army. We would stress that the young Christians in the construction units, indeed even the conscientious objectors in prison, are not trying to make a point against the state, but in favour of disarmament. We support those young Christians who are demonstrating by their words or their deeds that even the efforts for peace being made by our state do not make Christian striving for disarmament superfluous.

Conference of Governing Bodies of the Evangelical Churches in the GDR
Chairman
Bishop Dr Werner Krusche

SOURCE: *Mecklenburgische Kirchenzeitung*, 28 March 1982.

The Significance of Opposition

39. ROBERT HAVEMANN

In fact, until the famous declaration against Biermann's expulsion, not a single bourgeois intellectual in the GDR came out openly and publicly in support either of Biermann, or of our position, or of any unambiguous criticism of the SED's policy. None of these people, many of them very pleasant, as well as intelligent and artistically highly gifted people, dared to make a stand like Wolf, nor to stand beside him, because they were afraid their own work would suffer the same ban as was being very visibly imposed on him. By the manner in which they composed and wrote their books, their poems, novels and whatever else, they attempted to escape the party's criticism, as one takes shelter from a light shower, just remaining within the bounds of permissibility, and acting as an ideological safety valve for opposition in the GDR. Basically almost all of them shared our opinion, and showed it by keeping actively in touch with us and us often meeting them. Wolf's birthday parties in particular always saw a gathering of a very large number, a hundred or more literary people, writers, actors and artists of every kind, all celebrating his birthday. He sang his songs, and it was one big demonstration of shared feelings, of solidarity with Wolf, which always made me very happy, and him too. Of course, State Security always had information about all these things, and did everything they could to intimidate people, and in some cases they frequently succeeded.

SOURCE: *Ein deutscher Kommunist*, p. 23f.

40. LETTER FROM WILHELM GIRNUS AND ARMIN ZEISSLER (EDITORS OF *SINN UND FORM*) TO GÜNTER KUNERT

The reader rightly wonders: what does Günter Kunert mean here? Normally, after all, he has a high regard for exactitude and precision of expression. Exactitude, as understood here, is the closest possible matching of facts with their projection on to the linguistic plane – in other words, with what he says. Do we understand you aright in thinking that what you are trying to say with this little word 'symmetrical' is that throughout the world industrialisation produces its 'symmetrical' mirror-image in the form of 'equal' destruction of the environment? Industrialisation would thus necessitate the destruction of the natural foundation of our lives. Regardless of geographical, technological, economic, social and political conditions? Switzerland equals Belgium, West Germany equals Brazil, the Soviet Union equals the USA? Hence: 'Down with industry! Back to nature forever!'? Can Günter Kunert really be a devotee of such medieval obscurantism? Is it perhaps even something he hoped he could be proud of?

There are too many facts that contradict such a sweeping assertion. Let us just mention one example, even if it seems relatively insignificant: the Swiss watch industry (it lives off hydro-electricity and spews out no poison). You smile? Just small fry? Why should one not regard it as the ideal small-scale model for future industrialisation?

Reply from Günter Kunert

Dear Wilhelm Girnus,

I was surprised, indeed somewhat moved, to read your letter-like addendum to my brief essay on Ritsos and your objection to the little word 'symmetrical': eschewing all factual argument, you leave whatever conclusions are to be drawn entirely to the reader's own degree of 'enlightenment'. And that presumes that the reader shares your alternative way of thinking. I'm not so sure about that. At all events I'm grateful to you for at least not using the hybrid cliché which serves to divorce the problem from reality and sidetrack it into what is called the 'class viewpoint', as a way of permanently neutralising it: namely that when science and technology are in the hands of 'progressive forces', they could not possibly have the same negative effects as under capitalism. There is no need particularly to labour the point that this unmistakable piece of ideologese carries as much weight as a soap-bubble: it is refuted by the simple fact that a publicly owned industry, notwithstanding the distinctively different pattern of its organisation and ownership, does not pour pure manna into the rivers and lakes either, nor emit unadulterated oxygen. We must fear that, in defiance of all 'scientific' ideology, a socialist car produces the same poison as a capitalist one, and it has nothing whatever to do with who is driving.

In contrast to this 'symmetrical' result of a physical process which takes no account of political systems (and such processes are still immune to ideological influences), there is admittedly also an 'asymmetrical' one, to do with how well informed the public is. On the other side of the frontier they are reasonably aware of the problem, but on this side they suppress it, as far as possible – or impossible. Between ourselves: it is getting increasingly impossible.

We know, of course, that in Sweden, the USA and West Germany emission levels for internal combustion engines are prescribed by law, there is lead-free petrol, and the car industry has actually been made to show greater concern for the environment and is already experimenting with new fuels (such as hydrogen, which produces no toxic residues) – in this regard I really can't see anything 'symmetrical'. But there is one area where we can't fail to observe it with growing and justified anxiety: not so much in direct industrial manufacture, whose processes, as we have already said, are technologically virtually the same for all industrial societies and can possibly also, with great difficulty and at enormous expense, be put right; but rather – to give just *one* example – in industrialised agriculture, through which we are continuing to poison ourselves. It is specifically in this field that we are riding the well-known metaphorical tiger, and can no longer dismount. Not to beat about the bush: today's agriculture cannot manage without insecticides and pesticides, unless it is prepared to see its harvests hugely reduced, a further factor being that the pests themselves are developing greater resistance and higher doses of poison are required to exterminate them. The alternative to this latent and permanent poisoning is malnutrition for even more people and starvation for whole populations. What would in fact happen if the United States, which each year supplies hundreds of millions of tons of wheat not only to underdeveloped countries, but to 'symmetrical' ones too, to use this adjective for once in a favourable sense, if the United States for some unforeseeable reason had to do without pesticides? Catastrophic, worldwide starvation would be the result.

Faced with the choice of starving or poisoning ourselves, there appears to be no alternative solution. And that is only one aspect of the creeping catastrophe to whose general and specific symptoms we are closing our eyes. We must even fear that all those involved are deceiving themselves in their fight against exhaust gases from cars and industrial effluent: we imagine we are taking decisive steps to preserve or restore the ecology of the environment, and fail to notice that in a more important respect we have lost the ground from beneath our feet.

And in saying all this, I am taking no account whatsoever of the problem of atomic energy, whose technology will never be 'clean' as long as nuclear fusion does not advance beyond the theoretical stage. But I would like to deal with the passage in your addendum in which you offer me the really pretty feeble consolation of Swiss hydro-electricity for the watch industry. Unfortunately, I've already got a watch, and I'm sure other people have too, and in low-lying areas there's not much scope for mountain rivers and waterfalls anyway; and at the end of the day, therefore, even those who can directly exploit natural energy sources (such as the Italians with their volcanic power-stations), but above all the peoples of this earth who have no resources at all will be subject to the law of transvergence. (Please don't confuse this with convergence: I'm not talking about any growing similarity of antagonistic systems!) What this means is that, amongst other things, the effects of climatic change resulting from enriching the atmosphere with carbon dioxide and suspended particles will be worldwide, and thus become a transcendent, or rather transvergent phenomenon, against which *frontiers* will provide no defence. Let me pick out some examples from the catalogue of analogous contingencies: the polar ice-caps melt and sea-level rises by a few metres, which would entail the loss not just of populated areas but in particular of the most fertile land in the river basins. Or the much-feared destruction of the ozone layer by aerosol propellants, which would result in increased and thus dangerous penetration of hard radiation. To say nothing of the damage done to our greatest oxygen-producer, the ocean. And every one of these a product of human exertion, for which Swiss plumbing skills will scarcely provide us with an adequate remedy.

But worse than this is the fact that these far from rosy prospects are conjoined with a particular characteristic of homo sapiens, which could be described as his proneness to 'blind spots'. Even if we stopped using insecticides and pesticides which were recognised as being harmful, such as DDT, which for decades was scattered round the world with gay abandon, until people noticed that it was permanently absorbed into human fatty tissue, and new chemicals were spread on the fields instead – are we in fact any better informed about *their* effects? If we recall the very recent history of practical applied chemistry and its products, which initially were always presumed to be absolutely harmless – which in all too many cases proved to be mistaken, because the cumulative effect was unknown, experiments with a thousand rats never being as effective as those with 50 million human beings – then the suspicion will begin to dawn on us that every chemical used to combat one threat to our existence may itself harbour another threat.

Or else the suspicion does not begin to dawn!

The most glaring example of our unsuspecting nature is, of course, the car. The early years of motorisation gave not the slightest hint what this Pandora's can on wheels contained within it: poisoning of the environment, destruction of the physical fabric of cities, mutilation of the countryside with housing, concreting over of the land we need, hundreds of thousands of accident victims each year and – particularly crucial at the present moment – the burning up of the non-renewable raw material oil, instead of its carefully considered processing into essential products. For that is our fate: for all our forecasting, planning, extrapolating and other fashionable variants of the haruspications of old, it is not given to us to know the future, not even scientifically, and experiments, tests and simulations of the real thing can do absolutely nothing about it – in every real-life situation, so innumerable are the imponderables that arise, which may in their effect achieve catalytic proportions, that things which were intended to benefit us all, turn out to be an unmitigated curse.

But in our emotional inertia, in our cowardice, which has its origins in our need for personal security and our anxiety for social status and physical safety, in the laziness of our thinking, with its fear of possible conflicts: we let everything run its course, consoling ourselves and others with the idiotic formula that mankind, which has survived everything so far, will also survive present perils.

But that's the very thing we can't be certain of. And even if we could: speaking of mankind's survival presupposes, in the familiar inhuman way, that many members of the race will not share in this survival. You can't make an omelette without breaking eggs, can you, my dear Wilhelm Girnus? But in case that should be the ultimate in wisdom, we must ask ourselves whether this so-called progress has been worth the expense. For my own part, at least, I am inclined to be rather doubtful.

SOURCE: *Sinn und Form*, no. 2, 1979, p. 410f.; no. 4, 1979, pp. 850–3.

41 REVIEW OF AN ANTHOLOGY OF STORIES BY YOUNG WRITERS

Klaus Steinhaußen (ed.), *Kein Duft von wilder Minze* (Halle-Leipzig, 1980)

Approaches to literature by young authors and opinions on the subject vary considerably. Angelika Holan pointed to the discrepancies in how literature specialists deal with it in an article in *Sonntag*. By and large critical objections are more frequent than attempts at analysis. Thus Inge von Wangenheim, in *Genosse Jemand und die Klassik*, speaks of a 'loss of substance' that has occurred, as the torch is passed on to the 'third generation, the grandchildren'. Jurij Brězan sees in literature by young authors a challenge to certain socialist–realist principles: 'It is no secret that a not exactly insignificant minority of talented young writers in particular not merely does not accept as a model the literature we have produced and which goes by the name socialist realism, but is deliberately cultivating the image of being in conflict with it . . . If such an attitude produced great literature – well, great. But unfortunately this has not happened so far'.

If we are to give the public a more subtle assessment of literature by young authors, it is our duty to approach it in a more serious and analytical manner. The younger generation of authors is giving voice to a variety of attitudes to life, and their experiences differ, as do their conceptions of practical conduct.

With *Kein Duft von wilder Minze*, which he has edited, Klaus Steinhaußen is trying to bring young prose writers to the public eye. It contains fifty-eight stories, as these works are described on the jacket, by forty-six authors.

What tendencies can we discern in these literary productions? They are the work of authors aged between seventeen and thirty, whose basic experiences were gained at a different period in the development of socialism and whose writing emanates from a reality which for the preceding generation was still a goal to be achieved. Not merely are the war and fascism history for them, but the development of the GDR is as well. They have no direct experience of the complexity of the post-war years nor of the sharp conflict entailed in laying the foundations of socialism. They have grown up in peace, provided for by their parental home and school, watched over and protected. In many cases they were presented with a harmonious picture of social processes and frequently given the illusion of a life without conflicts. One must presume that this gives rise to many of the difficulties they have in understanding the dialectic in socialism.

Clearly we are concerned with an idyllic view of things when questions to do with the meaning of life, and the chance of realising one's own potential and one's own expectations of happiness are placed so squarely in the context of human life in its 'small dimensions' and are scarcely affected by society. There is no conception that the struggle between imperialism and socialism is increasingly coming to a head, nor any awareness that in the struggle for the preservation of peace the utmost effort is required from mankind, from progressive forces.

For literature to 'embrace life' – a target that Hans-Joachim Krenzke (1946) set himself – it must take account of the great issues of the time. But it is on this very point that we find virtually nothing of interest or value.

In most of the stories the problems centre on the authors' egos, and they fail to reflect objective social conditions. In those stories which are told in the first person, the authors either do not want or are unable to maintain any real detachment from their heroes.

These authors fully intend to be useful, to bring about change and get involved, to have an effect and produce results, and to set the reader thinking so that people may live and behave with more awareness and responsibility, and be more sensitive to other people. The trouble is, the directions they give are too imprecise. The topics chosen by writers tell us something about their relationship with reality and the extent to which reality can also be incorporated in literature. Experience shows that it does not take long to say all there is to say if one writes in purely subjective terms, and sometimes the urge to do so runs its course with the very first book. The works I have just discussed show that far too often they still lack the necessary experience of the world for any kind of objective portrayal.

SOURCE: Ingrid Pawlowitz, 'Kein Duft von wilder Minze', *Weimarer Beiträge*, no.9 (September 1982) pp.137–143.

42. WHAT IS EMANCIPATION?

An astonishing number of writers in the GDR are female. It was with this observation that a conference of the League of Culture began two years ago. The list of names then followed – familiar ones, and ones that were unknown at the time: Anna Seghers, Christa Wolf, Brigitte Reimann, Gerti Tetzner, Helga Königsdorf, Irmtraud Morgner, Rosemarie Zeplin, Doris Paschiller, Charlotte Worgitzky, Renate Apitz, Brigitte Martin . . . The list could be continued.

In 1981 the Soviet literature specialist, Tamara Motyliova, confirmed that our suspicions were correct: the large number of female authors is a particular feature of the literatures of the socialist countries. We must now ask whether something particular has thereby also been achieved. What women bring to literature when they write about themselves, their experiences, the problems in their lives, their conflicts: are these different from those of men? Do women have something to say which would not otherwise have been said in literature?

For some people, even to ask this kind of question is one-sided. After all, everybody who writes should have something new and personal to say. Isn't the question as to how men and women see each other, and how they treat each other, of secondary importance, at least in socialist society?

After all, surely the 'women's question' is characteristic of a class-society, surely it is the product of the historical division of labour, which allocated to women the responsibility for the reproduction of the man's labour power – in the family (unpaid housework, bringing up children, satisfying the needs of the man, including his sexual needs). Men, on the other hand, had their social function in social production, in politics, art, public life. Images and behavioural norms were determined by this division, as were men's and women's strategies for living. With their responsibility for the family women particularly developed their maternal qualities, their powers of sympathy, their adaptability and the skill of caring for others, strategies for living and qualities relating to people, and dependence on receiving personal recognition. Men's qualities and norms on the other hand, being formed by their job, are characterised by being related to objects, striving for achievement, rationality. That was the point of historical departure when the building of socialism was first embarked on. But how do things look now, more than thirty years later? What has changed in how people actually live, in the norms and the expectations we have of each other, now that men and women have legal and economic equality, and almost 90 per cent of women go out to work? Literature can give us some answers.

'Natural' and 'Unnatural' Women

The traditional images are still there – and I almost think, increasingly so – in literature, as written by both men and women. An absolutely typical case is John Erpenbeck's *Der blaue Turm*. The main character, a woman, hates 'cold, analytical, practical reason', being herself emotional and warm-hearted. The expression of feminine feeling, however, appears as an embarrassing cliché, even in the language used. In bed with her lover: 'The miracle occurred, we really became one, he ploughed my body powerfully and tenderly.' This is not just kitsch, but male dominance, right down to the vocabulary. It is as though, in the images they have of women, men think in almost biological terms. It is supposed to be in women's 'nature' to be clinging, sensitive to others and sympathetic, maternal and responsible for all the warmth and humanity in life.

The antipathy aroused by Christoph Hein's *Der fremde Freund* is no doubt partly to be explained by the fact that his main character is a thoroughly 'unnatural woman', in complete contrast to this widespread cliché: a woman of about forty, incapable of emotion, terrified of close contact with others, who refuses to let anything or anybody approach her, surrounds herself with armour plate and lives contentedly inside this 'skin'. The atrophying of human qualities that Hein describes is not specific to either sex. The fact that he links it to a woman is, however, a device that intensifies the shock. Don't a great many people have very deeply rooted notions of what a woman's 'nature' is? The discussion surrounding Charlotte Worgitzky's *Meine ungeborenen Kinder* proves it.

But how do women themselves see this when they write?

Love and Partnership

Ever since the appearance of Gerti Tetzner's *Karen W.* and Helga Schubert's *Lauter Leben*, the social investigation of the everyday life and psychological situation of women has become more precise. The findings are in some cases disturbing (but this is not only true of books written by women). Firstly, concerning the world of emotion, love, attraction. Rita in Christa Wolf's *Geteilter Himmel* once asked: 'How far, and for how long, and against what vagaries of fortune can love provide security?' The answer, to judge by more recent literature, appears clear: it can provide none at all. Many books take the breakdown of partnerships, a situation of disappointment, as their starting point. Love itself, however, is often excluded – and when it does appear, as in Rosemarie Zeplin's *Schattenriß eines Liebhabers*, it appears above all as overwhelming physical attraction. Also often excluded is the pain of love that has been destroyed. It is as though women, above all, no longer wanted to permit those feelings to exist which are so frequently injured, not even to confess to having them, as though they wanted to eradicate them, or at least minimise them. This is not possible, without further deepening wounds and inflicting new ones on oneself: reduction of the capacity to experience, increased self-centredness, an embittered view of the environment and one's own life. An example: Helga Schütz' *Julia oder Erziehung zum Chorgesang*. Julia leaves Ulrich because he has got 'someone else', and tries to 'drop out' of her whole present life, her well-kept home, her singing in the choir. 'I'm rescuing an injured past to take it with me into an empty future.' The certainty of life has been lost, but the actual pivotal points of the crisis can no longer be clearly made out, and the narrative itself therefore becomes blurred. You must not actually admit to feeling pain, and the result is an impression of vague complaints and accusations. But even amidst these weaknesses, one thing is still clear: women are beginning to interrogate themselves, to make their experiences public, to acquire self-confidence. The manner in which they are doing so demonstrates the difficulties.

Job and Family

Throughout, the basic theme: the daily lives of working women who have a family, the double burden of job and home, the demands of the job (including qualifications), and the need to give attention to one's children and one's husband. And very often, as a background accompaniment, the question: 'why, for all the equality between men and women, are there more dissatisfied women than men?' (Brigitte Martin, *Nach Freude anstehen*.) Emancipation seems to have become a burden. Too much is being asked of the women portrayed in literature, and they feel it, they feel guilty 'because you can only half-do everything'. In its extreme form, this appears very much as in Brigitte Martin's book, which has only this one theme: it's no fun any more being a woman, because everyday life is so hard and women bear the burden of this everyday life almost alone. There is substance behind these statements in literary form. Women do most of the housework. Men can spend more time on their careers, qualifications, and political work. But in the process old expectations and behavioural patterns are also to some extent reproduced.

Brigitte Martin raises a further problem: lack of time means lack of attention to one's children too, especially in the case of single mothers. Social institutions such as school and after-school care of children cannot automatically replace what has historically developed as the function of the family. That is where the children experience social relations in a context of intimacy, where they learn social behaviour and behavioural norms, where they experience unstinted love and acceptance. Disturbed family ties, lack of social experience in the family circle and lack of attention have an effect on children. Sibylle Muthesius' book, *Flucht in die Wolken*, tells of this. Many books in recent years appear to suggest that the demands of a job endanger interpersonal relations, family cohesion and children's health. This message admittedly describes an aspect of the subjective situation of many women, but it does not dig deep enough. The conflict is often reduced, as for example in the case of Brigitte Martin, to a problem of time. The woman is shown as a victim of demands which cannot be reconciled. But in this way the problem is only one-sidedly and superficially identified, because all too often it is isolated from the substantive demands of a job. It is misrepresenting the historical situation not to see the job at the same time as an opportunity for women, as a broadening of her relationships, and as a new possibility for her to develop her personality – and for the children too.

Questioning the Self and Questioning the World

It is particularly the demands made at work that break through the centuries-old limitations on the spheres of female activity, and permit women to experience relationships in other spheres. It is specifically the contradiction between the traditional behaviour patterns which were oriented towards husband and family, and the new ones which are directed towards material work and achievement, that gives rise to significant personal conflicts. The conflict, for instance, between the demands made by a family and a job, both of which one loves. In the absence of this kind of enrichment, the result is often extreme one-sidedness. It is indirectly accepted, and at the same time lamented, that the private sphere is allotted to women. This, however, often results merely in a reversal of the old clichés. Men are portrayed as slightly stupid and idiotic. The longing for a strong, dominant man, who could solve all the problems, is concealed – sometimes only barely concealed – behind the arrogant facade of an anti-male posture. With many women the search for their own selves is often still marked, in our literature, by earlier history, in that women continue to appear above all in the role of victim. But they have long been 'protagonists' as well. Helga Königsdorf tells of this kind of variant of female behaviour in her story 'Das Krokodil im Haussee' (in: *Der Lauf der Dinge*). 'Mummy was strong.' 'Our family stuck together.' One very soon realises that the family is, of course, not sticking together, Mummy's strength is a specific form of terror, and she in fact looks after the members of her family by violating them. Feminine cunning has become a strategy for dominating, the awkward neighbour is crushed, order has been restored. – One of the few stories in which the obverse of so-called feminine weakness is reflected, and in which, in the process, the mere reversal of the over-LORD relationship is reduced to its essential point: the overlord relationship is a relationship of oppression.

What Is Meant By Emancipation?

Stories about self-determination of women are one-sided if this is sought merely in separation from men. Emancipation then appears as emancipation from men and from the standards of 'male society'. It is still necessary to transcend the old choices: between the demands and objective rationality of a career on the one hand, and the 'humanity' and emotionality of women on the other. The stories and books that I find most interesting are those which actually deal with the one-sidedness of this separation, and which put it in perspective. Renate Apitz' stories, *Evastöchter* (especially the story about Wibke Winter), are of this kind, as are the new stories by Helga Königsdorf. What is required for this kind of writing is not just precise observation of oneself, but something that maybe women in particular have been able to develop more strongly (for the reasons given at the beginning): the capacity to attend to other people, to open oneself – and others – up. This was demonstrated by Maxie Wander's transcriptions, '*Guten Morgen, du Schöne*', and more recently by Irina Liebmann's *Berliner Mietshaus*: Irina Liebmann has written down what was told her by the residents of a block in Prenzlauer Berg, and has placed this transcription of conversations in a setting of research into the history of the building and the flats. The result is a fascinating hybrid of verbal photography and narrative, reportage and portraiture. The very ordinary life-stories narrated here tell us some fundamental things about our earlier history and our present – especially by virtue of their apparently totally sober authenticity. A complete contrast – and these then represent two extremes of the most recent writing by women – is offered by Irmtraud Morgner's novel of witchcraft, *Amanda*. Fantasy taken to its utmost, imagination, documentary material, anecdotes, humorous stories, quotations: all assembled into a novel. Central to its theme are the relations between the sexes. Discussed often wittily, but very often also with relentless persistence, by witches and others who no longer wish to be witches. It seems to me that concealed behind the many – all too many – varied episodes, problems and documentary pieces about education, it is this coquettish anti-male attitude that prevails. The basic narrative idea – the female being that is divided between Amanda and Laura, as told by Trobadora Beatrix, who has turned into a voiceless siren – is too contrived, and is at the same time riddled with references to the crisis of the environment, the problems of growing old, the theory of scientific understanding, the upbringing of children, etc. The fantastic for its own sake, untamed by narrative discipline. Quite unlike the fantasy, the fantastic, in Helga Königsdorf's *Die Wahrheit über Schorsch*. Here it is employed as a means of alienation – as previously in the fall from the balcony in *Bolero* – to make the reader sit up in astonishment at something quite ordinary. I have rarely read, in the space of so few pages, such an objective account of how deeply the conflict between traditional norms, codes of behaviour, expectations and changed demands can cut. The first-person narrator is no longer capable of love, and in the end she makes do with the dream-image of her ideal man, alongside her real-life husband (whom she keeps for fear of what people may say). A powerful tale of how difficult it is to meet old and new demands at the same time.

The very fact that so many women are writing is evidence of historical progress. No two ways about it.

We have explored the question of how the progress of emancipation in real life is portrayed in our literature. The books mentioned tell of our everyday lives, but often in a very one-sided manner. Everyday experiences are an important subject for literary investigation, but it has always been one of the – self-imposed – tasks of literature to scrutinise these everyday experiences, to imbue them with a philosophy, and so make them a vehicle by which we collectively come to understand ourselves. But here, in a certain sense, literature does not seem to be setting itself high enough standards, it seems to be too easily satisfied with itself.

SOURCE: K. Hirdina, 'Worüber Frauen schreiben', *Für Dich*, no.29, 1983, p.9f.

43. CHRISTA WOLF

Yes: economically and legally we have equality with men, and a high degree of independence through equal opportunities for training and the freedom to make our own decisions about pregnancy and birth, and no longer are we kept apart from the man of our choice by barriers of estate or class; and now we discover (if it really is love we are looking for, and not property or a two-way service contract) just how deeply the history of class society, or patriarchy, deformed those who were subject to it, and how very long it will take for human beings – men and women – to emancipate themselves. Many women still have to hide their feelings, so as to give their love an exchange-value for the immature yearning for love of many men ('You have to put on a bit of an act with men, or you frighten them off').

Maxie Wander's book testifies – without setting out to do so – to something very significant: only when men and women stop quarrelling over the week's wages, or about how to pay for an abortion, or about whether a wife can 'go out to work' and if so, who will look after the children; only when women are paid as much for their work as men; when they stand up in court to represent themselves; when, as girls, they are no longer trained to be 'feminine', at least in school, or as unmarrried mothers no longer condemned by public opinion: only then will they begin to make important discoveries, which concern them not in general, as human beings belonging to the female sex, but personally, as individuals.

The social contradictions, which previously tended to grind them down, or crush them, now appear to them in the subtler form of a personal conflict, and they find for themselves no ready-made role to resolve it. They now face numerous possibilities, and numerous mistakes and dangers. This book provides examples of how differently older and younger women react to the situation. In the words of the 47-year-old youth worker ('Karoline'): 'The things we take for granted today, they were a luxury for us, bread every day, to be able to buy shoes, just being treated like human beings. That's why this social system has to be *mine*.' 'Erika', the 41-year-old assistant drama consultant, wonders: 'Perhaps that's what emancipation is: things that used to cause disaster aren't a problem any more today. That a woman can say: if you won't play ball, I'll go my own way. Though it's not easy.'

Although it isn't easy, these women are beginning to turn the plots of classical tragedies upside down: 'He has the same rights as me, because I could live without him too.' Simply exchanging roles doesn't make them happy. 'I behaved like a man, making use of men's privileges': female philandering, which has the same result – or the same cause – as male philandering: incapacity for love. Although it isn't easy, women are repressing the need for protection they have learned and are standing up for themselves; they discover that it isn't always their fault if they are not sexually satisfied; they find out they have to 'understand with their whole bodies'. (We should nurture this discovery, which is still very fragile, and far from being unchallenged; it might, perhaps, help at least to call into question the merciless, inhuman rationalism of such institutions as science and medicine.) Although it's very difficult, they find out that women can love each other too, and be tender to each other. When the man in their arms, who is so strong when out in the world, indulges in infantile behaviour, they no longer wish to cover his retreat. So they take flight from the 'confines of the bedroom' to which they are 'banished' with their husbands; they are no longer resigned to the atrophied emotions from which many men suffer, in consequence of being forced for generations to conform to 'suitable' modes of conduct; they refuse the role of motherhood and they get divorced.

They pay for their independence with almost unbearable suffering, often with isolation, always with an extra workload, usually with a bad conscience towards husband, children, home, job, and the state as super-man. Only when we – our daughters, grandchildren – no longer have a bad conscience shall we really act with a good conscience, only then shall we be able to help men to become aware of that compulsive urge towards submissiveness and self-assertion which, for historical reasons, has become second nature for many of them, and which they fiercely defend. Only then will men be really willing to understand their women. 'I have never yet known one who wanted to get behind what I am really like and why I am like that.'

These women do not see themselves as opponents of men – unlike certain women's groups in capitalist countries, who are criticised for their often fanatical hatred of men. But how can they be expected to retain a sovereign calm and as far as possible a sense of humour, when they lack even the most elementary basis for an independent existence? Particularly if there is no strong working-class movement, women are driven into sectarian groupings which are directed against men, thinking that they have to use the same weapons to fight men that men have for centuries used against them. But – fortunately – they do not have such weapons; they have a pervasive sense of powerlessness; deprived of rights, they attempt to deny men access to their sense of identity; their route towards finding themselves often leads them to withdraw into their own sex; they must find it difficult to encompass the whole of society in their schemes. And yet: how much solidarity among themselves, what efforts to appreciate their own situation, what spontaneity and ingenuity in their self-help projects, what imagination, what variety. I cannot believe that we in the GDR have nothing to learn from them.

And indeed there are many signs, not least in this book, of the dissatisfaction many women are beginning to feel in our country: what they have achieved and are of course benefiting from, is no longer enough for them. They no longer start by asking what they have got, but who they are. They feel their new role beginning to become rigid, and that they can suddenly no longer move within the institutions; they take great pleasure in life, and their hunger for reality is insatiable. And so, tentatively still, they are taking on the new taboos, since changes are always pushed forward most vigorously where they were most far-reaching. The opportunity which our society gave them – to do what men do – has predictably faced them with the questions: what *do* men actually do and is that what I want in fact? It is not just that they ask critical questions of institutions – the younger ones particularly of the schools; it is not just that they rebel against being denied responsibility at work, which produces an air of resignation: 'If someone is not allowed to see the whole picture, he cannot be made responsible, nor can he do his work properly either.' They begin to ask themselves what their lives have made of them and what they have made of their lives.'If you continually gear yourself up to maximum performance, you destroy something important in your personality.' 'If I don't work I become alienated from myself.' 'You can't be happy if you're as divided as I am.' 'I'm completely dried up.' In contrast, rejection of the new slogans of younger women: 'Men and women are mad to be worried about spontaneity.' And, a remark made by a waitress that could have come from Kleist: 'But suddenly I feel so remote from people.'

That is the voice of the minority. There would be no point in campaigning against it with other sentences, though these can certainly be found. It is the expression of a new attitude to our times and to life in general (shared by young men too, incidentally). Women, who have matured through coming to terms with substantive and significant experiences, are proclaiming a fundamental demand: to live as a whole person, to be able to make use of all their faculties and abilities. This demand is a great challenge for a society which, like all communities in our time, imposes many and varied constraints on its members, and to some extent has to do so; nevertheless, it has itself awakened this demand, whether knowingly or not; it can no longer respond to it *only* with schemes for the advancement of women, nursery places and family allowances: nor by putting more women on those committees, where, as everywhere in this man's world, including our country, the 'important questions' are decided by men. Ought women even to want to be integrated in larger numbers into that hierarchically functioning machinery? To take on roles which over the centuries have done so much harm to men? Though there are indeed women like that lecturer and parliamentarian ('Lena', 43), tearing down the 'facade' of such roles and breaking through self-imposed taboos: 'I automatically lessen the distance between us, until people confide in me. I regard this whole charisma of authority as a farce, and no rational person has any need of it. Everybody in public life faces this contradiction. One will always be torn two ways between thinking in terms of authority and being oneself'.

Let us hope people will recognise the importance to all of us of women's sensitivity to such contradictions. Conditions in our country have enabled women to develop a self-confidence which does not at the same time imply the desire to rule, to dominate, to subjugate, but the ability to co-operate. For the first time in their history they are defining their otherness – an enormous step forward; for the first time they are displaying not just creative imagination: they have also developed that cool objectivity which men used to consider a typically male quality.

I am not claiming that women are by nature any more immune than men to political delusions or flights from reality. It is just that a certain historical phase has enabled them to help define certain principles of living for men too. Naturally, we become aggressive and anxious if old images have to be shattered – especially those of ourselves. But we shall have to get used to women no longer seeking just equal rights, but new patterns of living. Reason, the senses, the desire for happiness are what they have to offer, as against mere utility and pragmatism – that kind of 'rationality' which deceives itself. As if mankind could at one and the same time spend a growing proportion of its wealth on weapons of mass destruction, and be 'happy'; as if there could be 'normal' relations between human beings anywhere on earth, as long as half of mankind is undernourished or starving. Those are delusions. It seems to me that women, who value their new and hard-won hold on reality, are more likely to be immune to such madness than men. And that there is therefore hope in the productive energy of these women. 'The really big things', says one of them in this volume, 'are not in my power anyway, and I don't worry about them'!

Two of her companions join in a dialogue with her. One of them, 'Ruth', a 22-year-old waitress, says: 'I sometimes wonder: what sort of society are we really building? Everyone has a dream, and mine is: human beings will treat each other like human beings, there will be no selfishness any more, no envy and no mistrust.

A community of friends. And surely there'll be someone out there who agrees with me.' And the physicist ('Margot', 36) who now just has to paint, said: 'I would paint my vision: the fear of how human life can degenerate, and one's inner being be eroded by things. Human beings living in millions in their concrete cells, and none of them able to contact the others . . . Isolation again.'

Those are the alternatives we face, men, women, and especially the children. How can we women be 'liberated', unless all human beings are?

SOURCE: Foreword to Maxie Wander, '*Guten Morgen, du Schöne*', 14th ed. (Darmstadt and Neuwied, 1983) pp. 13–19.

Chronology of Events

1971

3 May 1971	Walter Ulbricht asks to be relieved of his post as First Secretary of the Central Committee of the SED. Erich Honecker is elected new First Secretary
15–19 June 1971	At the Eighth Party Congress the idea of a 'socialist human community' is dropped
24 June 1971	Erich Honecker elected chairman of the National Defence Council
5 August 1971	Honecker meets Brezhnev and Podgorny to discuss further co-operation between the GDR and the USSR
17 December 1971	Honecker's 'no taboos' speech

1972

26 May 1972	Traffic Agreement signed between GDR and FRG
October 1972	New SED plans to solve the housing problem by 1990
8 November 1972	The way is cleared for West German journalists to open offices in East Berlin

21 December 1972	Basic Treaty signed as a first step towards 'normalising' relations between GDR and FRG
1973	
21 February 1973	A new regulation against foreign journalists slandering the GDR, its institutions and leading figures
1 August 1973	Walter Ulbricht dies at the age of 80
18 September 1973	East and West Germany are accepted as members of the United Nations
2 October 1973	The Central Committee approves a plan to step up the housing programme
1974	
1 February 1974	East German citizens are permitted to possess Western currency
20 June 1974	Günter Gaus becomes the first 'Permanent Representative' of the FRG in the GDR
7 October 1974	Law on the revision of the constitution comes into effect. Concept of one German nation is dropped and closer ties with the Soviet Union stressed
1975	
1 August 1975	Helsinki Final Act signed
7 October 1975	Treaty of Friendship, Co-operation and Mutual Aid between GDR and Soviet Union
16 December 1975	*Spiegel* reporter Jörg Mettke expelled after another *Spiegel* reporter publishes a story on compulsory adoption in the GDR
1976	
29–30 June 1976	Conference of 29 Communist and

	Workers' Parties in East Berlin. Eurocommunist ideas put forward by Spanish and Italians and published in *Neues Deutschland*
10 July 1976	33 East Germans from Riesa make public their petition calling for support in their bid to leave the GDR
31 August 1976	Dr Karl-Heinz Nitschke is arrested in connection with the Riesa petition, and all other signatories are urged to withdraw their applications to leave the GDR
September 1976	Reiner Kunze's critical work, *Die wunderbaren Jahre*, appears in West Germany with the permission of the East German Copyright Office. Kunze is subsequently expelled from the Writers' Union
29 October 1976	Erich Honecker is elected Chairman of the Council of State
16 November 1976	The singer/writer, Wolf Biermann, is deprived of East German citizenship while on a concert tour in West Germany. The following day the Biermann petition is sent to Honecker. Some supporters of Biermann are subsequently arrested
18 November 1976	Stefan Heym decides not to attend a writers' meeting in West Berlin for fear he will not be allowed back into the GDR
26 November 1976	Havemann placed under house arrest. In December the East German Foreign Ministry requests West German journalists working in the GDR to refrain from contacting him
22 December 1976	The West German television reporter, Lothar Loewe, is expelled from the GDR

1977

14 April 1977	The writer Reiner Kunze and his family leave the GDR for West Germany
23 August 1977	Rudolf Bahro arrested after extracts from *Die Alternative* appear in *Der Spiegel*
26 August 1977	Professor Hellmuth Nitsche (who wrote to President Carter on human rights violations in the GDR), Dr K.-H. Nitschke (Riesa Petition), Gernulf Pannach, Christian Kunert and Jürgen Fuchs (who protested against Biermann's expatriation) are released from prison and go to the West
4 October 1977–9 March 1978	Belgrade follow-up conference to Helsinki. Lengthy criticism of communist states' record on human rights, particularly from the USA delegation
7 October 1977	Clashes between police and young people on the Alexanderplatz in East Berlin after a rock concert. Reports of some deaths
12 December 1977	The writer Hans Schädlich leaves the GDR for West Germany. He lost his post at the Academy of Sciences after protesting against Biermann's expatriation
30 December 1977	*Der Spiegel* publishes the first part of the 'Manifesto', allegedly written by middle-ranking and senior SED functionaries calling themselves the League of Democratic Communists of Germany. After publication of the second part the *Spiegel* office in East Berlin is closed down by the East German authorities

1978

31 January 1978	Before the UN Human Rights Committee in Geneva, the GDR claims that GDR law allows restrictions on civil rights such as freedom of movement and retaining GDR citizenship
6 March 1978	In discussions with the League of Evangelical Churches in the GDR, Honecker acknowledges the church as an independent organisation with social relevance in socialist society
29–31 May 1978	Eighth Congress of the Writers' Union not attended by many who signed the Biermann petition
14 June 1978	Conference of Governing Bodies of the Evangelical Churches agrees on its letter to the parishes, objecting to the introduction of pre-military training in schools
30 June 1978	Bahro sentenced to eight years' imprisonment
1 September 1978	Pre-military training introduced as a new subject in schools for fifteen and sixteen-year-olds

1979

5 April 1979	GDR citizens are no longer permitted to pay for goods with Western currency at Intershops. Currency must first be exchanged at a bank for coupons. Some East Germans express their disapproval on West German television
14 April 1979	A new regulation requires Western journalists to obtain permission to conduct interviews of any kind
26 April 1979	Heym's statement on the East

	German Copyright Office published in the West
9 May 1979	House arrest for Havemann ends, but proceedings started against him for alleged currency offences
May-June 1979	Havemann and Heym are fined heavily for publishing work in the West without permission. Heym is expelled from the Writers' Union together with eight others who protested against these moves. Heym gives a statement on the legal case against him and the West German television reporter who records it is expelled from the GDR
28 June 1979	Reform of the Penal Code, increasing maximum penalties for agitation against the state, establishing illegal contacts, public vilification. Law on taking up illegal contacts extended to apply to GDR writers who publish critical work in the West. Removal of 'subjective element' from para. 106
6 October 1979	Nico Hübner and Rudolf Bahro are released from prison as part of an amnesty to celebrate the thirtieth anniversary of the GDR. They both go to the West
December 1979	SED review of its members results in 3944 expulsions from the party
1980	
July–August 1980	Strikes in Poland over price rises escalate into demands for free trade unions
11 November 1980–9 September 1983	Madrid follow-up conference to Helsinki
1981	
9 May 1981	Appeal from the Social Service for Peace group, containing criticism of

	the 'militarisation' of East German society
12 September 1981	Klaus Gysi rejects Social Service for Peace and suggests that anyone who is not satisfied with the Construction Unit option is bent on confrontation
13–14 December 1981	Peace Meeting of writers and scientists in East Berlin. Criticism from writers of the authorities' actions against activists in the unofficial peace movement.
	Martial Law declared in Poland
1982	
9 February 1982	The East German minister, Reiner Eppelmann, is taken into custody after publishing the Berlin Appeal
13 February 1982	Peace Forum in the Kreuzkirche attended by over 5000 East Germans
March 1982	New military service law makes it possible for women to be called up in case of need Official ban on the Swords into Ploughshares badge
9 April 1982	Robert Havemann dies
19–20 June 1982	Politburo member Kurt Hager talks of possibility of an alliance between Marxists, Christians and pacifists in the GDR
24–28 September 1982	Synod of the Evangelical Church in Halle takes peace as its theme. The symbol Swords into Ploughshares is dropped 'for the sake of peace'
1983	
January 1983	East German Catholic bishops publicly criticise the introduction of pre-military training in schools

11–16 April 1983	International Karl Marx Conference in East Berlin. Western European and Japanese communist parties argue that the Soviet Union is not necessarily a model for all countries and that no ideology should become a state philosophy. Proceedings published in *Neues Deutschland*
22–23 April 1983	Second peace meeting of writers (in West Berlin)
May 1983	Petra Kelly, Gert Bastian and other West German Greens demonstrate for pacifism on the Alexanderplatz and are taken away by police
23 July 1983	Around 200 East Germans hold a silent demonstration in Jena as part of their campaign to leave the GDR
1 September 1983	Some 70 people attempt to form a human chain between the American and Soviet embassies in East Berlin to 'remind both nuclear powers of their responsibility for world peace'. Security police break up the demonstration
	In summer 1983, 57 East German doctors form the Initiative against Nuclear War and argue that medical aid is useless in a nuclear war
17 September 1983	500 women attend a meeting in the Lichtenberg Auferstehungskirche and discuss the link between armaments and the male mentality
December 1983	Cruise and Pershing missiles stationed in the Federal Republic. Willi Stoph states in the *Volkskammer* that the GDR government's main aim is to prevent a nuclear holocaust. This involves speeding up preparations for stationing long-range Soviet nuclear missiles in the GDR

12 December 1983	Ulrike Poppe and Bärbel Bohley are arrested after involvement in peace initiatives and setting up a non-state nursery. Released on 24 January 1984

1984

20 January 1984	Six people from East Berlin enter the US embassy there in connection with their attempt to leave the GDR. They are eventually allowed to go to the West. Others who try the same tactic soon afterwards are ejected from the embassy
24 January 1984	Twelve East Germans enter the West German Permanent Mission in East Berlin and are allowed to leave for West Germany
March 1984	Evangelical Church Synod at Görlitz calls upon the government to create the conditions in East Germany which will encourage its citizens to stay
6 April 1984	35 East Germans leave the West German embassy in Prague after five weeks and return to the GDR when they receive an assurance that they will be permitted to move to the Federal Republic
15 May 1984	*Neues Deutschland* reports that in response to the stationing of American missiles in Western European countries long-range missiles have now been stationed in the GDR
27 June 1984	The West German Permanent Mission in East Berlin is closed after 55 East Germans enter in their attempts to move to the West. They leave the Mission three days later
17–21 July 1984	END Conference in Perugia attended by East German peace activists. They criticise political repression in the

	GDR, excessive church influence on the unofficial peace movement, and point out that the number of peace activists in the GDR has fallen dramatically as a result of people being allowed to leave the country for the West
October 1984	Up to 130 East Germans enter the West German embassy in Prague
9 November 1984	The West German authorities announce that 36 123 East Germans moved to the Federal Republic in the first nine months of 1984
1985	
15 January 1985	The last six East German citizens leave the West German embassy in Prague and return to the GDR after receiving an assurance that they would not be prosecuted and that their applications to leave the GDR would receive attention. At one point the number of East Germans in the embassy had reached around 350

Bibliography

Journals

DDR Report
Deutschland Archiv
Einheit
GDR Monitor
Kirche im Sozialismus
Neues Deutschland
Problems of Communism
Sinn und Form
Der Spiegel
Temperamente
Weimarer Beiträge

Books and Articles

Ammer, T., 'Bürgerrechtsbewegung in Riesa – ein Versuch', *Politische Studien*, no. 234, 1977, pp. 381–90.

Amnesty International Briefing EUR 22/01/82.

Arens, U., *Die andere Freiheit: Die Freiheit in Theorie und Praxis der Sozialistischen Einheitspartei Deutschlands*, 2nd ed. (Munich, 1980).

Bahro, R., *Die Alternative* (Hamburg, 1980).

Bahro, R., 'Ein deutsches Ereignis' (manuscript, 1982).

Bahro, R., *Ich werde meinen Weg fortsetzen*, 2nd ed. (Cologne; Frankfurt, a. M., 1979).

Bahro, R., *Plädoyer für schöpferische Initiative* (Cologne, 1980).

Bauer, A., H. Paucke, 'Einheit und Kampf zwischen Natur and Gesellschaft', *Deutsche Zeitschrift für Philosophie*, no. 5 (May 1979) pp. 593–602.

Bäurich R., *Manifest eines Christen im Sozialismus* (Bad Oeynhausen, n.d).

Baylis, T. A., *The Technical Intelligentsia and the East German Elite* (Berkeley; Los Angeles; London, 1974).

Belwe, K., *Mitwirkung im Industriebetrieb der DDR* (Opladen, 1979).

Bericht des Zentralkomitees der Sozialistischen Einheitspartei Deutschlands an den X. Parteitag der SED (Berlin, 1981).

Berliner Begegnung zur Friedensförderung (Darmstadt and Neuwied, 1982).

Beyme, K. von and Zimmermann, H., *Policymaking in the German Democratic Republic* (Aldershot, 1984).

Biermann, W., *Demokratisierung in der DDR?* (Cologne, 1978).

Biermann, W., *Nachlaß I* (Cologne, 1977).

Bilke, J. B., 'Menschenrechte im SED-Staat', *Aus Politik und Zeitgeschichte*, 15 November 1980, pp. 3–19.

Böhme I., *Die da drüben* (Berlin, 1982).

Brown A. and Gray J. (eds), *Political Culture and Political Change in Communist States*, 2nd ed. (London, 1979).

Bühn, K., 'Gedanken zur Verbesserung der kommunistischen Erziehung im Staatsbürgerkundeunterricht', *Pädagogik*, no. 10 (October 1980) pp. 806–9.

Bundesministerium für innerdeutsche Beziehungen (ed.), *DDR Handbuch*, 2nd ed. (Cologne, 1979).

Bundesministerium für innerdeutsche Beziehungen, *Zehn Jahre Deutschlandpolitik* (Bonn, 1980).

Bundesministerium des Innern, *Document no. VtK 15 934000 VII.*

Burens, P. C., *Die DDR und der Prager Frühling* (Berlin, 1981).

Büscher, W., Wensierski, P., and Wolschner, K., *Friedensbewegung in der DDR* (Hattingen, 1982).

Büscher W., and Wensierski, P., *Null Bock auf DDR* (Reinbek, 1984).

Bussiek, H., *Notizen aus der DDR* (Frankfurt a. M., 1979).

Bust-Bartels, A., *Herrschaft und Widerstand in den DDR-Betrieben* (Frankfurt a. M.; New York, 1980).

Childs, D. *The GDR: Moscow's German Ally* (London, 1983).

Curry J. L. (ed.), *Dissent in Eastern Europe* (New York, 1983).

Ehring K., and Dallwitz M., *Schwerter zu Pflugscharen* (Reinbek, 1982).

Eisenfeld, B., *Kriegsdienstverweigerung in der DDR – ein Friedensdienst?* (Frankfurt a. M., 1978).

Faust, S. *In welchem Lande lebt Mephisto?* (Munich and Vienna, 1980).

Finn, G., and Fricke, K. W., *Politischer Strafvollzug in der DDR* (Cologne, 1981).

Francke, G., 'Neue Erfahrungen mit den Oranienburger Familiengesprächen', *Organisation,* no. 3 (May/June 1982) p.9f.

Fricke, K. W., *Opposition und Widerstand in der DDR* (Cologne, 1984).

Friedrich-Ebert-Stiftung, *Die Friedensbewegung in der DDR* (Bonn, 1982).

Fuchs, J. *Gedächtnisprotokolle* (Reinbek, 1977).

Glaeßner, G.-J., *Herrschaft durch Kader* (Opladen, 1977).

Goss, A. J., *Deutschlandbilder im Fernsehen* (Cologne, 1980).

Götting, G., *Die CDU und die Aufgaben der achtziger Jahre* (Berlin, 1983)

Göttinger Arbeitskreis (ed.), *Studien zur Deutschland-Frage*, vol. 3 (Berlin, 1979).

Gundermann, H., *Entlassung aus der Staatsbürgerschaft* (Frankfurt a. M.; Vienna, 1978).

Gyöngyösi K. M., *et al.* (eds), *Der Bahro-Kongreß* (Berlin, 1979).

Hager, K., *Zur Theorie und Politik des Sozialismus: Reden und Aufsätze* (Berlin, 1972).

Havemann, R., *Berliner Schriften*, ed. A. Mytze (Munich, 1977).

Havemann R., *Ein deutscher Kommunist* (Hamburg, 1978).

Havemann, R., *Ein Marxist in der DDR*, ed. H. Jäckel (Munich and Zurich, 1980).
Heuer, U. J. *Gesellschaftliche Gesetze und politische Organisation* (Berlin, 1974).
Heuer, U. J. *Recht und Wirtschaftsleitung im Sozialismus* (Berlin, 1982).
Heym, S., *Collin* (Munich, 1979).
Heym, S., *5 Tage im Juni* (Frankfurt, a. M., 1977).
Heym, S., 'Plötzlich hebt sich der Boden', *Der Spiegel*, no. 22, 31 May 1982, pp. 94–100.
Heym, S., *Wege und Umwege*, ed. P. Mallwitz (Munich, 1980).
Hirdina, K., 'Worüber Frauen schreiben', *Für Dich*. no. 29, 1983, pp. 9–11.
Honecker, E., *Die Kulturpolitik unserer Partei wird erfolgreich verwirklicht* (Berlin, 1982).
Höpcke, K., 'Zwei gegensätzliche Ströme von Texten', *Forum* (February 1979) p. 4f.
Hübner, N., 'Letter from Berlin', *Encounter* (July 1978) pp. 84–8.
Jäger, M., *Kultur und Politik in der DDR* (Cologne, 1982).
Jakobs, K.-H., *Das endlose Jahr* (Düsseldorf, 1983).
Jänicke M., *Der dritte Weg: Die antistalinistische Opposition gegen Ulbricht seit 1953* (Cologne, 1964).
Johannes, G. and Schwarz, U. (eds), *DDR. Das Manifest der Opposition* (Munich, 1978).
Jones, W. T., 'The Literary Climate in East Germany', *Index on Censorship*, no. 3 (May/June 1979) pp. 17–25.
Keßler, H.-J., and Miermeister, J., *Vom 'Großen Knast' ins 'Paradies'?* (Reinbek, 1983).
Komitee gegen die politische Unterdrückung, *Freiheit heißt die heiße Ware* (Cologne, 1978).
König H., 'Die Verantwortung der FDJ für Kultur und Kunst in den Kämpfen unserer Zeit', *Junge Welt*, 22 October 1982.
Kuczynski, J., 'Brief an Hermann Kant', *Neue Deutsche Literatur*, no. 10 (October 1980) pp. 156–65.
Kusin, V., 'Typology of Opposition', *Soviet Studies*, no. 1 (July 1973) pp. 125–9.
Lemke, C., 'Departure from Conformity? Political Socialization and Political Change in the GDR' (manuscript, 1984).
Loest, E., *Der vierte Zensor* (Cologne, 1984).
Loewe, L., *Abends kommt der Klassenfeind* (Frankfurt a. M., 1977).
Lolland, J., and Rödiger F. (eds), *Gesicht zur Wand!* (Stuttgart, 1977).
Löw, K., *Die Grundrechte: Verständnis und Wirklichkeit in beiden Teilen Deutschlands* (Munich, 1977).
Lübbe P., *Der staatlich etablierte Sozialismus* (Hamburg, 1975).
Ludz, P. C., *The Changing Party Elite in East Germany* (Massachusetts, 1972).
Ludz, P. C., *Die DDR zwischen Ost und West* (Munich, 1977).
Ludz, P. C., *Deutschlands doppelte Zukunft*, 3rd ed. (Munich, 1974).
Ludz, P. C. 'Experts and Critical Intellectuals in East Germany', in

E. J. Feuchtwanger (ed.), *Upheaval and Continuity* (London, 1973) pp. 166–82.

Ludz, P. C. 'Die Neuordnung der Führungsspitze der DDR', *Europa-Archiv*, no. 4 (1977) pp. 113–20.

Ludz, P. C., 'An Overview of Survey Research in the German Democratic Republic', in W. A. Welsh (ed.), *Survey Research and Public Attitudes in Eastern Europe and the Soviet Union* (New York, 1981).

Mampel, S., *Die sozialistische Verfassung der DDR: Text und Kommentar*, 3rd ed. (Frankfurt a. M., 1972).

McCauley, M., *The German Democratic Republic since 1945* (London, 1983).

Mleczkowski, W., 'Grenzprobleme regimekritischen Denkens', *Liberal*, no. 21, 1979, pp. 552–4.

Mleczkowski, W., 'Der neue Moralismus – Zur politisch-geistigen Alternative in der DDR', *Liberal*, no. 4, 1979, pp. 262–77.

Mleczkowski, W., 'In Search of the Forbidden Nation: Opposition by the Young Generation in the GDR', *Government and Opposition*, no. 2 (Spring 1983) pp. 175–93.

Naimark, N., 'Is it true what they're saying about East Germany?', *Orbis*, no. 3 (Fall 1979) pp. 549–77.

Neugebauer, G., *Parteien und Staatsapparat in der DDR* (Opladen, 1978).

Papiere aus Osteuropa zur Vorbereitung der END-Konferenz in Perugia, vom 17.–21. Juli 1984

Pelikán J., and Wilke M. (eds), *Menschenrechte: Ein Jahrbuch zu Osteuropa* (Hamburg, 1977).

Picaper, J.-P. *DDR-Bild im Wandel* (Berlin, 1982).

Programm und Statut der SED.

Roos P. (ed.), *Exil: Die Ausbürgerung Wolf Biermanns aus der DDR* (Cologne, 1977).

Rudolph, H., *Die Gesellschaft der DDR – eine deutsche Möglichkeit?* (Munich, 1972).

Sandford, J., *The Sword and the Ploughshare*, (London, 1983).

Schapiro, L. (ed.), *Political Opposition in One-Party States* (London, 1972).

Schmitt, K., *Politische Erziehung in der DDR* (Paderborn, 1980).

Schütz G., *et al.* (eds), *Kleines Politisches Wörterbuch*, 3rd ed. (Berlin, 1978).

Schütz G., *et al.* (eds), *Kleines Politisches Wörterbuch*, 4th ed. (Berlin, 1983).

Schweigler, G., *Nationalbewußtsein in der BRD und der DDR*, 2nd ed. (Düsseldorf, 1974).

Shtromas, A. Y., 'Dissent and Political Change in the Soviet Union', *Studies in Comparative Communism*, vol. 12, nos. 2 and 3 (1979) pp. 212–44.

Strafgesetzbuch der Deutschen Demokratischen Republik (mit den Änderungen vom 28.6.1979).

Timmermann, H., *Reformkommunisten in West und Ost: Konzeptionen,*

Querverbindungen und Perspektiven (Berichte des Bundesinstituts für ostwissenschaftliche und internationale Studien, no. 31, 1980).

Tökés R. (ed.), *Opposition in Eastern Europe* (London, 1979).

Verfassung der Deutschen Demokratischen Republik vom 6. April 1968 in der Fassung des Gesetzes zur Ergänzung und Änderung der Verfassung der Deutschen Demokratischen Republik vom 7. Oktober 1974.

Vogel B., *et al., Wahlen in Deutschland* (Berlin, New York, 1971).

Vogt, H., *Parlamentarische und Außerparlamentarische Opposition* (Opladen, 1972).

Wallace I. (ed.), *The GDR under Honecker, 1971–1981* (Dundee, 1981).

Wander, M., '*Guten Morgen, du Schöne*', 14th ed. (Darmstadt and Neuwied, 1983).

Weber, H., *Kleine Geschichte der DDR* (Cologne, 1980).

Weber, H., *Die SED nach Ulbricht* (Hanover, 1974).

Wettig, G., *Die Folgen der KSZE aus östlicher Sicht* (Berichte des Bundesinstituts für ostwissenschaftliche und internationale Studien, no. 7, 1977).

Williams, R., *Problems in Materialism and Culture* (London, 1980).

Wolf, C., *Voraussetzungen einer Erzählung: Kassandra*, 6th ed. (Darmstadt and Neuwied, 1984).

Wolfschütz, H., 'Gespräch mit Stefan Heym', *GDR Monitor*, no. 8 (Winter 1982/3) pp. 1–14.

Zweite Berliner Begegnung: Den Frieden erklären (Darmstadt and Neuwied, 1983).

Postscript

In July 1985 Reiner Eppelmann and the writers Sascha Anderson and Rüdiger Rosenthal signed an open letter to the FDJ, calling for basic rights to be observed in the GDR, and arguing that every limitation of human rights posed a threat to peace. On these issues they were at odds with mainstream thinking within the Evangelical Church: at his February meeting with Erich Honecker Bishop Johannes Hempel had stressed that the various 'open questions' between state and church were secondary to the cause of maintaining peace. Despite the priority given to peace, however, Evangelical Church representatives such as Hempel and Manfred Stolpe, as well as the regional synods, have settled into a routine of fairly vigorous criticism of militarisation and of the human rights situation in the GDR. Synods have also kept alive the proposal for social service for peace as an alternative to military service.

Critical intellectuals have not disguised their disapproval of the call from Honecker and Klaus Höpcke for works of art which focus on the active hero rather than the observer, and which take the working class as their subject-matter. Bernd Schirmer must have had some support from the intellectual community in order to get into print with the reply that it was childish to expect writers to think in terms of positive and negative models, of good and bad.[1] On the occasion of his seventieth birthday in April 1985 Stephan Hermlin was awarded the Grand Star of Friendship between Nations despite the rather blunt things he had to say about officials who claimed the right to criticise intellectuals in the name of the masses.

Soon after, the irrepressible Stefan Heym cast a shadow over the official East German celebration of the fortieth anniversary of the 'liberation of Germany' by pointing out that in 1945 the

Soviet Army had been more concerned with defeating the Germans than with liberating them.[2]

The final tally for East German citizens moving to the Federal Republic in 1984 was around 41 000. In March 1985 *Neues Deutschland* gave considerable prominence to reports claiming that more than 20 000 East Germans who had moved to the West over the years now wanted to return to the GDR. West German sociological surveys tell a different but not altogether positive story: in follow-up interviews conducted one year after their move to the West most East Germans were found to have become integrated in terms of jobs and material possessions, but their social integration was far from complete.[3]

At the end of July 1985 foreign ministers from the thirty-five states represented at the CSCE came together in Helsinki to mark the tenth anniversary of the Final Act. In the run-up to the meeting Erich Honecker and Foreign Minister Oskar Fischer stressed that the Helsinki Agreement had reaffirmed the political and territorial realities of post-war Europe, but they had nothing to say on the human rights aspect of Helsinki. Weighed against this is the renewed impetus given to the discussion in the GDR on the rights and freedoms of the individual. The legal theorist Eberhard Poppe has recently referred to the 1977 constitution of the USSR and 'progressive international documents' – including the Helsinki Final Act – which prompted the GDR to place greater emphasis on the basic rights of the individual. For Poppe this was an indication of the mature stage socialism had reached: now that class antagonisms had been overcome, it was possible and necessary to protect the development of the individual's personality and freedom.[4]

When it comes to critical intellectuals' freedom of expression, however, there have been some recent reminders of how sensitive the authorities can be: Franz Loeser, formerly a professor of philosophy at the Humboldt University but now in the West, has pointed out that the editor of *Deutsche Zeitschrift für Philosophie* was fired after publishing an article in which Loeser defended the progressive side of religious faith and defied any Marxist to call the 'Swords into Ploughshares' motto reactionary. Gabriele Eckart also ran into trouble when the plan to publish her controversial account of life in an agricultural collective was dropped. Disillusioned, she applied to leave the GDR for the West.

But the difficulties encountered by individuals should not direct attention away from shifts in SED policy which would seem to be in part a response to pressure from below. The founding of the *Gesellschaft für Natur and Umwelt* in 1980 can be seen as an attempt by the party to channel the growing concern for the environment into politically acceptable activity. Although in many ways the society trivialises the fears of the unofficial ecology groups, the rapid growth in its membership (to 50 000 in just four years) suggests that this was a shrewd and successful move by the SED. Reports of co-operation between church ecology groups and the society confirm the party's wish to avoid confrontation and to embrace milder forms of criticism.

A July 1985 law on local representative bodies seemed to be a further step in this direction: local authorities are now obliged to pay closer attention to suggestions, problems and complaints from East German citizens.

Such developments seem to lend support to what Western commentators describe as a drift in communist politics towards 'consensual legitimacy', meaning that party policies take popular expectations increasingly into account.[5] One is thus led into a broader discussion of what kind of society the GDR is and to consider what a study of opposition can add to this discussion.

The mid-1970s saw a revival of totalitarianism theory in the Federal Republic, a revival which continued into the 1980s with Karl Dietrich Bracher's *Zeit der Ideologien*. Advocates of this approach to understanding Eastern European communism tend to look to the classic study of totalitarianism by Brzezinski and Friedrich (*Totalitarian Dictatorship and Autocracy*, 1956), in which the essential features of a totalitarian system are set out. One of these is an official ideology which claims absolute validity and permeates every sphere of society. Bracher thus takes the suppression of opposition in favour of ideological and political unity as a key element of totalitarianism.[6] If one looks at the role ideology has played in the Honecker period, particularly *vis-à-vis* opposition, this emphasis on its supremacy seems inappropriate. Ideology has in fact also been used to accommodate and defuse opposition trends. More generally totalitarianism theory tends to assume that the system it seeks to characterise cannot change, a notion which fails to take into account the distinct phases East German society has gone through. Moreover, it is clear that potential dissent has been a factor in bringing about the progression from one phase to the next.

Western political scientists have also considered to what extent the term 'pluralism' may be applied to the political systems of the Soviet Union and the other Eastern European states. In the case of the GDR it is only useful to speak of pluralism in the limited sense of a range of views and some degree of autonomy from central control. Pluralism in the sense of a variety of groups exerting equal influence on policy-making is scarcely in evidence.

Frederick Barghoorn has looked at dissent in the Soviet Union after Krushchev and noted that the suppression of dissent led to protests based on 'relative deprivation'. This refers to the difficulty a regime has in 'reversing the past' by embarking upon a campaign to reduce the level of citizens' political, social and economic expectations.[7] In the case of the GDR under Honecker opposition has helped to raise the level of popular expectations, and if reports that Honecker is to bow out as party leader in 1986 are correct, his successor will have to rank these expectations among the less negotiable facts of political life in the second half of the eighties.

References

1. *Weimarer Beiträge* (February 1985) pp. 222–38.
2. See Harald Kleinschmid, 'Gespräche mit DDR-Schriftstellern zum 8. Mai', *Deutschland Archiv*, no. 6 (June 1985) p. 663.
3. See K. Pratsch, V. Ronge, 'Arbeit finden sie leichter als Freunde', *Deutschland Archiv*, no. 7 (July 1985) pp. 716–25.
4. E. Poppe *et al., Politische und persönliche Grundrechte in den Kämpfen unserer Zeit* (Berlin, 1984).
5. See Henry Krisch, 'Political Legitimation in the GDR', in T. H. Rigby and F. Fehér, *Political Legitimation in Communist States* (London, 1982) p. 113.
6. *Zeitgeschichtliche Kontroversen* (Munich, 1976) p. 43.
7. F. Barghoorn, 'Regime—Dissenter Relations after Khrushchev', in S. G. Solomon, *Pluralism in the Soviet Union* (London, 1983) p. 138.

Index